PRAISE FOR HARVEY COX AND

When Jesus Came to Harvard

....

"[Cox] weighs in on the contemporary Jesus boom with his usual sagacity and wit, finding America's latest and greatest obsession alive and well among Christians and Buddhists, believers and unbelievers, and even in the secular citadel of Harvard."

— STEPHEN PROTHERO, author of *American Jesus*

"Stimulating." — *Boston Sunday Globe*

"Elegantly organized . . . Cox pulls off a near miracle as he gathers disparate scholarly and religious views of Jesus, while demonstrating respectful, deep knowledge of Jewish, Muslim, and Buddhist traditions, and various Christian teachings." — *Seattle Times*

"Want to know what Jesus would do? Harvey Cox's book *When Jesus Came to Harvard* might help." — *Chicago Tribune*

"An acute observer of faith and culture . . . He covers a dazzling array of subjects . . . Cox's exuberant probing of the Gospels is wise and humane." — *San Francisco Chronicle*

"Cox is intelligent and provocative, but also kind and reverent . . . [presenting] a postmodern Christian's vision of Jesus which just might inspire readers thirsting in the secular city."

— *Raleigh News and Observer*

"Provocative . . . erudite yet accessible." — *Hartford Courant*

"Weaving together movie themes, politics, poetry, and Eastern philosophy, Cox makes a powerful argument." — *Library Journal*

When Jesus Came to Harvard

....

Making Moral Choices Today

HARVEY COX

A MARINER BOOK
HOUGHTON MIFFLIN COMPANY
Boston • New York

First Mariner Books edition 2006

Copyright © 2004 by Harvey Cox
ALL RIGHTS RESERVED

Library of Congress Cataloging-in-Publication Data
Cox, Harvey Gallagher.
When Jesus came to Harvard : making moral
choices today / Harvey Cox.
p. cm.
Includes bibliographical references and index.
ISBN 0-618-06744-2
1. Jesus Christ—Example. 2. Jesus Christ—Person
and offices. 3. Christianity—Forecasting. I. Title.
BT304.2.C69 2004
232.9'04—dc22 2004054069

ISBN-13: 978-0-618-71054-6 (pbk.)
ISBN-10: 0-618-71054-X (pbk.)

Printed in the United States of America

Book design by Robert Overholtzer

MP 10 9 8 7 6 5 4 3 2 1

"The Annunciation" by Samuel Menashe is reprinted by permission of the author from *The Niche Narrows* (Talisman House, 2000). "Demiurge" by D. H. Lawrence, from *The Complete Poems of D. H. Lawrence*, edited by V. de Sola Pinto and F. W. Roberts, copyright © 1964, 1971 by Angelo Ravagli and C. M. Weekley, executors of the estate of Frieda Lawrence Ravagli, is used by permission of Viking Penguin, a division of Penguin Group (USA) Inc. "Those Who Carry" by Anna Kamienska (translated from the Polish by Tomasz P. Krzeszowski and Desmond Graham) is reprinted with permission from Flambard Press. "Crucifixion" by Anna Akhmatova (translated by Stanley Kunitz) is reprinted courtesy of Darhansoff Verrill Feldman Literary Agents.

I would like to dedicate this book to every one of the countless students who, during more than four decades of teaching, have pushed, provoked, and sustained me. I learned as much from them as they did from me, at the Andover-Newton Theological School, the University of Michigan, the Naropa Institute, Brandeis University, and the Seminario Bautista de Mexico, but most especially at Harvard College and Harvard Divinity School.

> *"Children are like arrows in the hand of a warrior . . .*
> *Happy is the man who has his quiver full of them."*
>
> —PSALMS 127: 4,5

Contents

When Jesus
Came to Harvard

Introduction

THE JUXTAPOSITION of the two nouns in the title of this book may seem odd. Harvard, although it was originally founded in 1636 as a school for the training of ministers, has long since shed its religious identity. For nearly a century now it has been a modern research university, often thought of as quite rich, somewhat snooty, and famously secular. Jesus, on the other hand, who lived two thousand years ago, is associated in most people's minds with simplicity, humility, and the spiritual life. He is the central figure in the world's largest religion. What does Nazareth in Galilee have to do with Cambridge, Massachusetts?

Two major trends in the past few decades have rendered this apparent contradiction less improbable. The first is a growing anxiety on the part of large numbers of people that we have entered an era of conflicting values and colliding worldviews, and that this moral divide is disrupting not only local communities and national states, but also whole cultures and civilizations. I have my doubts about this description. Much of it is based on a distorted picture of the past, drawn more from nostalgia than from history. When was the world, or America, ever free of venomous rivalries? Still, the perception certainly exists, and in cases like this, perception has more influence than reality on the way people think and act.

The second trend is also a perception, namely, that after centuries of steady decline, religion has made a startling comeback in virtually every part of the world. But this is also a dubious idea. It is true, of course, that a century ago scholars were confidently predicting that the rapid spread of science, urbanization, and literacy would inevitably crowd religious traditions to the edges of modern societies. There, it was said, they would gradually languish, or petrify into the quaint curios of a previous era. But seldom in history have such self-assured predictions been so dramatically refuted. Have the gods who were solemnly declared dead returned to bury their pallbearers? Or perhaps, as I believe, were they never dead at all, just transforming themselves into new shapes more in keeping with the changing times?

Now some scholars are interpreting the alleged crisis of values and the presumed resurgence of religion as cause and effect. This analysis comes in two versions. On the one hand, some observers claim that, confronted with new and vexing ethical challenges — everything from cloning and organ merchandising to mass famine and terrorism — people are confused and uncertain. Add the growing public distrust of political and business elites, and it is no wonder that these dazed victims of modernity are retrieving the spiritual traditions that for millennia had provided a sense of meaning and orientation.

Other analysts, however, turn this picture on its head. They insist that this same alleged revival of religion is actually fomenting the conflict. Some even declare that we are heading for a protracted war between Judeo-Christian and Islamic civilizations, mainly because their core religious values are allegedly at odds. In this diagnosis, religion (or at least someone else's religion) is not a healing balm but a toxic pathogen. In either scenario, however, both religion, whether as Good Samaritan or as Beelzebub, and the moral crisis — either real or illusory — are once again claiming the public's attention. And this is just as true in the quiet shadows of Harvard Yard as it is elsewhere.

I found myself caught up in these swirling currents in the early 1980s when the faculty of Harvard College asked me to teach a course on Jesus in the newly introduced Moral Reasoning division of the undergraduate curriculum. The faculty had created this program after deciding that the university could no longer ignore a growing embarrassment. Why were we hearing so much about insider trading, sleazy legal practices, doctors more interested in profits than patients, and scientists who fudged the data? Worse still, why were some of these culprits our own graduates? Why were so many well-educated people doing bad things? Was something missing from the education we were giving our students?

We knew we were equipping them with a good command of the humanities and the sciences. They were familiar with the causes of the Civil War and they could write coherent summaries of their chemistry experiments. But we began to see that we were giving them virtually no preparation for how to apply their educations in a morally responsible manner. They were becoming experts on facts but novices on values. So the faculty decided that henceforth every student would be required to take at least one course in moral reasoning in order to graduate. It was a small step, intended to do something about a malady that afflicted not only our students but also our whole society. That was when a faculty committee asked me to teach a course that would focus on the moral example and teachings of Jesus.

I had my doubts about the idea. I wasn't sure that morality was something one could teach in the classroom. I suspected that it was probably better taught by religious institutions and families, and to younger children rather than to adolescents. I also had other questions. What is the relationship, if any, between moral reasoning, moral conviction, and just plain moral courage? For example, would it be theoretically possible for a student to develop such highly refined skills in moral reasoning that he or she got an A in the course but cheated on the exam? Was there a danger that we could turn out a generation of graduates who could debate moral issues with flair and proficiency but who lacked any real conviction about them? Wasn't this the very thing — he called it sophistry — that had so angered Socrates about the education being given to the youth of Athens in his day? And what about moral courage? Is there any way to nurture guts in a lecture hall?

I had still other reservations. To give the students a wide choice, there were to be several courses on moral reasoning. But by introducing what appeared to be a wildly disparate congeries of course offerings, was the faculty inadvertently replicating the same cafeteria view of morality they wanted to avoid: "Let's see; do I prefer Immanuel Kant's emphasis on duty or John Stuart Mills's utilitarianism? Aristotle or Aquinas?" Didn't this barrage of options contribute to the nebulous relativism the faculty wanted to challenge?

When I vented my reservations over coffee to colleagues who were already teaching other courses in moral reasoning, they tried to be reassuring. They told me that all we could hope for was to teach students how to think clearly about moral issues. They argued that if we helped them to talk through choices and understand moral arguments, they would develop skills in this area just as they honed their observational skills in the laboratory, their musical skills in the bands and choirs, and their physical skills on the playing fields. I was not convinced. I felt that, without some common grounding, moral arguments would eventually go nowhere, and the students might find themselves even more deeply mired in the moral blurriness around them.

I could also foresee another problem. Our students represented every religion and none, and they held sharply different views on many ethical questions. Consequently, the faculty had suggested that I try to show how Jesus' moral vision might commend itself not just to students who accepted the traditional Christian doctrines about him, such as the Incarnation or the Resurrection, but also to those who did not. I told them that I could try, but that an argument about this question had been going on for a long time. On the one hand, many people believe that unless one accepts the religious claims about Jesus, his moral teachings make little sense, and these people have a certain point. Jesus did often personalize his teaching and even place himself at the center of his message. On the other hand, it is obvious that millions of people who do not embrace Christian doctrines have been inspired and instructed by the moral example and teaching of Jesus. Mahatma Gandhi is the most famous example. I thought I could present the claims of both these groups, but I still had some doubts about undertaking the course. The more I reflected, however, the more I found the prospect attractive, and eventually, despite my reservations, I agreed.

I am glad I did. It was evident from the outset that this was not going to be just another course. Starting with the first semester, large numbers of students enrolled, and after a few years seven or eight hundred were taking it each year. Soon visiting fellows, postdoctoral scientific researchers, midcareer diplomats, city planners, and journalists attended as well. The burgeoning enrollment came as a surprise to the people both inside and outside of Harvard who had considered the university to be a sturdy bastion of secularism. Why were so many students crowding into a course that had the words *moral* and *Jesus* in the title? Those who were so surprised had obviously misjudged both the mood of the current student generation and the changing temper of the times. After the course had run for three years, the president of the university took me to a local French restaurant for lunch and asked me to explain what was going on. I told him that there were many factors at work. After all, students were required to take one course in moral reasoning, and as one candid chemistry major explained, when I asked him why he had selected my course rather than one of the others, "Well, I had never heard of that guy Descartes [he pronounced it "des-carteeze"], but Jesus . . . well, at least I'd *heard* of him." Also, at that time no other courses touching on Jesus were offered to Harvard undergraduates (there are now). When I consulted old catalogs I discovered the last course of lectures with "Jesus" in the title had been offered by the late Professor George Santayana, who had left Harvard in 1912. Oddly enough, a course on Jesus was something of a novelty.

The reason for the seventy-year disappearance of Jesus from the Harvard College catalog typifies something that was happening in many other American colleges during those decades. Higher education, even in schools that had been founded by churches, had become more secular and more specialized. Science, rather than theology, had become the queen of the disciplines. Religion was consigned to seminaries and divinity schools. Harvard, which had been founded by pious Puritans, had long since left its religious purpose behind. The Divinity School had been pushed to a remote corner, and the late President James B. Conant even thought seriously about giving it away. "Objectivity" was believed to be the only legitimate approach to teaching anything, and religion — it was thought — could never be taught objectively. I am sure that during those years Jesus was often mentioned in courses on ancient history and in art and music history. But there was no course specifically about him until mine was introduced in 1982. No wonder there was so much student response. In seventy years, quite a backlog of interest had built up.

Soon so many students were signing up that the registrar had to move the lectures to Sanders Theater in the towering red brick Memorial Hall, where crowds gather to hear the Boston Symphony Orchestra and visiting rock bands. When the class got so large, I had to search out unlikely venues for the multiplying section meetings of fifteen students each, some of which I led or attended so I could keep close tabs on what they were thinking. That is why some discussion sections were eventually scheduled for a notorious campus eyesore, an unsightly frame construction that was once the ROTC building. It was a depressing setting, a nondescript frame edifice stuck between the zoology lab, an abandoned nuclear accelerator, and a parking lot on the farthest edge of the Harvard campus. It was an allegedly temporary structure, which the university had been promising to tear down ever since I was a student, but had not gotten around to demolishing. Still, it eventually became the place where some of the most memorable moments in my life as a teacher took place.

Jesus and the Moral Life was my first sortie into teaching undergraduates, most of them between seventeen and twenty-two years of age. Previously I had worked mainly with graduate students. At first this made me apprehensive. I wanted to connect the material I was teaching to their lives, but the fast-paced youth culture they inhabited seemed foreign and a little intimidating to me. The songs I knew were not theirs, but the ones their parents sang. The movies they saw were the ones I avoided. The last rock group I appreciated was the Beatles. I was not at all sure I could talk about Jesus in a way that would make any sense in their world.

As soon as the course started, however, I lost my misgivings and began to look forward to the class meetings, especially the discussion sections. The students were highly likable. Yes, the faculty required them to take one course in moral reasoning, but they were scarcely an immoral lot. They were bright, talkative, hard-working, and extremely intent on "doing the right thing." They did not exhibit the symptoms of some widespread moral crisis. Still, I could tell they felt puzzled. Their courses in cultural anthropology, philosophy, psychology, history, and sociology had led many of them to believe that morality was a "sometimes" thing. It varied from age to age, from society to society, and from person to person. Who are we to question the relaxed sexual customs of South Sea islanders, or the mores of the Neskilik Eskimos who encouraged their old people to wander off to die in the snow? How can we sit in judgment on the Roman legions that razed Jerusalem or the conquistadors who burned Tenochtitlán? Why should we find fault in classmates whose "personal lifestyle" includes taking drugs or sexual promiscuity, as long as they don't bother us or cause us to violate our own consciences? At least in science courses students were encouraged to be rigorously honest observers and not to tweak the data. But in the laboratories they also quickly picked up the widespread, though sometimes tacit, opinion held by some in the scientific community that people engaged in research should not worry too much over the possible applications of their experiments. In short, they were receiving an excellent, but amoral — *not* immoral — education.

All the same, the students themselves strongly felt that something was missing. "I just *know* genital mutilation is wrong. I know it, but I can't tell you why," said a typical senior in one of the discussion sections in that obsolete ROTC depot. These students, like increasing numbers of people in the modern world, sensed — however vaguely — that there was something fundamentally inadequate about moral relativism. They were sickened by the devastation some technologies have wreaked on nature. They winced at the posturing of politicians and the deceptions of the media. They recognized that advertising is saturated with calculated sham. Still, when it came to sorting through real ethical choices in conversation with other people, they seemed awkward and stifled. When they tried to locate a common moral vocabulary, they stammered and squirmed, then often just gave up. Sometimes they shook their heads and settled for, "Well, it all depends on where you're coming from." But the next minute they realized that some things — torturing children, for example — were "just plain wrong" no matter *where* you were coming from. They resented anyone else trying to impose their ethical standards on them, and most were reluctant to impose theirs on someone else. "Live and let live" was their Golden Rule. In short, they were what I would call benevolent but uncomfortable relativists.

But they were also restless about where such benevolent relativism leads. Genital mutilation was an easy target. Of course, no one in any of my classes ever defended it. But how do we discuss issues that are much closer to home? Bill Gates was a kind of folk hero for many of them. However, when a newspaper article reported that his personal wealth (about $46 billion at the time) was more than the entire wealth of the lowest 40 percent of American families, some felt that was wrong. Others did not: Hadn't he earned it? They argued a short while, but then gave up. Not only could they not agree, they were stymied about *how* they could even discuss such a question. Is it enough just to say, "This goes against my gut feeling"? Should they try to persuade a friend to have (or not have) an abortion? What right do we have to tell the Brazilians not to destroy their rain forests or the Pakistanis not to test nuclear weapons? Are terrorism and torture wrong in all circumstances, or just in some? Above all, how are we to come to any decisions as a nation if "it all depends on where you're coming from"?

Still, there was something likable and innocent about the students. If they were confused relativists, they were certainly gentle ones. They loved to make fun of the hype they saw in TV commercials. But, above almost anything else, they loathed the thought of being looked upon as judgmental or "holier than thou." The virtue they admired most was tolerance. They were living examples of the old Native American adage, "Never judge a man until you have walked a mile in his moccasins," which implies, of course, that after that mile you will not want to judge him at all.

We are all fortunate that tolerance, at least on paper, is a widely accepted virtue in America. There are many places on earth where it is not. In a society as mixed as ours, without tolerance we would constantly be at each other's throats. It is a sine qua non. But a thoughtful and mature approach to the moral life requires something more than tolerance. It pushes us from insisting on the "right to decide" to considering what *is* the right thing to decide. The students were grappling with this slippery transition. Like many adults I know, they were alert and articulate on many subjects, but they lapsed into incoherence when they tried to discuss moral choices — whether about cloning or the death penalty or world hunger or euthanasia — with people who did not share their own religious or secular starting points. I was grateful that they wanted to "do the right thing," but I was also glad they were coming to realize that a nation with 250 million separate moral codes is an impossibility, and a world with 6 billion individuals each doing his or her own thing would become unlivable.

The students who had a serious religious commitment were not much better off than the rest. They seemed to have a clearer notion of what was right or wrong *for them,* and in most cases thought it was right for everyone. But even in such instances they were usually reluctant to impose that belief, especially by law. They also found it hard to explain why anyone else should follow such a moral practice voluntarily without at the same time buying into the religious premises on which it was grounded. So when it came to the question of how their own religiously based ethical standards could operate in a religiously and morally pluralistic world, they were just as puzzled as the others. In the end, even the most religious students had to settle for a kind of mutual tolerance, do-no-harm stance, which they increasingly recognized was important but just not enough.

As soon as I began to teach the course I discovered something I should have known all along: Students are not so different from the rest of us. We all often have difficulty finding our moral bearings in a world that forces us to make decisions our ancestors never had to face. They had to make ethical choices too, of course, but they did not have genetic engineering, nuclear weapons, organ transplants, the Internet, or morning-after pills. I also learned during the course that the faculty's guess had been correct: Many people — and not all of them conventionally religious — believe that Jesus of Nazareth should somehow help us to make good moral choices, but they are puzzled about how to find the connection.

There is no generation gap here. We all need to think clearly about today's changed moral environment and to reexamine how, or whether, religion relates to this new situation. Many of our fore-bears lived in fairly homogeneous communities in which morals were guided by tradition. But today all of us — whether we are seventeen or seventy — live in a world of competing and conflicting codes of behavior. The traditional ethical signposts are not as clear as they once were; nevertheless, there is still a persistent belief that knowing more about Jesus might help, especially if he does not need to be understood within a constricting theological framework. The problem is how to do it.

As we grapple with this question, it makes little difference whether we are personally religious or not, whether we are old or young or in the middle. We are all in the same boat. We need a fresher and wider conversation about religion and moral choices, and about how the two relate.

I was determined the students in the course should have a chance to thrash through real-life moral decisions with each other, so in addition to attending my lectures they all took part in a small weekly discussion section. These sometimes furiously animated sessions gave students a forum to explore what "doing the right thing" might mean in their own lives. They also enabled these normally articulate students to practice finding the words to discuss their varying views about moral questions. While they were hostile to know-it-all moral absolutism, they were equally frustrated with the limp moral relativism they saw around them. They wanted something else. And they expected, or at least hoped, that by exploring the life and teachings of Jesus in a setting with no holds barred and no questions excluded, they just might find some help in making sound decisions while avoiding both inflexibility and flabbiness.

The class was a microcosm of the world. It was usually evenly divided between men and women. Some came from well-to-do families, but most — due to the university's generous scholarship program — came from modest homes. Some were raised by devout parents, but many were not. In addition to those from Christian backgrounds, many Hindus, Jews, Muslims, Buddhists, and agnostics (and at least one student who claimed to have invented his own religion) signed up. They came from Santa Barbara and Bangor, from St. Petersburg and Seattle, and from several different countries, including Brazil, Nigeria, and the People's Republic of China. They represented a broad variety of ethnic and racial groups. Some brought at least a degree of familiarity with the life of Jesus to the course, but others knew virtually nothing about the Bible. It was a mixed and motley group. Still, they all seemed eager to escape the moral confusion around them, and they had all enrolled in a course on Jesus and the moral life. So we had at least a couple of things in common.

Some of the students had heard that the answer to virtually any moral dilemma could be found simply by asking, "What would Jesus do?" Most had also come to realize that this formula doesn't always work. Because he lived twenty centuries ago and in very different circumstances, Jesus never had to face many of the vexing choices they did. They were aware that the centuries separating Jesus from us constitute a real quandary. But during the course they learned that Jesus was a rabbi, and that he did not just hand out answers. Rather, he demonstrated a way of approaching moral decisions that they could use themselves. They saw that if we draw on the powers of our imagination, as Jesus made people do with his cryptic sayings and piercing parables, his message does indeed say something important to us today. The question is how we translate his method and his message into our current idiom.

In recent years myriad volumes have appeared about the "search for the historical Jesus," but this is not one of them. If anything, it is almost the opposite: It is about a "search for the contemporary Jesus." Its purpose is to bring to light for the twenty-first century the moral significance of a man who lived two thousand years ago. Therefore, the plan of the book is quite straightforward. The chapters follow the life of Jesus as it is recounted in the four Gospels, from the Christmas narratives to the Easter accounts. The book focuses on the stories he himself told and the stories other people told about him. It recalls how my students tried to think through the moral choices they were facing in the light of these stories, which they did — again like most people — sometimes with puzzlement and suspicion, sometimes with appreciation, but always with intense curiosity. It describes how their varied and often unexpected responses enlarged and deepened my own thinking. And it recounts how, in the light of these very old stories, we confronted a range of very contemporary choices. These were decisions they were already facing or ones they knew they would soon encounter — choices we all face, one way or another, as life unfolds.

My hope for this book is that it will reach far beyond Harvard Yard and spark a much more inclusive exploration, that it will open a door for readers of all ages and all religious backgrounds, or none, to become co-searchers in this urgent quest. It does not assume any more knowledge of religion or the Bible than most of my students had. But it invites anyone who is equally dissatisfied with both moralistic fundamentalism and do-your-own-thing relativism to take a fresh look at a certain first-century rabbi from an obscure corner of the Roman Empire called Galilee. His life is sometimes described as the most important single moral influence in history, but the actual nature of that influence is frequently difficult to discern. The premise of this book is that despite all the sacred formulas and pious bumper stickers, and behind all the doctrines and dogmas about him, rightly understood, that Galilean still has a powerful, even imperative, moral significance for our times.

He Was Then, We Are Now

TWENTY CENTURIES — sixty generations — have passed since Jesus of Nazareth lived. The people who met or heard him then numbered only in the hundreds, or a few thousand at most. The Romans did not consider him significant enough to record his execution in their annals. He wrote no books. No monuments were erected in his memory. Yet today countless people believe that he has an important moral significance, not just for his time, but for ours as well. Still, they are often perplexed and frustrated about just what that significance is. Many experts, from TV evangelists to university researchers, claim in self-assured tones to speak authoritatively about Jesus. But they have so many different and conflicting interpretations of him, they cannot all be right.

One way I tried to close the then/now gap was to introduce the students to a number of recent figures for whom Jesus was the principal inspiration. We studied Gandhi, who never became a Christian but tried to base his life on the Sermon on the Mount. We read about Martin Luther King, who found in Jesus the model for his own nonviolence and a racially inclusive community. We talked about Dorothy Day, the founder of the Catholic Worker Movement, who tried her best to follow Jesus' pattern of poverty and simplicity. I told the class about Dietrich Bonhoeffer, the German pastor whose determination to follow Jesus in Nazi Germany led him to join the conspiracy to assassinate Hitler and who was hanged by the Gestapo just hours before the Americans arrived at his concentration camp in Flossenburg. Many students chose to write their term papers on one of these twentieth-century disciples of Jesus. In a world full of celebrity idols with oversize clay feet, they seemed to be looking for credible moral heroes. Jesus obviously provided a powerful example of someone who took the side of the dispossessed, spoke truth to power, and was willing to pay the price of his convictions.

But there was still something missing. Even the most thoughtful students had a hard time finding in Jesus' life and teaching much concrete guidance in making the day-to-day decisions they faced. One day a candid junior who was active in the local Lutheran church asked me a simple question: "Why does nearly everyone we study in this course end up getting crucified, shot, or hanged?" He was referring to Jesus, Gandhi, King, and Bonhoeffer. But he was not being flip. He told me he had no ambition to get rich or famous, and that he was genuinely inspired by Jesus' concern for the outcast people of his day. But, he said, he did want to find a satisfying job someday, get married, raise a family, and be a good citizen of his community and of the world. Naturally, he wanted to do the right thing. But he did not feel up to confronting the Roman legions.

Sometimes the most devout students told me they prayed to Jesus for guidance about their choices, and I believe they did. But when they looked to him as a living example of how to make moral decisions, they were often puzzled. The Sermon on the Mount seemed compelling to them, and I am sure many would have at least tried to "turn the other cheek," and even to love their enemies. But were they really supposed to take Jesus' admonition literally, sell everything they had, and give it to the homeless people in Harvard Square? Did I seriously expect them to "take no thought for the morrow," as Jesus taught, when I had assigned term papers and scheduled a final exam? In short, they found Jesus powerfully attractive, but it was hard to make a moral connection with him.

It was not just the Christians who found Jesus both appealing and puzzling. The Jewish students who knew their own religion recognized him as a fellow Jew in the tradition of the prophets, like Isaiah and Jeremiah. Buddhists immediately saw him as a *bodhisattva*, one who chooses to forgo entering nirvana so he can help all sentient creatures to do so as well. Muslims also considered him one of the prophets and frequently reminded me that he receives a prominent role in the Qur'an. They all considered him a virtually incomparable model of courage and self-sacrifice. But as a guide to thinking through today's issues, he seemed somehow unavailable. A middle-aged visiting scholar from India, a Hindu economist who audited the course, once told me he found Jesus extraordinarily admirable and could well understand why Gandhi had followed his example. Like the mahatma, he said, he also had a picture of Jesus on the wall of his room. But, he added, the life of Jesus had ended at the age of thirty-three. He had never entered what the Hindus call the "householder" stage of life, nor the ascetic or "sunyasi" phase, which comes with advanced years. How could one follow him into one's fifties and sixties and beyond? Since I myself was entering that last phase I knew immediately what he was saying. Still, I saw little point in telling him that the German philosopher Friedrich Nietzsche had once speculated about the same question and had suggested that if Jesus had not died so young, he might eventually have outgrown his youthful exuberance, calmed down, and become a different kind of person. Who knows? Still, it is hard to imagine Jesus collecting Social Security or playing shuffleboard in Fort Lauderdale.

During the years I was teaching the course many people hoped that the widely heralded "Jesus seminar" and the search for the "historical Jesus" might produce an answer to the mystery of who he really was. Now, they thought, at last they could know the true Jesus, shorn of all those confusing myths and legends. But they were quickly disappointed, the more so since the project appeared at first to be such a promising one. There are, however, understandable reasons for both its waxing and its waning. The "Jesus seminar" began with an intriguing question: What can we say about Jesus if we restrict ourselves solely to currently accepted methods of historical research? What profile of him emerges if we scrape away the many layers of myth that have encrusted his figure over the centuries? What happens if we treat the New Testament Gospels no differently from other contemporary ancient sources, such as the Dead Sea Scrolls and the Gnostic Gospel of Thomas? What is added when we turn to the archaeology of ancient Palestine; what can anthropology teach us about the structure of colonized peasant societies like the one Jesus lived in? It sounded like an exciting enterprise that might yield a morally relevant Jesus, at least for those who wanted to emulate him. For a few years this quest for the historical Jesus captured much of the class's, and the public's, attention.

There is little doubt that the notoriety many weekly newsmagazines and TV shows lavished on the project helped make it more widely known. The media had previously suspected that featuring stories about Jesus was a guaranteed way to win readers and viewers, and they were right. Even after two thousand years, Jesus of Nazareth remains an enormously fascinating figure and continues to be an integral part of the collective human psyche in large parts of the world. This is true whether or not one is a Christian or even conventionally religious. Atheists and agnostics have written appreciative books on Jesus. Nearly everyone believes he *ought* to have some moral significance, but much confusion and conflict remains about just what it should be, and about what "following Jesus" in this or that situation would actually mean. Much of this disagreement has arisen from the radically different portraits of him that interpreters have made over the years: the gentle carpenter, the fiery prophet, the divine lover, the miraculous healer, and the pale mystic. In recent years Jesus has even appeared as a rock singer in *Jesus Christ Superstar,* a circus clown in *Godspell,* the husband of Mary Magdalene in *The Da Vinci Code,* and a helpless victim beaten to a bloody pulp in *The Passion of the Christ.* But many people wondered still, who was he *really?* Now, with the scientific historians of the Jesus seminar eagerly at work, perhaps this question would at last be answered. No wonder the public was fascinated.

In addition, we live in an era of spins and cover stories, of doctored accounts and "now it can be told" journalism. People often discount official versions of anything and suspect they are being deceived or duped. Consequently, when ordinary people learned, not from the pulpit but from the local kiosk, that the biblical Gospels were written many years after the events they describe, that they were pieced together from earlier sources, and that they were edited for particular audiences, they wanted to find out "the inside story." Now the Jesus seminar's quest for the historical Jesus, which hit its stride during the early 1990s, was there with the answers. It assured the public that thanks to carbon dating, computer databases, and a strictly scientific approach to the question, at last we could know who the "real Jesus" was. Naturally the public curiosity was kindled. At a time when historical revisionists were overturning previously sacred versions of everything from the legends of Jesse James to the Vietnam War, the public's fascination with the search for the "Jesus of history" was understandable. Besides, it sold lots of magazines. So why did the disappointment set in so quickly?

It soon became obvious that the historians carrying on the quest were coming to a bewildering set of contradictory conclusions about who Jesus really was. Some depicted him as a wandering sage, others as a charismatic preacher, and still others as a religiously inspired social revolutionary. Their disagreement baffled and annoyed those who believed the search was a genuinely scientific undertaking, the religious equivalent of the genome project, and that it would produce a clear and final answer. But it turned out that the answer to the question, "Who was this Jesus, really?" was as hard to answer as it had ever been. Why had such a mountainous scholarly effort produced such a molehill of results?

This impatient dismissal of the historical Jesus project was not entirely fair. Despite widespread discrepancies among the researchers, some things were not contested. All agreed that Jesus really had existed, and that he was a first-century Palestinian Jew living under the heel of a Roman occupation that — like many such occupations before and since — had split its captive people into feuding sects and warring factions. They also agreed that he was a rabbi who taught the imminent coming of the kingdom of God, and gained a following as a teacher and a healer in Galilee, especially among the landless and destitute, but that he aroused the ire of the nervous ruling religious circles and the tense Roman authorities. When he and some of his followers arrived in Jerusalem for the Passover holidays he caused a stir in the Temple, was arrested, interrogated, and executed by crucifixion, a form of death by torture reserved by the Romans for those suspected of subverting their imperial rule. But after his death, his followers insisted that he had appeared to them alive, and they continued to spread his message even in the face of harsh persecution.

Beyond this tiny historical capsule of raw data there is an ocean of additional material about Jesus that does not pass muster with scientific historians. Much of it is in the Bible itself. But there are also teachings and sayings attributed to Jesus and stories about him in the sources called the apocryphal Gospels that the early Christians chose not to include in the New Testament. There are also numerous legends about Jesus — for example, that he journeyed to India or Tibet or Japan during the "silent years" between his twelfth birthday and the three years preceding his early death, a period the Gospels simply skip over. But there is no historical evidence whatever for any of these intriguing travelogues. The sum of the matter is that although we do know something about the "historical Jesus," meaning the bare facts that can be uncovered by contemporary historical research, this method does not yield very much, and probably never will. Even carbon dating and archaeology have their limits. Still, the search for the historical Jesus had not really failed. It had done much of what it set out to do. It had simply not lived up to its inflated advance billings or the exaggerated expectations of its audience.

This is not, however, the main reason why the celebrated quest for the historical Jesus frustrated so many people. It was disappointing not because it produced so little, but because what little it produced seemed so irrelevant. It not only uncovered Jesus as a historical figure, it also *left* him as one. Paradoxically, this subverts what the same scholars believe was the central message of the historical Jesus. They all agree that Jesus insisted his hearers respond to the presence of God in the "here and now." The best that historical reconstruction can do, however, is to leave Jesus in the "there and then." He is still the robed, bearded figure of the Sunday school books and the Jesus movies — romantic, tragic, heroic — but no closer to us than Socrates or Julius Caesar. He is fascinating but inaccessible, living in a strange world very different from ours, grappling with issues unlike those we confront.

Despite the failure of the quest for the historical Jesus to satisfy the unrealistic expectations it engendered, some people continue to hope that eventually historical research — one more frayed old scroll dug out of one more cave — will clarify who Jesus really was. Others still think that asking, "What would Jesus do in this situation?" will resolve any dilemma. The problem with the first hope is that, except for the barest essentials, historians will always disagree about Jesus, and a whole cave full of scrolls will not tell us for sure who he "really was." Consequently, when we read their differing accounts of his life or see a film or TV show about him, we often feel we are catching a fleeting glimpse of an elusive, distant figure on the other side of a wide abyss. The problem with simply asking what Jesus would do is that we grapple with many choices today that Jesus never had to face, so trying to speculate on what he would do when faced with a controversial modern dilemma is anyone's guess. The students in the course knew this all too well. They recognized that Jesus never had to endure a series of exhausting job interviews, cope with an unintended pregnancy, or (as far as we know) weigh the consequences of breaking up with a girlfriend. Looking ahead in their own lives, they knew Jesus never had to worry about a fifteen-year-old son he suspected might be taking drugs, or decide how to tell his parents about a sweetheart they would surely not approve of, or agonize over whether to place his failing mother Mary in a retirement community, or consent to disconnecting his father Joseph's life-support system if the cancer had spread to all his organs. On issues like humanitarian military intervention, reproductive cloning, or doctor-assisted suicide, students could find no clear answers in his life and teaching — or else they found a range of conflicting ones. Try as they would, they continued to see Jesus on the other side of a wide chasm. He was still then, and they were clearly now.

These students were not alone. Similar questions stalk anyone who lives in a society without a widely accepted moral frame of reference. Many thoughtful people now insist that we should "put values back into education." They may be right. But if we do, whose values shall we teach? *Which* morality: that of the American Civil Liberties Union, or that of the Christian Coalition? In a Jewish Yeshiva, an Evangelical Christian college, or an Islamic Qur'an school these questions answer themselves. But even then, one has to ask how students and adults who learn these religion-based codes will fare in a wider, pluralistic world in which tensions between different religions and value systems often contribute to the discord.

Students do not live on another planet. As they struggled to converse about moral decisions, I heard echoes of the same goodwill and the same confusion one might detect in conversations overheard in restaurants, at family gatherings, on TV panels, at the pizza shack, and at the neighborhood bar. All of us, whether adolescents or adults, are up against the same predicament. We are trying to "do the right thing" in an age in which the old road maps don't persuade everyone, and sometimes don't even persuade us. But what is the "right thing," and is Jesus any help in discerning it?

I think the people who believe Jesus has an important moral relevance for the twenty-first century are right, despite the wide historical ravine that separates his time from ours. But I also believe we have tried to discover that relevance mostly in the wrong way. Little by little I have become convinced that there are two key components to bridging the chasm between him and us, and that the two are closely linked.

The first is to remember that even before acquiring the rich array of titles Christian history has assigned to him — Lord, Master, Savior, Lamb of God, and many others — Jesus was a rabbi. He taught and applied Torah, the Jewish law, albeit in an unprecedented historical situation and with an original twist. He never delivered an easy answer to a hard question but, in time-honored rabbinical fashion, asked another question or told one of his unforgettable stories. He would not allow people to escape the responsibility of making their own decisions. Instead he enlisted them in a way of thinking that would nurture and extend their moral insight. This is exactly what the best rabbis have always done, and still do.

The second key to spanning the gap between Jesus and ourselves is to recognize that while he passed on the moral tradition of his own people in the light of novel demands, he did so by relying more on narrative and example than on precept and principle. He realized that the missing dimension in nearly all moral reflection is imagination. Of course we need reasoning to lead a moral life, but we need — even more — the capacity to intuit what is important and what is not, to envision alternative possibilities, and to see beyond what sometimes appears to be an impasse. We need to appreciate not just how other people see things but how they feel about them, and to do this our most potent resource is still the human imagination, awakened by compelling narratives.

It is not impossible to bridge the gap between Jesus and ourselves. The secret lies in recovering the link between the rabbinic story-teller on the one hand, and our own human imaginations on the other. Taken together, these two elements can still make him our contemporary and jog the slumbering moral consciousness of our times.

Rabbi Jesus on the Scene

One of the Pharisees, called Nicodemus, a member of the Sanhedrin, came to him by night. "Rabbi," he said, "we know you are a teacher sent by God; no one could perform these signs of yours unless God were with him." — JOHN 3:1

THE QUEST for the historically verifiable Jesus still leaves us peering across a wide chasm. The Nazarene remains a first-century man. We are left with the problem of how he can become our contemporary, and whether his teachings and his example — his moral wisdom — can speak to us in the twenty-first century. This is a question the search for the historical Jesus should never have been expected to answer. But the core of the portrait that emerged from that search — that Jesus was a rabbi — does help us take the next step.

Far too few people are aware that Jesus was a rabbi. Forgetting this important fact about him began within a few years of his death, when so many Gentiles began to pour into the movement he had started that they soon far outnumbered the Jews who had been his first followers. As the movement spread from Palestine throughout the Greco-Roman Mediterranean basin, the people who were joining knew little and cared less about rabbis. They tried to understand him in terms drawn from their own culture. They have bequeathed us a rich array of symbolic interpretations.

There is no reason to discard these ancient appellations, such as the "divine logos" or "being of one substance with God." They demonstrate how people in other ages understood and responded to him, as do the more recent interpretations of Jesus that have arisen among Christians in Africa and Asia, where he is referred to as a cosmic ancestor or as an expression of the *tao*. This in turn helps us understand the relevance of Jesus for our own time and place. But it does not mean that we should be searching for some moral lowest common denominator. What years of discussing Jesus and the moral life with students from a wide variety of backgrounds taught me is that we do not need doctrinal agreement on Jesus to confirm his moral validity. But it also taught me that we lose something vital if we merely jettison these doctrines and images. They all have a story to tell. Still, the time has come to recognize again that long before this luxuriant history of religious interpretations began, Jesus was a rabbi. He spent his earthly days interpreting and applying Torah, the Jewish law, mainly by telling stories and by living his own life as a vivid demonstration of what he taught.

Jesus was neither the first nor the last rabbi. We have to understand him not just against the *background* of the Jewish law and religious practices of his day, which the historical Jesus researchers have done extremely well, but also through the *foreground* of the two thousand years of rabbinical teaching and storytelling that have passed since. Familiarity with this venerable Jewish tradition reminds us that rabbinical moral reasoning is an ongoing enterprise. The Talmud is made up of texts, commentaries, and commentaries on the commentaries, all directed toward helping people make decisions in the light of an ongoing moral tradition. And the process continues today. If we want to discover the morally relevant Jesus, this is where we must start, but it is only a preliminary step.

Rabbis tell stories, stories are narratives, and narratives awaken the imagination. Still, although the imagination is an indispensable factor in the moral life, most writing and teaching on ethics leave it out completely. Instead they focus on the idea of virtue or on principles and values, all of which are important in their own way. What is often missing is the most fundamental question: What kind of person do I want to be? Answering this requires the capacity to put oneself in situations one has never experienced, to see and especially to *feel* a moral question from the viewpoint of people of a different class or race or gender or age, even from a different historical era.

When it comes to a moral dilemma, any moral dilemma, we always face three steps. The first is the most important: We must recognize it as a moral issue, not just an investment decision, or a clinical issue, or a political choice. The second step is to find an answer to the question: What should I do? Then comes the third, and undoubtedly the hardest step: to summon the courage to do it. A well-cultivated imagination can inform all these steps. It helps us recognize the moral issues wrapped in all kinds of choices. It helps clarify what the right choice is, and it motivates us to take the action that choice calls for. But how do we acquire and nurture such an imagination?

This is where stories and the imagination come in. The Jewish philosopher Edith Wyschogrod has observed that, for all their importance, neither ethical principles nor moral theories actually *motivate* anyone. What motivates people are stories, narratives, accounts of situations in which choices must be made and stands taken. In a perceptive discussion of the significance of literature for ethics, the philosopher Martha Nussbaum writes that narratives tell us "to notice this and not that, to be active in these and not those ways." They lead us into "certain postures of the mind and not others." Narratives speak to the inner spirit. They link the moral reasoning we do in our heads to the courage and empathy that must come from the heart. In short, they help us to become the people we want to be.

This clarifies the connection between Jesus the rabbi and the moral imagination. He spent his brief lifetime telling stories and enacting them. Even his provocative entry into Jerusalem and his death by torture became part of the narrative of his life. Meeting him always seemed to shake people up. He constantly pushed them to think beyond their own immediate interests, to picture themselves in a variety of situations in which choice and action were required — in short, to use their imaginations. What do you do when you find a stranger lying bleeding by the roadside; when no guests show up for your big banquet; when a sassy and rebellious son you thought had left for good shows up on your doorstep broke? Jesus also put people in uncomfortable situations by the way he lived. He violated the social and religious taboos of his day. He ate with people a respectable rabbi was not supposed to eat with. He kept company with shady characters and social deviants. He lived in such a way that anyone who encountered him had to reexamine the meaning of life and look at the world from a new point of view. His words were deeds and his deeds were words.

But this is still just the beginning. To understand the relevance of Jesus for the issues of *our* day, we do have to grasp how he responded to the issue of *his own* time. This is where the historical Jesus researchers have been extremely helpful, because we also have to know, to use a favorite phrase of my students, "where he was coming from." Jesus was indeed a first-century Palestinian Jew living under Roman occupation. But it was as a rabbi that he had to cope both with the Roman tyrants and with the destructive divisions among his own people. He was no stranger to moral chaos, political rancor, and religious strife. That is *who* Jesus was and *where* he was. But where was Jesus "coming from"?

Jesus was coming from the ancient religious tradition of his own people. Each year at Passover he undoubtedly celebrated the exodus from Egypt at a seder dinner with his family. The Gospels report that he went to synagogue on the Sabbath "as was his custom," but not just to pray. He also went to teach. He was so familiar with the prophets like Jeremiah and Amos and Isaiah that he linked his own calling with theirs. Like many of us, as a child he may have had to memorize the Ten Commandments, which biblical scholars see as the distillation of the entire Jewish moral and religious tradition. The "Lord's Prayer" that he taught his followers was actually a familiar Jewish prayer. To understand him we have to read more than the Gospels. We have to become aware of both Jewish life in the first century and what Christians now call the Old Testament, the only "Bible" Jesus ever knew.

When we become familiar with Jesus' Bible, we can see why the Gospels do not provide all the concrete ethical guidelines people often expect to find in them: Both Jesus and most of his hearers *were already aware* of these guidelines. Rabbi that he was, Jesus had no interest in introducing a new law. In fact, he insisted that "not even one jot or tittle" of the old one was to be abrogated. But as a rabbi, Jesus took another step. He spun out parables and told stories to demonstrate the *present* reality of something close to the heart of the Jewish tradition called the "reign of God," which most Jews at the time believed would begin only with the coming of the Messiah. The concept of the reign of God is central to his life and teaching, but he did not invent the idea. He obviously assumed that most of his hearers already knew what he was referring to. What Jesus added was that this long-expected time of God's presence in daily life was now dawning. It was no longer to be postponed. Rather it was here and now, "in the midst of you," demanding an urgent and immediate response, though it was still partial and still hidden. It was no longer something you could only wait and pray for. It was something you looked for in the world around you, even in the most unlikely places.

Jesus does provide an excellent example of moral reasoning, but not in the way most people expect. He forced people to think for themselves by using stories and what we might now call case studies. Like the generations of rabbis who came after him, he did not offer answers that would apply to everyone and for all time. Nor was he interested in general moral theory. He dealt with issues on a case-by-case basis. In this respect Jesus was much like the rabbis who composed the Talmud. They also were not interested in theoretical questions, and their arguments often ended not with a single answer but with the opinions of two or even more rabbis. Usually when anyone asked Jesus a hypothetical question, he responded in typical rabbinical style with an anecdote or — just as rabbinical — with another question. He used his stories to make people grapple with moral issues, but not in a vacuum. He expected them to think about these questions in the light of both the moral tradition and the life trajectory that had brought them to this decision. Both Jesus and the rabbis assumed that anyone who is drawn into such a process learns something invaluable and is in a better position to make informed choices in the future. Also, since no two human situations are identical, every answer is by its nature a provisional one. The next situation one meets might be somewhat similar, but sufficiently different to warrant a quite different response. The answer to any moral dilemma is important, but it is not as important as the *way* one learns to respond. There will be another moral quandary tomorrow, and another the next day.

Once the importance of imagination is brought back into moral reasoning, it is possible to look at the simplistic formula "What would Jesus do?" in a new light. If it means trying to mimic Jesus' behavior in some mechanical way (he did this, so I should do that), this formula clearly does not work very well as a moral guideline. There are just too many decisions it does not encompass. But if it means combining the rabbinical insight that no two cases are exactly the same with the exercise of moral imagination, then the question "What would Jesus do?" does make some sense. It pushes us, as Jesus pushed his listeners, to put ourselves in unfamiliar, even threatening, situations. It requires us to look again and again at not just what Jesus himself did, but at what those who have been touched by his life and message have done over the years.

Looking at the life of Jesus makes it clear that stories were the principal means he relied on to evoke effective moral engagement. I think that stories are just as powerful a technique today. But one troubling question remains. If Jesus was indeed a rabbi, rooted in the Jewish tradition, what made him so popular and at the same time so controversial?

Jesus became divisive for at least two reasons. First, as Gandhi once observed, he not only taught, he also followed his own teachings. He insisted that God — not Caesar, not Herod, and not the priestly elite — was the only real source of moral authority, and he acted out this conviction in such a provocative way that the ruling powers decided they had to eliminate him. In addition, Jesus taught that all people, including those who had not been born within the Jewish tradition, could play an equal part in the human moral enterprise. This offended some, though probably a minority, of his fellow Jews. But it eventually became one of the sources of the disagreement that resulted in the division between what we now call (but no one did then) Christianity and Judaism; that is, between those Jews and Gentiles who followed him (only later called Christians) and the Jews who did not.

The apostle Paul, one of the most prominent voices in early Christianity, was also a widely respected teacher of the Jewish law. He echoed Jesus' emphasis on welcoming the outsiders in slightly different words. He wrote in his Epistle to the Romans that although the Jews do indeed have the Law, the Gentiles have the same thing "through their own innate sense." The Law is, he says, "engraved on their hearts." Paul, of course, had never met a Buddhist or a Hindu. He had no way of knowing that not only had God inscribed the Law in the hearts of distant peoples, but that these peoples had also inscribed it in their own sacred books and codes, their own equivalents to the Torah. For Jesus and for Paul, there was a luminous core within their own Jewish religious tradition that pointed beyond itself.

Jesus' belief in a common human moral capacity is often misunderstood. He did not teach some abstract universal moral code. Nor did he mean that now everyone could, in effect, become Jews in an ethical sense. In speaking to his fellow Jews, he often held up Gentiles as exemplars of the moral life, a practice some of his hearers resented, although Jewish sages have taught the same thing many times. For example, he once said of a Roman centurion, "I have not found faith like this in all of Israel." His famous story of the Good Samaritan cast a religiously suspect man in the role of moral prototype. He seemed to believe that the interaction of peoples from different traditions need not result in moral confusion. It should be welcomed because it could itself become a stimulus to faith and morality.

This is an important insight for us in our morally and religiously diverse world. When individuals schooled in different spiritual traditions meet, they often come away frustrated by the encounter. Such meetings sometimes push their participants into either a defensive circling of the wagons or a spineless retreat into relativism. The first freezes into a kind of moral fundamentalism; the second melts into skepticism. Both strategies result in the belief that further conversation is pointless, so why bother?

Jesus, however, demonstrated how neither response is necessary. If his example means anything, such cross-cultural encounters should be viewed not as obstacles but as opportunities. He demonstrated this first by entering the actual worlds of the people he met, whether they were despised Roman centurions, avaricious tax collectors, learned Pharisees, or Samaritan women of shady repute drawing water from the town well. Then he engaged them not with arguments (even though this is what some of them wanted), but with conversation, and — of course — with stories. What emerged was neither a behavioral code he wanted to impose nor one they might be trying to defend, but something new — an enlarged moral universe that included both of them. His knack for coping creatively with such polyglot diversity is an important reason why Jesus remains an indispensable example of moral reasoning in our morally multilingual world today.

Once I began to understand Jesus as a rabbi and notice the critical role imagination played in his life, the hulking ROTC building where we held our discussion sections no longer seemed so gloomy. Here were individuals from highly disparate moral and religious traditions, hearing each other out and responding to the stories Jesus told in the light of their own diverse life histories. I think the rabbi from Nazareth would have been delighted. He had, after all, affirmed the validity of his own tradition but also the innate moral capacity of all human beings. And he believed that provoking an animated conversation with different kinds of people was not something to be avoided, but on the contrary could contribute to a shared ethical vision. Further, he believed that kindling the human imagination with engaging stories was the best way to create that moral interface. Let us now step into the fascinating world of those stories.

A World Full of Stories

This is the disciple who is testifying to these things and has written them, and we know his testimony is true. But there are also many other things that Jesus did; if every one of them were written down, I suppose that the whole world itself could not contain the books that would be written. —JOHN 21:24

A WISE JEWISH RABBI named Reb Zebulun once said, "Today we live, but by tomorrow, today will be a story. The whole world, all human life, is one long story." He was right. We live in a world full of stories. Some people go down in history as great storytellers. Others are the kind about whom people tell stories. Only a few people are both, and Rabbi Jesus was one of them. The four Gospels are the main source both of stories by Jesus and of stories about him. They are like collections of pearls strung together on a narrative string. About half of their content consists of the words of Jesus, and the other half of what other people said about him. For centuries, however, just what *kind* of literature the Gospels are has been a matter of continuing dispute.

I grew up in a small town in Pennsylvania. My parents, who were not themselves churchgoers, sent my brother and sister and me to the Baptist Sunday school next door. There I was taught by earnest Sunday school teachers to think of the Gospels as historical accounts, like the ones we read in our textbooks at school, only divinely inspired and totally accurate. Later, in college and seminary, I learned from practitioners of the historical-critical approach to the Bible that much of it consists of myth and legend; but that did not bother me as much as it seems to bother literalists. I still loved the stories of the Bible, and besides, at the same time I was studying Sophocles, Shakespeare, Milton, and Herman Melville. They had created stories too, and many of their stories — like the Gospels — were inspired by real historical figures, such as Richard III and King Oedipus. It seemed quite sensible to me that stories did not need to be verbally inspired in order to be taken so seriously that they made a difference in your life. That the Bible is in part a collection of stories, albeit many of them based on history, is no reason to distrust its spiritual validity. In many ways it actually enhances that validity.

This is the approach to the Gospels I used in the course, and I believe it is the best way to discover the moral meaning of Jesus. It is one reason for my dissatisfaction with attempts by so many fine scholars to uncover the definitive picture of the "historical Jesus." The problem is not only that equally well-trained researchers come up with such disparate portraits. It is also that their fealty to the current canons of historical research often inadvertently obscures the story quality of the Gospels. Their project is in part a symptom of the peculiar modern fascination with viewing everything through the lens of a scientific method, which has the unfortunate result of exacerbating our tone deafness to other and subtler ways of grasping reality.

When I stood before a classroom of modern students I soon found I had to cope with this modern deficiency. "What!" they sometimes exclaimed, about one or another biblical narrative. "It's only a *story?*" Once, for example, I mentioned in passing that archaeologists had determined that the ancient city of Jericho never had walls. This meant, I said, that the "tumbling down" of the walls, dramatically recounted in the book of Joshua — and celebrated in song and story — had to be read as a gripping, imaginative re-creation of the Israelite past. It was written, after all, eight centuries after the event it celebrates. I added that learning this had not in the least diminished my confidence in the Bible. In fact, it had enlarged it. An informed reading of the Joshua chronicle plunges one into the spiritual struggles of the Jewish people at a critical moment in their history, not of the time the book depicts, but of the time it was composed. The same thing could be said about Tolstoy's *War and Peace.* It tells us far more about what was going in Tolstoy's Russia at the time he wrote it, half a century after the Napoleonic invasion it portrays. It does not claim to be an accurate chronicle of the war. It is a novel, and therefore it reveals a different but equally valuable picture of the human condition and the Russian spirit in particular.

One student, however, told me after class that he did not agree. If you can't trust the Bible for historical facts, he said, then how can you trust it for religious or moral truth? It was, he believed, all of a piece. I was glad he had brought up the question. I knew it was on the minds of other students as well, but he was the only one who had the courage to raise it, so I asked him to voice it again the next time the class met. As I had anticipated, when he did so many other students agreed with him. This led to a valuable discussion about the many various types of literature found in the Bible and about the relationship between modern conceptions of historiography and other modes of communicating truth. Thank God for students with the cheek to disagree rather than just scrawling things in their notebooks and coughing them back up on exams.

But the class discussion also forced me to ask a more basic question: Why do people often use the phrase "only a story"? Why are many students — and many adults — troubled and upset when they learn that historical writing, as we know it today, only developed in the modern period, and that most of the classics that nourish the human spirit — including the Bible — consist not just of history, but also of poetry, legends, myths, and sagas? Could it be because we have been taken in so often by puffs and cover-ups? We have understandably become so wary of reporters who fake their sources, of duplicitous advertising and campaign handouts, that we want to make sure we are not being hoodwinked yet again. This is why it is important to recognize that the biblical narratives are not mere concoctions. They were not churned out by a public relations office or a marketing division. They represent the selective and imaginative appropriation of the past by generations of people who were trying, as we still do, to make sense of the present and prepare for the future.

There are, of course, thoughtful people who admire, even prefer, stories that have no basis whatever in empirical history. The Italian novelist and critic Umberto Eco, for example, has written that if he were a visitor from another planet, discovering any race that could dream up the story of Christ — "of universal love, of forgiveness for enemies, of life sacrificed that others may be saved" — would fill him with admiration. Even if Christ were only the subject of a great story, he goes on,

> the fact that this story could have been imagined by humans, creatures who know only that they do not know, would be just as miraculous (miraculously mysterious) as the story of a real God being made flesh.

Eco says that such a story would "even move and ennoble the hearts of those who do not believe."

The French-Canadian novelist Yann Martel voices the same idea. He creates characters that squirm with discomfort beneath the primacy of reason in modern Western life, because it "kills mystery" and produces spiritual hunger. They are looking for God, and almost any god will do. In one of his novels, *Self*, he writes,

> Occasionally I would intuit how much grander the march for life would be if God *were*. At such moments the truth or falsity of God's being seemed irrelevant. It was a fiction of such magnitude, why not believe it? What was gained by a truth that left one with an empty feeling?

In a later work, *Life of Pi*, Martel deliciously inverts the stale plot of the Western youth who goes East to seek spiritual wisdom by making his hero a young South Indian who goes on the quest. But the hero has a similar suspicion. He believes that "agnostics lack imagination and miss the better story."

I sympathize with Eco and Martel. But I cannot agree. The fact that human beings could create such stories, or that they make us feel better, is not quite enough for me. I am too earthbound for that. I need to know that *something* actually happened in the same human history I live in, and that the story I am now reading arose from people trying to make sense of that history. Religion tries to find meaning in the jumble of life. It does not have to be factual. But it has to be true. "True" in a story means something different from "true" in a news account or the lab report. A true story is one that is true to life at its deepest and most complex.

There are, of course, good stories and bad ones. The good stories inspire compassion, hope, and generosity. The bad ones demean or demonize people; or they purport to close questions that should remain open; or they discourage further embellishments, additions, or refinements. This suggests that the people who plead so eloquently for the restoration of myth and story should be more discriminating than they sometimes are. The great twentieth-century scholar of comparative religion, Mircea Eliade, was a persuasive advocate for the "return of myth." But his apparent unwillingness to apply moral criteria to myths resulted in his embrace, in his early years, of the ultranationalist anti-Semitic myth that was rampant in his native Romania at the time.

Religious narratives, like all narratives, can be either toxic or salubrious. But within the larger world of stories they occupy a special place. As with all stories they are sometimes based on historical events, often only dimly remembered by way of legends, songs, and sagas, such as the tales of the patriarchs and kings in the Hebrew scriptures. They are sometimes complete inventions, like the stories of Jonah or Esther, and other times they are the distillation of imaginative visions, like the wheels and chariots of the prophet Ezekiel or the scorpions and dragons of St. John, the writer of the book of Revelation. But what sets religious stories apart from other stories is that they point beyond themselves to a crucial dimension of human existence that defies reduction to empirical proof or disproof. Religious stories are often woven into rituals that enlist not just the mind but also the body and all the senses into the narrative.

They link individuals and communities to vital parameters of life —
pain, death, destiny, meaning, value — in such a way that they provide the most basic sense of direction and orientation. Religious
stories cannot be proven to be true or false by either historical or scientific research. They become untrue when they no longer adequately link a person or a people to this ultimate dimension. This
means that religious stories are sometimes a perplexing genus to
understand in an age that insists on sharp distinctions between the
objective and the subjective, fact and value, prose and poetry. Still,
they provide an indispensable component to what it means to be
truly human, and it is hard to imagine human life without them.

In any case, confronted with the discomfort of my students about
stories, and at a university whose motto is "Veritas," I had to ponder
again the stubborn dilemma of why, in our era, factualness has
become synonymous with truth. Is it because "bits" and "information" are crowding out narrative as the preferred mode of commu-
nication? If that is so, it is bad news indeed. It will eventually lead to
a severe impoverishment of both the mind and the spirit. We need
facts, if only to protect us from frauds, but we also need stories, to
enable us to make sense of the facts.

Jerome Bruner is one of the greatest twentieth-century scholars
of how human beings learn. After years of research he came to
the conclusion that narrative — along with science and logic — is essential to us for organizing our experience. Without narratives we
would not be able to cope with the fragments of segmented information that constantly surge around us. Narratives provide a
framework that enables us to know our world. Without a narrative
thread, the fabric of the world is no more than rags and tatters. It
would make just as much sense, maybe more, to say, "Well, that's
just a fact" rather than "that's just a story."

When bad stories crowd out good ones, soon narrative itself begins to putrefy, but without narrative, moral reasoning becomes impossible. To be able to discern what kind of person you want to be
or what you should do in a given situation, as I discovered with my
students, you have to have some idea of "where you are coming

from." The philosopher Alasdair MacIntyre has suggested that the only way to answer the question, "What am I to do?" is to ask, "Of what story or stories do I find myself a part?" Maybe our obsession with fact is a symptom of something deeper that has gone wrong. It may stem from the increasingly manic pace of modern life and the overload of messages and signals that assail us from every side, day and night, and undermine our capacity to organize the important aspects of our lives. No wonder people have turned in such large numbers to meditation, and are seeking out retreat centers where they can slow down and allow their thoughts and experiences to catch up with each other. Even computers buzz and beep as they take the time they need to process, organize, and retrieve the information bits we pour into them.

Not only is there a glut of stories, they often contradict each other, and — as I discovered with my students — people are often unaware of how the divergent stories that shape their lives affect their opinions on moral issues. This was one of the sources of frustration in our class discussions. Students sometimes left the old ROTC barracks convinced that there was just no point in talking about moral issues. But this is just what I did *not* want to happen, so gradually, and painfully, I devised a way to help them uncover the often hidden sources of their disagreements.

I had noticed that the students were often unknowingly disagreeing at different levels of the dispute, and that consequently their arguments seemed to race past each other and never meet. No wonder they were sometimes exasperated, and simply gave up on the very possibility of moral discourse. But that way leads to relativism and even cynicism, just what the Moral Reasoning division of the core curriculum was supposed to avoid.

The approach I finally turned to is one that helps the parties in any dispute to pause, take a step back, and try at least to agree on where their disagreement lies. It does so by sorting out any disagreement into four levels. The first level was the factual. What exactly is "partial birth abortion"? Who, precisely, is cutting down the trees in the Amazon Valley? Is it or isn't it technically possible to monitor nuclear weapons production? Fortunately, in a research university, the facts were not that hard to come by. But agreeing on the facts was only the beginning of the process.

The second level took us to what is usually taught in most courses on moral reasoning. Is the case you are making consistent and coherent? Is it logical? What are the counterarguments, and how do you respond to them? This, I came to believe, is an essential but — on its own — wholly insufficient approach. It often ends just where the real sources of disagreement begin.

The third level moved us beyond what most conventional moral reasoning courses cover. It focused on loyalties. What, I asked them to consider, are your fundamental life commitments — to family, nation, faith community, ethnic group, gender? How do these loyalties, even if you hold them in varying and changing degrees, influence your thinking about moral questions? I did this not to suggest that loyalties provide sufficient grounds for making a moral choice (intensely loyal Nazis did horrendous things), nor to imply that students should abandon their loyalties, which only produces an isolated individualism. I raised the question to coax to the surface what are often submerged factors in moral disputes, and thus make it a little easier to see where the disagreement actually lay.

But there was also a fourth level, and it often turned out to be the most significant. It was the level of "grand narratives," what some have called "worldviews." This is the level that is most deeply embedded in people, often starting in childhood. It comprises not philosophical concepts, however, but stories. The British theologian Don Cupit has written, "Stories are interpretive resources, models and scenarios through which we make sense of what is happening to us and frame our action. Unlike the forms and concepts of philosophy, stories are stretched out in time . . . They shape the process of life. It is through stories that our social selves, which are our real selves, are actually produced." I would add only that these formative narratives are often buried very deep within us, sometimes in fragments, and we are often unaware of the unspoken implications of our primordial stories.

The students found this fourfold approach valuable. By trying first of all to identify at what level they disagreed with each other on any given issue, they were sometimes able to step back and lower their voices a notch or two. They stopped resembling stags butting their antlers together in a mountain meadow, and the tone of the conversation often became less overwrought. Even if they still could not agree on the issue itself, they drew some satisfaction from finding out why they disagreed. They discovered for themselves what the Indian novelist Arundhati Roy reminds us of in the epigram she cites from John Berger at the beginning of *The God of Small Things*: "Never again will a single story be told as though it's the only one." The students learned they would have to live out their days in a world full of different and often contradictory stories.

The students also made another helpful discovery. They noticed that although with a little effort these levels could be distinguished, in any moral disagreement they were always intertwined, and they influenced each other. Worldviews and loyalties color what counts or does not count as a "fact." But a stubborn irreducible fact will sometimes cause someone to modify a long-held loyalty or even a worldview and the stories that convey it. Comparing narratives can even result at times in a new and composite narrative. This is exactly the way religious narratives have evolved over the centuries. The Bible itself is a composite of narratives that were at times thought to be incompatible. Fortunately, our course was one in which all four levels of moral discourse were in play, and a number of different master narratives were represented. When Hindus and atheists and Muslims discuss the stories of Jesus with Christians, few come out with exactly the same story they went in with.

Still, this approach requires people to be able to tell their stories and to listen to those of others, and this is a skill we have to learn. Does our present oversupply of conflicting stories make it more difficult for us? The German writer and critic Walter Benjamin thought so. In an essay entitled "The Storyteller," Benjamin once wrote, "The art of storytelling is coming to an end." Less and less frequently, he lamented, do we meet people who are really able to tell a story properly. "It is as if something that seemed inalienable to us, the securest among our possessions, were taken away from us: the ability to exchange experiences." Benjamin traced this wasting away of storytelling as an indication that human beings were beginning to lose confidence in their own experience.

This idea in fact became a major theme in twentieth-century philosophy and literature. The reasons for the loss were not hard to understand. In the early decades of the century, millions of young men were thrown onto battlefields where the scale and horror of the weaponry — machine guns, heavy artillery, poison gas — and the scope of the death all around them were so unprecedented that most of them were incapable of grasping what was happening, to say nothing of describing it later. Then worldwide inflation stunned people who learned that the fistfuls of marks or francs they clenched in their hands could not buy even a loaf of bread. Then came another conflict, with its thousand plane raids and atomic bombs, which dwarfed the previous wars. This was followed by the advent of television, which has so diminished the frequency of personal interaction in civil society that what happens on the screen bleaches out what is going on next door.

Still, the picture Benjamin paints seems unduly grim. Perhaps we are not quite that bad off, at least not yet. People still relish a good story. My students could rattle them off easily, when they were about relatively superficial matters. But when it came to conveying their most important experiences to each other, they often lapsed into exasperated silence. This may be what Benjamin had in mind, and it could indeed be ominous. We need to tell our stories to make our own experiences real, not just to others but also to ourselves. Consequently, when we find it harder to make our experiences known to each other, to nourish our urgent human need to confirm and compare our lives, then experience itself shrivels.

This vicious circle contains an especially grave threat to the moral imagination and to moral reasoning. To be the kind of persons we want to be and to make sound moral choices, we need to converse with each other at a deeper-than-ordinary level. We need to be able to recognize a moral dilemma when it appears. We need to be able to tell ourselves, and then someone else, what the dilemma is, and how we came to find ourselves facing it. And we need to say this with some element of coherence. Then we need to be able to listen to other people as they narrate similar accounts, and to respond to them with a narrative that intersects sympathetically with theirs and carries the story forward. The original story now becomes a larger story, encompassing both the teller and the respondent. My narrative plus your narrative becomes our narrative.

This fusing of plot lines is an important feature of human interaction. A skilled storyteller often begins by describing where and when he or she first heard the story. Isaac Bashevis Singer, for example, one of the great raconteurs of the twentieth century, nearly always begins his stories by describing the setting in which he, or his narrator, heard it. Sometimes it is a rabbi's stuffy study in Poland, sometimes a late-night cafeteria in Manhattan. But wherever it is, the setting draws both the teller and the hearers into a larger and older conversation. The stories enshrined in the scriptures and spiritual traditions of the human race are also like this. They are usually placed in particular settings, and — taken as a whole — they constitute a vast deposit of question and response covering an endless range of moral quandaries. If we were ever to lose our capacity to tell and hear stories, we would lose touch with this wisdom as well. Human beings stand erect, but so can gorillas. Human beings know they are going to die, but maybe elephants do, too. Human beings communicate with language, but the clickings and groans of dolphins do something very close. But is there any other creature that tells stories? I doubt it.

Walter Benjamin may have been intoning a dirge for storytelling prematurely, but his diagnosis remains perceptive. Today narrative is beset by three interrelated crises. The first is that the importance of storytelling has been unfairly demoted. Even though we would scarcely be human without them, narratives are under attack everywhere. Some "postmodern" philosophers think we must learn to get along without them. For years writers and filmmakers have been experimenting with novels and movies without discernible plots. Appreciating these plotless concoctions has become a skill that sophisticated people try to cultivate. It can even make those who have honed this capacity feel superior to the people who stubbornly insist on asking, about a film or a novel, "But what was it *about?*"

Still, I wonder if there is not a more profound message in these storyless inventions. Maybe their frustrating lack of plot is a backhanded tribute to plots. When they are not there, we miss them. Walter Benjamin has suggested that it is only with the decline of narrative that we have come to appreciate it. We now see how essential it is — something previous generations did not notice because they took it for granted.

The second threat narratives face today is, paradoxically, that there are too many of them. Rather than storyless, we are story-sated. We have docudramas, documentaries, and "mockumentaries"; historical fiction and fictionalized history; press releases and cover stories; before-and-after testimonies for diet pills, self-help books, exercise machines, or God. We are drenched with stories. Some have the ring of truth; others are transparent inventions. Some brilliantly illuminate the deeper reaches of our humanity; some numb and stupefy us; others can be forgotten the next minute. But all dance with seemingly equal license on the horizon of our consciousness. Anything can suddenly pop up unbidden on the screen of our awareness, and we are often puzzled about how to sort the event from the spin, the important from the trivial, the wheat from the chaff. Without some clarity about one's own ongoing story, and the larger narratives of which it is a part, one can easily drown in a swirling sea of conflicting claims and counterclaims.

This leads immediately to the third element of the crisis in narrative. How do we make our way, crafting our own personal stories in the midst of so many others? "Like it or not," Paul Elie writes, "we come to life in the middle of stories that are not our own." At the same time, the intricate link between one's personal story and the older narratives of one's people and of the human species as a whole has become more elusive. There was a time when ethnic communities, religious traditions, families, and neighborhoods helped us to envision our place in the bigger picture. But the fragmentation of perception and relentless leveling that global market culture has brought on have taken a serious toll. They have undermined the power of these institutions to mediate meaning. Individuals must now try to manage on their own much of what recurrent rituals and twice-told tales once did to help us see ourselves within a larger frame.

This change, however, is not just a loss. Elie also says, "As ever, religious belief makes its claim somewhere between revelation and projection, between holiness and human frailty; but the burden of proof, indeed the burden of belief, for so long upheld by society, is now back on the believer, where it belongs." Our religious traditions no longer do the work of meaning making for us. We now see them not as infallible authorities that tell us who we are, but as resources we can turn to selectively to help us become the people we want to be. This can be a welcome gain, but it is a daunting task, and one that is never done. Also, the work of fashioning and refashioning our own biography is impossible to do alone. We need a present-day equivalent for the ritual settings in which the classical narratives were once sung, enacted, and interpreted. But given the altered cultural context, today's equivalents must welcome a degree of sorting and selectivity rarely found in the older ones, and encourage people to exchange their personal accounts in the light of the larger narrative.

Is this happening anywhere? I think it is, and under surprisingly disparate conditions. The swapping of stories at twelve-step programs and the custom of giving testimonies at some religious and political gatherings come to mind. The practice in many Jewish Passover seders is to struggle — over the sweet wine and unleavened bread — about the current significance of the ancient account of the exodus. I also like to think that our weekly discussion sessions in the ROTC building provided a similar opportunity.

The battle to preserve and rejuvenate narrative has not been lost.

But the only way we can defeat the threat Benjamin dimly foresaw is to respond to the three-pronged attack. First, we must stop derogating the role of narrative and reinstate it to its rightful place as an essential component of being human. As the French philosopher Paul Ricoeur says, all life has a narrative shape, and our calling as human beings is to live a life worth recounting.

Second, we must recognize that what has happened to storytelling in our era is not a death rattle, it is more like logorrhea. We are swimming in stories, even when we do not recognize them as such. Even in the face of the blinding flurry of facts, alleged facts, and isolated bits of information that inundate us, stories live. They have a resilience Benjamin may not have appreciated enough. But there are good ones and bad ones, and our task is to sort out the salutary from the toxic.

Third, in order to do this sorting out, we need venues and occasions where we can strengthen each other's capacity to integrate what is still worthwhile in the grand narratives of our peoples into our own lives. Then, grounded in these archetypes, we can sort out the timeless from the transient, truth from propaganda, that which unites from that which divides.

Narrative may still be an endangered species, if not exactly as Benjamin thought it was. What we must do is to recognize the real threat to its existence and resist it. We do this best, I think, by becoming storytellers ourselves. It is not that hard. It comes naturally, because it is a part of the way our brains work.

Rabbi Jesus was one of the greatest storytellers of all time. Like us, he lived in a world of contending and conflicting narratives. The stories he told, and the stories people told about him, still live on when many of their rivals have long since fallen silent. Who now sings of the glory and might of Caesar? Who now intones the dark mysteries of Isis or Mithra? But the stories of this Palestinian rabbi have been repeated and heard again and again throughout twenty centuries by more people than we could count. To enter into his story world is to take the first step toward understanding his spiritual and moral relevance for us today.

I

STORIES THEY
TOLD ABOUT HIM

The Ballad of the Begats

[1] The book of the genealogy of Jesus Christ, the son of David, the son of Abraham. [2] Abraham was the father of Isaac, and Isaac the father of Jacob, and Jacob the father of Judah and his brothers, [3] . . . and Judah the father of Perez and Zerah by Tamar . . . [5] And Salmon was the father of Boaz by Rahab, and Boaz the father of Obed by Ruth, and Obed the father of Jesse, and Jesse the father of David the king. And David was the father of Solomon by the wife of Uriah . . . [18] . . . and Jacob was the father of Joseph, the husband of Mary, of whom Jesus was born, who is called the Christ. — MATTHEW 1:1, 2, 3, 5, 18

MOST STUDENTS like to hit the ground running. Even though they often slow down as the term proceeds, they start off with a burst of energy. Mine were no different. Many of them began reading the Gospel accounts of Jesus even before the first official meeting of the class.

That was always a mistake. The Gospel of Matthew, the first in the New Testament, opens with a long and seemingly incomprehensible genealogy. The impatient students immediately felt discouraged, and they were not alone. Gandhi once wrote that when he first tried to read the Bible he got completely bogged down in all the "begats." The students had the same problem, and no wonder. The genealogy of Jesus runs on for eighteen verses in Matthew and twenty-one in Luke (I have quoted only a fraction of it above), and it mentions several figures even those familiar with the Bible know little about. How could I rescue my students from the Gandhi syndrome and keep their eyes from glazing over as they read these endless lineages?

★ ★ ★

First, I told them, don't read them, sing them. Most ancient genealogies, including the ones in the Bible, were not intended by
their writers to be historical records. This is not their real point (in
fact, the genealogies in Matthew and Luke are not consistent). Their
purpose is to conjure an aura, to position the person who comes at
the end of the long sequence, in this case "Jesus who is called the
Christ," in a generational narrative and thereby to establish his significance. The ancestral flow charts in the Gospels are more like the
ballads an ancient bard might chant around a campfire while strum-
ming on a lute. I suggested they try crooning them aloud — quietly,
and in the privacy of their own rooms — to get in the proper frame
of mind. Understood this way, Matthew and Luke's genealogical tables are treasures. Not only do they tell us much more than first
meets the eye, they even hint at some racy subplots. When I told the
students this, it sent them scurrying back to check out some of the
figures mentioned.

People today sometimes ridicule these genealogies, but when
they do they are missing something about even twenty-first-century
human beings. We have never outgrown the yen for roots and the
respect they allegedly entitle us to. In a given year, how many people send for one of those widely advertised coats of arms that can be
tacked up over the mantel to demonstrate that one's family stems
from a Scottish laird or from Languedoc nobility? The cross-swords,
heraldic lions *rampant,* and fleurs-de-lis cannot help but impress,
even though the ancestors of those displaying them next to the
bowling trophies were more likely to have fertilized onion patches
as serfs on the baronial estate than to have dined at the lord's table.
We all want roots, and if we don't know what they are, we look for
them. And if we can't find them, we sometimes invent them.

The New Age has a new, but actually quite old, way of tracing
genealogies. It consists of striving to get in touch with one's previous lives. This, of course, implies a belief in reincarnation, which
both Judaism and Christianity have rejected, at least officially. But
it serves as a more individualized version of the ancestral escutch-

eons. Once again, however, it is significant that when people go through the necessary steps to retrieve their previous personae, the ancestors they conjure turn out to be courtesans in Cleopatra's palace or captains in Napoleon's legions. It is hard to find anyone who has discovered a previous incarnation as a scullery maid or a swineherd.

With this in mind we can derive some enjoyment and insight from the way Jewish stories position the most famous rabbis in dynasties. For example, the great eighteenth-century rabbi and scholar Nahman of Bratslav, born in 1772, is remembered not only for the inspired work he did on the Kabala, but also because he was the great-grandson of Israel ben Eliezer, the Baal Shem Tov, on his mother's side, and the grandson of Nahman of Horodenka on his father's. More recently, Rabbi Abraham Joshua Heschel, who was born in 1907, was descended on his father's side from Dov Baer of Mezhirich, and from Levi Isaac of Berdichev on his mother's. In this latter case, the scholarly lineage continues in a way that would have surprised previous generations of rabbis. Heschel's daughter Susannah is a professor of Jewish studies at Dartmouth College. With this blood coursing through their veins, how could these people not have been great scholars?

The genealogies that Matthew and Luke chart for Jesus of Nazareth, however, are different from those of most other rabbis. They are particularly fascinating because of the way they use the same form to make a quite different kind of statement. They mix together patriarchs, prophets, kings, and nobodies. They name both men and women in a way that at first appears to be random. What are these creatively composed pedigrees trying to tell us about this Galilean rabbi?

They seem to say two somewhat contradictory things. First, Jesus is the heir, not just of the patriarchs, but also of the kings. They place him firmly in the line of Abraham, Isaac, and Jacob, but they add that he is also descended from Jesse and the great King David. Then, in Matthew's version, there follows a list of royal ancestors with names like Hezekiah, Manasseh, and Josiah. Three groups of fourteen generations each are registered, perhaps encrypting the numerical equivalents of the letters in the Hebrew name for David.

But when Matthew the genealogist comes to Joseph, it is evident that he has a second purpose. And he also, therefore, has a problem. He has traced the regal line as it had to be traced, through the fathers. But he also wants to claim that ultimately the significance of Jesus, however impressive his princely bloodline, does not rest on this royal lineage. It comes directly from God. Consequently, after we pick our way through thirteen generations, we find at the fourteenth that Joseph (who is listed in the royal line) is referred to discreetly as "the husband of Mary," not the father of Jesus. So what happened to the noble DNA?

Again, the literal mind must blink at this inconsistency. But Matthew's genealogy was never intended to be the kind of family tree index available in archives of research libraries. Matthew was not filing a legal brief that might be subpoenaed in a court dispute about an estate. He was composing a musical overture to announce the significance of Jesus and to preview some of the motifs that would soon be heard. The genealogy he skillfully constructed for the Nazarene carpenter is a *parable*, the first in a book that is replete with parables on nearly every page.

There is an even more curious element in this genealogy-cum-parable, something that must have come as a shock to its first-century readers, and this is the spicy part. As in the normal pattern, the genealogy follows the male line, but — inexplicably — four women are mentioned. The first two, Tamar and Rahab, are both Canaanites, non-Israelites. The third is Ruth, a Moabite. The fourth one's name is not mentioned, but everyone knows who it is: Bathsheba, the beautiful Hittite woman King David glimpsed on her rooftop while she was bathing. First he seduced her, and then he ordered her husband Uriah the Hittite murdered on the battlefield so he could have the lovely lady all to himself. There is something notable about these four women. All are Gentiles. And all of them are involved in plots that exude a whiff of sexual irregularity, subversion, or deception. They thicken the plot.

Tamar's story is told in Genesis 38, where we learn that Judah, the son of the patriarch Jacob, picks her out as a bride for his eldest son Er. But before she can bear a child, Er does something "wicked in the Lord's sight" (we are not told what it is), so God slays him. Judah then tells his other son, Onan, to sleep with Tamar, thus fulfilling his fraternal obligation and producing a child. But Onan is suspicious. Apparently his father's order came so soon after the brother's death that the child might be credited to him and not to Onan. So Onan "spilled his seed" on the ground (thus inspiring the odd term *Onanism*), whereupon God slays him as well, leaving Tamar twice-widowed and still childless. Now, however, Judah tells her that she should wait until an even younger son, Shelah, becomes old enough to make her a mother, and that meanwhile she should move out of his (Judah's) house and go to live in her own parental household, which she does.

The plot thickens again. Judah's wife dies. Shelah comes of age but Judah makes no move to marry him to Tamar. Instead, come sheep-shearing time, he sets out for a town called Timnath, where the sheep are pastured. Tamar tires of waiting, and hearing that Judah is on the way, acts fast. She takes off her mourning weeds, disguises herself, then sits by the side of the road like a prostitute. Judah notices her, but does not recognize who she is, and tells her he wants to have sex with her. She asks what he is willing to pay, and he promises her a young goat from his own flock. But Tamar tells him she must have a pledge until the goat arrives, and will settle for the seal he is wearing around his neck and the staff he is carrying. Judah agrees. They go off together. Then Judah returns home, and Tamar puts her mourner's clothes back on.

Shortly after this, Judah sends a friend with a goat to pay the "prostitute" and to retrieve his seal and staff. But the friend searches in vain and has to return and tell Judah that no one in the town of Timnath knows of any such *fille de joie*. Three months later word reaches Judah that his daughter-in-law Tamar, who is still a widow with no legitimate sexual partner, nonetheless has gotten herself pregnant. Furious, Judah orders that she be brought to him to be burned. As she is being dragged out, however, she displays Judah's seal and staff and tells the servants that the man by whom she is pregnant is none other than their master. Judah, who has now been caught in a compromising pose, admits that he is in the wrong and cancels the execution. Tamar then gives birth not to one baby but to twins, Perez (who is duly listed as one of Jesus' forefathers) and his brother, Zerah. With this kind of scandalous stuff inside the covers of the Good Book, who needs to waste money on true romance magazines?

Rahab and Ruth are also featured in stories guaranteed to appeal to the undergraduate appetite and to disabuse them even further of the mistaken notion that the Bible does not have its share of lust and derring-do. Rahab, unlike Tamar, is depicted as a bona fide harlot, not a counterfeit one. She plies her trade in Jericho in a boudoir conveniently located on the wall of the city. When Joshua, the Jewish military commander, sends his spies into Jericho, Rahab (having heard of the "greatness of their God," as the text puts it) shelters them. Even more, she hides them under stalks of flax when the agents of the king of Jericho come looking for them; she then gives the royal agents a false lead and lowers the spies to safety with a rope. Grateful, the Jewish spies promise that she and her family will be spared when the Israelites conquer the city, and they are. In rabbinical lore, Rahab is described as one of the four most beautiful women in the world, and she became the ancestress of Jeremiah and seven other prophets.

The story of Ruth is not as swashbuckling as that of Rahab, but it has a charm all its own. In fact, more than one biblical scholar has suggested that it is so simple, straightforward, and beautiful that it is an injustice to interpret or comment on it. Still, it is legitimate to ask why Ruth, a Moabite woman, appears in the genealogy of Jesus.

What happened was this: During a period of famine in Galilee an Israelite family — a father and mother and two sons — had moved from Bethlehem to Moab in search of food. While they were there, the two sons of the family married local Gentile women. Then all three of the men died, so the mother, Naomi, decides to return to her old homestead. One daughter-in-law chooses to stay in Moab. But the other, Ruth, has become so fond of her mother-in-law that she decides to stay with her, and to accompany her to a place she had never seen: thus the famous line, "Wherever you go, I will go. Your people will be my people, and your God will be my God."

When the two arrive back in the old country, however, the mother and daughter-in-law run into hard times. They are reduced to gleaning, picking up the discarded sheaves of barley left on the edges of the fields for the poor by the harvesters. Not content with this dismal lot, Naomi, apparently a wise and canny woman, sends Ruth to ask protection from a man named Boaz, a distant relative. For whatever reason, Boaz grants it, and even marries her. The text says Ruth crept into his bedchamber at night and "uncovered his feet," a transparent euphemism. The unstated subtext is that the impoverished but beautiful relative worked her charms on the rich landowner. According to biblical legend, the son they had became the ancestor of King David.

These stories all conclude with happy endings for marginal women. The heroines all take their place in a hit parade of biblical beauties who deployed their feminine magnetism to do the right thing. The star of the cast is no doubt Queen Esther, who does not appear in Jesus' genealogy. Her story is celebrated annually on the Jewish holiday of Purim. Living with her people in captivity, she was gorgeous enough to win the beauty pageant the Gentile king staged, became a part of his harem, and used her inside track to save her people from the fiendish Haman. This was something she could hardly have accomplished if she had stayed home polishing the candlesticks and baking matzahs. Or if she had been too skinny or too portly.

It is not hard to imagine the discussions these juicy stories behind the desiccated genealogies sparked in a classroom full of young people, for whom matters of sex and attractiveness are never very far out of mind. The discussions focused on how much, if at all, one is entitled to draw on one's physical allure or sexual charisma for a good purpose. Granted that it happens all the time, what are the limits, if any? These deliberations rarely if ever reached definitive conclusions. I doubt if they ever do, but I was glad that the course had again provided a venue in which a matter of considerable importance in the moral life could be openly thrashed out.

No doubt Matthew would have been surprised by the discussion his curious genealogical allegory stimulated among the students. His genealogy of Jesus begins at the first verse of the first chapter of the first book of what was much later to become the New Testament. But there was no New Testament then, only oral traditions and a variety of written documents about Jesus, most of which have long since been lost. Scholars date this Gospel at about 70 C.E., forty years after Jesus' death, when increasing numbers of people, including many Gentiles, were responding to his message. Most of his readers would never have known Jesus in the flesh. Matthew wanted to do two things. First, he wanted to connect the Galilean rabbi clearly with the previous history of the Jewish people, but at the same time to demonstrate that Jesus also represented something fresh, that a new community was forming that would unite Jews and non-Jews. He also wanted his genealogy, like an overture, to foreshadow Jesus' life, to forewarn the reader about what was coming. His is the first story *about* Jesus. Matthew packs piles of information about this unusual rabbi into his ballad. He is telling us that Jesus' Jewish dynastic credentials are second to none, but that the credentials are not what matters most about him. He tips us off that in his teaching, this rabbi will appeal to many of those whom the conventional teachers have overlooked or condemned: the ladies of shady repute, the socially marginal, and the Gentiles. These are the types of characters who will appear time and again as we trace the stories of Jesus in the Gospels.

❧ 5 ❧

Picking Just
the Right Woman

In the sixth month the angel Gabriel was sent by God to Nazareth, a town in Galilee, with a message for a girl betrothed to a man named Joseph, a descendant of David; the girl's name was Mary. The angel went in and said to her, "Greetings, most favoured one! The Lord is with you." But she was deeply troubled by what he had said and wondered what this greeting could mean. Then the angel said to her, "Do not be afraid, Mary, for God has been gracious to you; you will conceive and give birth to a son, and you are to give him the name Jesus. He will be great, and will be called Son of the Most High. The Lord God will give him the throne of his ancestor David, and he will be king over Israel forever; his reign shall never end." — LUKE 1:26–33

> She bows her head
> Submissive, yet
> Her downcast glance
> Asks the angel, "Why
> For this romance,
> Do I qualify?"
> — SAMUEL MENASHE, "The Annunciation,"

THE CRIMSON is Harvard University's daily undergraduate newspaper. I frequently scan it, but had paid little attention to the want ads and personals until one of my students called my attention to this item:

We are searching for an intelligent, healthy, and very attractive woman 19–30 years old of English-American descent. Must be 5'4"–5'7", small to medium build with brown/blue eyes.

She told me the ad was a solicitation for human female eggs to be used for in vitro fertilization. She said the *Crimson* often ran these notices and that the money they offered for one egg ranged from $5,000 to $50,000, a serious inducement for a young woman anticipating a large tuition loan debt, as many students now do. She wanted to know if she could write a term paper on the ethical issues raised by this growing practice. I asked her what part of the Gospel narratives had brought it to mind. She answered right away that it was the Annunciation, God's choice of Mary to be the bearer of a son. After all, she pointed out brightly, God must have been looking for someone very special, and Mary's pregnancy had begun without sexual intercourse, as would the pregnancies initiated by these seeds from Harvard Yard.

I was so taken aback by the idea that I said nothing for several seconds while she gazed at me expectantly. Finally, I agreed, but I reminded her that whatever other virtues the Virgin Mary had had, she was not a student in an elite university, and that even though she is often pictured in paintings of the Annunciation kneeling with a small prayer book in her hands, she probably could not read. I added that she was decidedly not of the ethnic background these ads usually sought, had probably not reached her late teens, and was already engaged to be married. But this was not the most unusual suggestion for a term paper I had ever received, so I asked how she planned to do it. She said she hoped to talk with several of her undergraduate female friends, all of whom had seen the ads, many of whom had considered them, and a few of whom had actually responded to them. She wanted to find out what they had thought of the ad, what moral issues had come to mind (if any), why they had decided one way or another, and what they would advise their friends to do. Furthermore, she added, smiling, her own name was Mary. That did it. I told her to go ahead and write it, and I would read it with great interest.

I knew, of course, that the biblical story of the Annunciation was not about in vitro fertilization. True, theologians over the years have made much of the fact that Mary had to *agree* to the angel Gabriel's proposition. She was not like Leda who was raped by Zeus in the form of a swan and then gave birth to Castor and Clytemnestra. Mary *chose* to be the bearer of a son whose father was not Joseph, her fiancé. But the question of why God chose this particular Jewish maiden to be the mother of Jesus is also an intriguing one. All things considered, the fact that this old story had — two thousand years later — stirred a young modern woman to investigate an important ethical issue demonstrates once again the power of narrative to stimulate the moral imagination. Stories do that. They start the mind and memory racing. They spark connections and associations. They recall similar experiences in the life of the hearer.

The fact that a biblical story that dates from two millennia could reach over the centuries and provoke this idea for a student's term paper demonstrates again how a story, once told, escapes the teller's control. It goes into free flight. It morphs into new versions and accumulates new meanings even though it remains fundamentally the same story. Stories possess an inherent resonance that few other forms of human expression have.

I wondered what new incarnation this ancient account would inspire for this sophomore Mary with her blue jeans and canvas book bag, so as the weeks passed I asked her now and then how she was doing. She said she was doing just fine. I grew increasingly curious about what she would find, so when the papers came in at the end of the term I shuffled through them to find hers and read it first. It was a dazzler. She was concentrating in the history of science, and had taken a number of courses in physiology and chemistry, so I had to consult my dictionary occasionally as I read. But it was clear she had done a thorough job. The young women she talked to who had in fact contributed eggs (more accurately, "sold" them) had almost all done so because the financial rewards were so attractive. In a few days some had made as much as the workingwomen who cleaned their classrooms and flipped their pancakes made in a year. Of those who did not respond to the cash-for-eggs invitation, it turned out that most had declined not for moral considerations, but because they had learned that the procedure was invasive, often painful, and that there were sometimes complicated side effects.

I could well understand their hesitation. The "donor" is first given drugs that prevent ovulation until the oocytes are mature. Hormonal level indicators are then administered, and when they register the maturity of the eggs, another drug is given that prepares the eggs for ovulation. Then, about thirty-six hours later, the ova are removed by a process known as egg aspiration, which literally means that they are sucked out of the womb. After that the "donor" can pick up her check and go home. The next steps do not require her presence. The egg is fertilized with semen in a laboratory and then implanted in the uterus of the woman who will carry it until birth.

I was interested to see that many of the women my student interviewed, even those who did not sell their eggs, saw nothing wrong with the process as such. A healthy human female produces between four hundred and five hundred eggs in a lifetime. She can bear only a tiny fraction of that number of children, so she is not losing any capacity to bear her own children. Moreover, many of the people seeking these eggs are childless and desperate. They want children badly, and many want the child to have at least some of their own genes, which this process allows because the husband's semen can be used. And, very important, the couple wants to experience the actual birth of the baby. Now science has made it possible for them to have such children, so why should anyone object?

But, my student researcher had asked, what about picking "very attractive" Ivy League women as the preferred producers of the eggs? Doesn't this seem elitist and a bit shady? "Why should it?" some of the women retorted. "We do that all the time when we pick out where to go to college, with whom to go out on dates, whom to marry? It isn't just our parents who are constantly sizing up potential mates on many of the same criteria that appear in the ads. We do the same thing." They saw no reason why ethical standards not generally used in shopping for mates (and thus for the qualities of the children) should suddenly loom into prominence in shopping for human eggs.

"But what about the cash-on-the-barrelhead feature of this transaction?" she had asked. I pressed the same point in the section meeting. "Doesn't transforming human oocytes into consumer commodities trivialize the inherent value of human life?" Our forefathers eventually became enraged at the sale and purchase of human beings, which we call slavery. Doesn't this human egg market slide toward the same cheapening of innate human worth? If the couple wants a child, and you have lots of extra eggs, why not *really* become a "donor" and contribute one?

"Well, that's easy enough for someone pulling down a good salary to say," some of the students shot back. "They don't have to start off in a career with $50,000 in student loans to repay." One student responded that she knew from her anthropology courses that in some cultures lavish financial inducements, dowries and the like, are part of the prenuptial bargaining. Some pointed out that there has been a recognized and accepted market for blood for decades; now there is a somewhat less acceptable market for kidneys and other organs. Some people sell a kidney, and they have only two. Some medical professionals are publicly suggesting payment for organs as an acceptable practice. At least one country, Israel, has now legalized this practice. What is an egg or two out of four hundred? Whether we like it or not, we live in a market society. Everything has its price. Maybe we should have a better system, but until we do, this is the way it works. This was the logic many of the women followed.

Only a few of the women my student talked with objected to the procedure as violating the means God (or nature) has decreed for having babies. A few more objected to the commercial aspect because it discriminated both against female students who needed the money but were of the "wrong" ethnic stock, and against childless couples without the fat bank account. One or two even said they would be more tempted to undergo the pain and discomfort for a childless couple with no money than they would for those who waved a pile of thousand-dollar bills at them.

The student concluded the paper in a fashion I had gotten used to seeing. She knew how she would respond to any such ad but she was hard put to ground her conviction in anything but her own feelings. She said she felt "very strongly" that she herself would never go through such a procedure, even though she could certainly use the money. But she admitted she did not really know *why* she wouldn't. It was something "very visceral" that made her sure she was not a candidate for egg donor (or seller).

I had hoped she might suggest more plausible reasons for her conclusions. But I gave the paper a good grade. Inspired, however improbably, by a biblical story, she had thoroughly aired a complex moral quandary. She had, I am sure, awakened the awareness of the women she had interviewed to the ethical dimensions of selling their eggs, whatever they eventually decided. She had also sharpened the tools she would be using herself when she ran into other complicated moral issues, as she certainly would throughout her life. In short, she had come away from the task of writing a term paper with just the kind of experience I think Rabbi Jesus would have wanted her to have. She was better prepared to go on to the next perplexity life would inevitably put in her path.

After I read her paper, however, I found myself wondering why indeed, among all the young women of Israel at the time, God did pick Mary. The Bible itself is silent about this, hinting that choosing her demonstrates that God is free to choose whom he will. But the reticence of the Bible has, of course, only fueled endless speculation about God's choice. In Jean-Luc Godard's controversial film *Je Vous Salue, Marie,* a twentieth-century Mary works in a filling station. The fourth-century theologian Athanasius taught that Mary was not only a pure virgin, she also had a "harmonious disposition" and "did not want to be seen by men." She always remained at home, worked like a honeybee, cared for the poor, and prayed to God "not to let a bad thought take root in her heart." Obviously

Athanasius is projecting his own image of the good, if not perfect, woman on the girl from Nazareth. But he is only one of many thousands who have done so. Mary, like Christ himself, has become a kind of Rorschach inkblot in which countless people have discovered their own mothers, wives, sweethearts, and other women they have admired. I once heard a radical priest in Latin America tell his congregation on the Feast of the Assumption, when Catholic tradition says that she was carried to heaven without passing through death, what he thought that doctrine meant. Its meaning, he said, was that since Mary was now "with God," and we know that God is present with the poor struggling against their oppressors, that was where she was, too.

A revolutionary Mary? The only scrap of evidence we have that suggests what kind of person the Gospel writers thought Mary was makes that priest considerably more credible than Athanasius. It comes just after the Annunciation, when Mary visits her cousin Elizabeth, who is pregnant with John the Baptist. This was when Mary herself sang the song that we know as the Magnificat.

And Mary said:

> "My soul tells out the greatness of the Lord,
> my spirit has rejoiced in God my Saviour;
> for he has looked with favour on his servant,
> lowly as she is.
> From this day forward
> all generations will count me blessed,
> for the Mighty God has done great things for me.
> His name is holy,
> his mercy sure from generation to generation
> toward those who fear him.
> He has shown the might of his arm,
> he has routed the proud and all their schemes;
> he has brought down monarchs from their thrones,
> and raised on high the lowly.
> He has filled the hungry with good things,
> and sent the rich away empty.

He has come to the help of Israel his Servant,
as he promised to our forefather;
he has not forgotten to show mercy
to Abraham and his children's children for ever."

(Luke 1:46–55)

Whatever else this is, it is not the portrait of a withdrawn, stay-at-home mom. She celebrates the scattering of the proud, the de-throning of the mighty, and the raising up of the debased. As her son eventually does in the Beatitudes, she not only blesses the poor and promises the feeding of the hungry, she also predicts bad times for the rich, who will be "sent away empty." Professor Elisabeth Schüssler Fiorenza, a colleague of mine who teaches New Testa-ment and early Christian history, voices her view of Mary in her characteristically robust language. "In the center of the Christian story," she writes, "stands not the lovely 'white lady' of artistic and popular imagination, kneeling in adoration before her son. Rather it is the pregnant young woman, living in occupied territory and struggling against victimization and for survival." All in all this sounds more like the description I heard from that radical priest than like that of Athanasius.

Since I was raised as a Protestant I was never taught to venerate the Virgin Mary. She was certainly never disrespected in our church, but doctrines like the Immaculate Conception and the Assumption were viewed with suspicion. We never crowned any statues of her, had Mary Day Processions, or repeated "Hail, Mary" prayers. We did not wear her medallions around our necks. Still, I continue to be impressed with the remarkable persistence of Marian piety, and not just among Catholics, into our own day. Hardly a year goes by with-out another major apparition of Mary somewhere in the world, and minor apparitions occur even more often. She appears in the clouds, in the leaves of trees, on a taco, and, recently in Tampa, Florida, in the window of a bank. Sometimes she dutifully confirms Catholic orthodoxy, but sometimes she criticizes the hierarchy for not giving sufficient emphasis to traditional devotions like praying the rosary.

She still seems to have a mind of her own, and to be the one to whom the misused and the marginalized still turn.

I strongly doubt whether, if human egg sales had been possible in those days, any of the elite families of Palestine would have sought one from Mary. She was not the type they were looking for. But apparently she was what God was looking for.

6

Exiles from Eden

God said, "You shall not eat of the fruit of the tree which is in the midst of the garden, neither shall you touch it, lest you die." But the serpent said to the woman, "You will not die. For God knows that when you eat of it your eyes will be opened, and you will be like God, knowing good from evil." — GENESIS 3:3–5

"How can this be?" said Mary. "I am still a virgin." The angel answered, "The Holy Spirit will come upon you, and the power of the Most High will overshadow you; for that reason the holy child to be born will be called Son of God." — LUKE 1:34–36

BUT WAS SHE REALLY A VIRGIN?" students asked every year. "And why should she have been?" They are good questions. The story of what has come to be known as the "virgin birth" of Jesus has undoubtedly played an enormous role in the history of Christianity. The phrase "born of the Virgin Mary" was incorporated into the earliest creeds. Devotion to "Our Lady" inspired everything from poetry to painting to cathedral building during the Middle Ages. Henry Adams once wrote that it was the Virgin "who built Chartres." The most prominent Catholic university in America, Notre Dame, is named for her. During the nineteenth and twentieth centuries the Roman Catholic Church added two official doctrines to its list of required beliefs, the Immaculate Conception of Mary and her Assumption. The first declares that Mary's parents were protected from sin during her conception so that she would not pass on the poison of original sin to her son. The latter teaches that Mary was taken directly to heaven without passing through the portal of death.

But there is an important difference between honoring, even revering, the mother of Jesus and taking the idea of the virgin birth as a literal biological fact. When the doctrine is taken literally it remains a hurdle — and I think an unnecessary one — for many of today's students and adults. This is why it is important to pay attention to the biblical story itself. It reports that when Mary, who was engaged to Joseph but not yet married, heard the angel's message she immediately asked the natural question: How can this happen when I do not have a husband? The answer she hears is that the Holy Spirit will be the father. But instead of emphasizing the divine fatherhood, much of the Christian tradition has instead focused on the virginal motherhood. To many people today this accent seems antisexual, even antihuman. These are understandable suspicions, so in discussing this passage, I thought my responsibility was to direct the students' attention back to what I think was the original intent of this story, namely to communicate two things.

First, Jesus participated in the natural continuities of human life. He started as a tiny embryo and emerged from a uterus through the painful exertions of a young woman. He did not, like Venus, spring full-grown from the brow of Zeus.

Second, in the Christian understanding, God yearns to share every aspect of human finitude, pain, joy, disappointment, and mortality.

Like the genealogies, the story of "divine fatherhood" (as I would prefer to call it, rather than the virgin birth) shows the early Christians struggling with how Jesus was both the same as us and different from us. But this is similar to stories from many other religious traditions, and because Jesus was a rabbi, it is the Jewish parallels that seem most pertinent. It is said in Hasidic lore, for example, that when Adam stood in the Garden of Eden at the trunk of the Tree of Knowledge, all the souls that would ever exist were gathered into his soul. But as he stood there, one soul detached itself from the rest and flew away upward. It was the soul of Rabbi Israel ben Eliezer, the famous Baal Shem Tov, the founder of the Jewish mystical movement called Hasidism. Thus, when Adam tasted the fatal fruit, the Baal Shem's soul did not take a bite.

When a truly great rabbi departs from this life, those who were touched by him often believe that the circumstances of his coming into this world must have been exceptional. Although he was clearly one of us, they muse, he must in one way or another have been spared some of the fatal flaws that weigh on the rest of us from birth. For many Jews and Christians the burden of those flaws is symbolized by the story of Adam and Eve.

There are many conflicting opinions about just what the story of this intriguing primal pair means. Has any other couple ever been subject to more interpretations and counterinterpretations? Not even Caesar and Cleopatra or Romeo and Juliet have provided the theme for as many cartoons as this seductively unclad couple, their nakedness always partially veiled by leaves and branches, with the serpent coiling in menace around the nearest tree. Does their nibbling on the forbidden fruit represent the opening scene of human history with all its victories and defeats? Was it really a "fortunate fall," as John Milton suggests in Book XII of *Paradise Lost*, because it set in motion so much good, including the redemption of the world? Was it a cautionary tale, proof positive that women are simply not to be trusted, as male exegetes for centuries have maintained? What, in fact, was their lapse, if that is what it was? Was it concupiscence? Disobedience? Sloth? Gluttony? However their story is spun, we just don't seem to be able to leave the two of them — or the three of them if you count the snake — alone.

Like everyone else, I have my own favorite interpretation of the story of Eden. I realize it is only one of many contenders, but I think it ultimately makes the most sense. A careful reading suggests that their fatal mistake was their refusal to be content with being human, and therefore mortal. Mere paradise, crammed with all that fresh air and ripe fruit, even having each other as loving partners, was not good enough for them. They wanted to shake loose from aging, death, and the other inconvenient liabilities of earthliness.

They longed for unlimited possibilities. They craved, as the serpent so succinctly whispered, "to be like God."

But whatever their ruinous slip-up, it is largely agreed that its pall still poisons our capacity for sanity and decency. Put another way, Adam and Eve are not prehistoric forebears. We have met them, and they are us. Their story is our story, projected back into mythic time. Dissatisfied with being merely human, we try to be more, to snatch control, and we end up spoiling it all. Illnesses often depress us not only because of the pain they bring but because they take the management of our lives away and put it in the hands of other people. We try, sometimes in subtle ways, to manipulate the people close to us — at work and at home — so that things proceed the way we ourselves want them to. We want our team, our tribe, our nation to be number one. We even fantasize about extending our lives far beyond the traditional three score years and ten, maybe indefinitely. Inevitably we realize we cannot possibly succeed in being in control of everything. But even after we have tried to mend our ways, and have succeeded in some small measure, we still have to live with the residues of the greed of the previous generations that polluted lakes and decimated forests, and with the rancid resentments provoked by our past wars. We still have on our hands the mess that previous generations of control seekers and we ourselves have created.

Ah, but what about those extraordinary messengers God sends to remind us that we are not ultimately intended for the mess? What about the prophets and the saints? On the one hand they have to live, as we do, within life's frustrating confines, littered with the muddle of previous generations of snatching and grabbing. Like us, they get tired and hungry. They get angry and are tempted. Like us, they die. But they do not seem to carry the mess with them, and they do not perpetuate it. They hint at an alternative. Are they, at least in part, exempt from the common infirmity that Adam and Eve represent? Do they signal another possibility for life, one that is fully human but not fated to forge yet another link in the iron chain of cruelty and heartbreak?

The Christian tradition of the divine fatherhood of Jesus and the Jewish tale of the miraculous exemption of the Baal Shem Tov from Adam's offense have a similar purpose. Both are attempts to show that the chain of cause and effect that perpetuates our human enmeshment in evil can be broken. *Adam* means *man,* and *Eve* means *life.* But neither Adam nor Eve was content with merely being human and being alive. The Baal Shem's soul, so it seemed to those who knew him, wasn't contaminated by Adam's futile attempt to be more than a man. The "Bisht," as he is fondly remembered in Jewish lore, reveled in *this* life and saw God in every pebble and every blade of grass. Likewise with the spirit of the rabbi from Nazareth: It is said that it was the Spirit of God who placed him in Mary's womb. Both, of course, were born, as St. Augustine once indelicately put it, "between urine and excrement." Both suffered painfully early in life. The Baal Shem Tov's father died while he was still a young child. The infant Jesus, like millions of children today, was roughly hustled by his terrified family into a refugee existence to escape a political tyrant. Neither eluded the bruises of life. But there was something about each of them that called to mind the ebullience of Adam before he looked around and decided that life as God had created it was not satisfactory.

Each of the two traditions, in its own way, reflects this echo of Adam. It is said, for example, of the famous Rabbi Shalom of Belz, that one day a friend, with his young son in tow, came to call on the rabbi and his wife. They were warmly received in a simple room with no decorations and a plain board table. On their way home, the visitor asked his son, "So, what impression did the holy rabbi and his wife make on you?"

"They seemed like Adam and Eve before they sinned," the lad answered.

"And the room, how did that seem to you?" his father asked.

"Like paradise," said the son.

"Good," said the father, "that is how they looked to me as well."

The rabbi from Nazareth mentions Adam and Eve only once, to pronounce the famous words now often used in wedding services:

"What God has joined together, let no man put asunder" (Matthew 19:6). But his followers could not resist going further and drawing comparisons. It is important to note, however, that the comparisons are almost all contrasts. Jesus and Mary become the counterparts, the antidotes, to Adam and Eve. The apostle Paul, for example, had little interest in the "innocent" Adam. He cast him in a negative light as the source or symbol of the human plight, the one through whom death and decay entered the world. Jesus was the "Second Adam," through whom God had given humanity a fresh opportunity. In medieval Christian art, the skull that lies at the foot of the cross in many paintings of the Crucifixion is that of Adam. The very spot where we all went wrong, as it were, is the one where we can start over. This is not a literal statement, of course. The idea of divine fatherhood suggests that the God who started off by creating humanity from without now decides to begin the long process of healing from within the damage his creatures have done to each other. Contrasting Adam with Jesus and Eve with Mary implies that although the primal couple portrays the conditions under which we live, they do not determine our destiny. The symbolic juxtaposition means that within each of us there is not only an Adam, but also a Christ; not only a malcontent who condemns himself to frustration and despair, but also a human being capable of living life to the fullness God intended. "As in Adam all die, so in Christ all will be brought to life"(I Corinthians 15:22).

Today the story of Adam and Eve is interpreted in many and various voices. The different ways the two traditions, Judaism and Christianity, handle it provide highly instructive examples of how the surface similarities of stories can sometimes hide significant differences. What seems admirable to me about the Jewish tradition is its unfailing suspicion of romanticism, its willingness to look life straight in the eye and, despite all, not to lose hope. Christianity, on the other hand, while recognizing our terrestrial nature, also frequently demonstrates a yen to probe its limits, to look for cracks in the ceiling through which the light of another dimension might peek through. At the popular level Christianity, somewhat more than Judaism, can be swayed by miracles, supernatural signs, and mystical apparitions. This is a generalization, of course. The two traditions are not consistent. Christianity has tended to put a greater emphasis on the power of sin and self-delusion to distort even our highest aspirations. And for centuries Jews have told stories about miracles and wonderworkers. There is a good deal of overlapping, albeit a difference in emphasis, between the two traditions.

Taken together, the stories of Adam and Eve and of Mary and the divine fatherhood of Jesus symbolize the ongoing struggle between limitations and aspirations that is the stuff of the human drama. They are not about the historical origins of *Homo sapiens* or an alternative mode of reproduction. The students did not always understand this. Occasionally one would ask to do a paper on the new experiments in gene splicing and genetic engineering to find out if a virgin birth is indeed scientifically possible. Unlike the student who wrote on the sales of female human eggs, however, I usually discouraged them because I thought their ideas seemed too influenced by a literal reading of the story of Mary and the angel. The people who are inventing these new ways to escape nature sometimes seem to be making exactly the *opposite* point that the virgin birth/ divine fatherhood tradition makes. They apparently want men and women to kick loose of natural processes, to soar into some existence not bound by finite limitations and inconvenient things like having to die. The divine fatherhood story, on the other hand, makes the startling claim that God chooses to move in the opposite direction, to leave his limitlessness behind and start over as a fertilized embryo. That move will entail floating in amniotic fluid, being wrenched out through a narrow birth canal, blinking at a terrifying new world, growing up, suffering, and dying.

This story is about what it means for human beings to inhabit a body. At some level we are all aware of this, and we also know that some of the most intimate and painful moral decisions we make center on our bodies. What kinds of things should I take into it, and what not? To whom should I give it, and to whom not? How should I care for it? What will I do when it slows down and begins to deteriorate? What do I think about the certain fact that one day it simply will not be?

I once believed young people rarely thought about these questions, that especially aging and debilitation, disease and death were far from their minds. But I was wrong. They think about them a lot. Some students have told me that they think about one or another of them nearly every day. But college provides few occasions to air these thoughts and to compare them with those of other people their age. One woman once asked the other students in the section if they remembered a childhood ditty that goes:

> Do you ever think
> when the hearse goes by
> that someday you
> are going to die?
> And the worms crawl in
> and the worms crawl out
> and the worms play pinochle on your snout.

Many did remember it. She said, however, that when she chanted it as a child, it never occurred to her that *she* was going to die. That seemed impossible. Dying was what old people did. But now, she said, whenever she hears the familiar line from John Donne's poem, "Ask not for whom the bell tolls / It tolleth for thee," she knows someday it will toll for her. And, she added, "I won't even be able to hear it."

The virgin birth / divine fatherhood story is about "incarnation." I rarely used the term in class, but what it means is the "enfleshment" of God, that God understands the ambiguity of our embodiment because God shared, and shares, that embodiment. None other than D. H. Lawrence, that consistent celebrant of life in the flesh, who continues to be a favorite of undergraduates, has captured the meaning of the Incarnation in his poem "Demiurge":

> They say that reality exists only in the spirit
> that corporal existence is a kind of death
> that pure being is bodiless

that the idea of the form precedes the form substantial.
But what nonsense it is!
as if any mind could have imagined a lobster
dozing in the under-deeps, then reaching out a savage and iron
    claw!
Even the mind of God can only imagine
those things that have become themselves:
bodies and presences, here and now, creatures with a foothold
    in creation
even if only a lobster on tip-toe.
Religion knows better than philosophy.
Religion knows that Jesus was never Jesus
till he was born from a womb, and ate soup and bread
and grew up, and became, in the wonder of creation, Jesus,
with a body and with needs and with a lovely spirit.

The story of the virgin birth of Jesus has often been badly misunderstood. It is misleading to emphasize the virginity of Mary so much that the real point of the story — the divine initiative — is obscured. It is especially disingenuous to claim, as some Catholic doctrines do, that Mary remained "eternally virgin" throughout the remainder of her life, which implies a deprecation of sexual intimacy in marriage. Jesus did, after all, have at least one brother, James, who led the first Christian congregation in Jerusalem. The birth of Jesus to Mary is not principally about virginity at all. Lawrence got it right. It is about God becoming flesh. Its point is a simple one: God needed and wanted a body. Even if Adam and Eve were not satisfied with being human, which means having a body, God went the other way to demonstrate — and maybe to satisfy himself — that being human, with all its limitations, is not so bad after all.

7

The Gurus and
the Usual Suspects

Jesus was born at Bethlehem in Judea during the reign of Herod. After his birth astrologers from the east arrived in Jerusalem, asking, "Where is the newborn king of the Jews? We observed the rising of his star, and we have come to pay him homage." King Herod was greatly perturbed when he heard this, and so was the whole of Jerusalem. He called together the chief priests and scribes of the Jews, and asked them where the Messiah was to be born. "At Bethlehem in Judea," they replied, "for this is what the prophet wrote: 'Bethlehem in the land of Judah, you are by no means least among the rulers of Judah; for out of you shall come a ruler to be the shepherd of my people Israel.' "

Then Herod summoned the astrologers to meet him secretly, and ascertained from them the exact time when the star had appeared. He sent them to Bethlehem, and said, "Go and make a careful search for the child, and when you have found him, bring me word, so that I may go myself and pay him homage."

After hearing what the king had to say they set out; there before them was the star they had seen rising, and it went ahead of them until it stopped above the place where the child lay. They were overjoyed at the sight of it and, entering the house, they saw the child with Mary his mother and bowed low in homage to him; they opened their treasure chests and presented gifts to him; gold, frankincense, and myrrh. Then they returned to their own country by another route, for they had been warned in a dream not to go back to Herod. — MATTHEW 2:1–12

IT IS MATTHEW, not Luke, who tells the next part of the familiar cluster of stories associated with the birth of Jesus, and it also presages something integral to the life of the Nazarene rabbi. Visitors, called in the Greek text *magoi,* appear at the barn doors bearing gifts. Many of my students also remembered putting on paper crowns and carrying cardboard scepters sheathed in shiny silver wrapping paper for this part of the Christmas pageant. But despite all the familiar carols about the "three kings," the tinfoil crowns, and thousands of paintings — some of them artistically marvelous — there is nothing in the Bible itself that says these visitors from the east were kings, or that there were three, or that they were all men, or that one of them was black (or that the other two were white).

The Revised Standard Version calls these visitors "wise men." The Revised English Version prefers "astrologers." Undoubtedly, however, Matthew wanted us to think of them as practitioners of religions other than Judaism, perhaps from Persia. In our current usage, the term *magoi* might best be interpreted as "gurus," spiritual masters from the east. To update the tableau for today we might include a Muslim dervish, a Buddhist lama, a Hindu *sunyasi,* a Confucian sage, and maybe a druid in the church school montage. The point is that these were teachers from other spiritual traditions. It was only much later, when Christianity became the religion of the empire, and still later the ideology of the monarchs of Europe, that these masters of wisdom were handed scepters and crowns and recast into royalty. The point of Matthew's plot is that although they were definitely not Israelites, they sensed that something was going on among these strange Hebrew people which was also important for them. They came to check it out. They brought gifts — gold, frankincense, and myrrh, the story says — and then went home again. *They did not stay.* They did not become disciples of this child, nor was there any indication that they should.

The story of the *magoi* has another dimension as well, and it is a patently political, even subversive, one. They have noticed a new star rising and see it as an auspicious sign. But when they first arrive from the east, they do not know where to look, so they inquire in Jerusalem for the whereabouts of the child they think may grow up to become the new king of the Jews. King Herod, who had been appointed king by the Roman Senate and was never that secure on his throne, is understandably disconcerted. He tries to find out from the visitors where the child is by lying to them that he too would like to pay homage to the baby. But the *magoi* see through his chicanery, elude him, and go home by a different route.

Here is a birth story that, like the genealogies, is replete with intrigue, conflict, and deception. Once again, like the ominous musical theme in a suspense movie, it alerts us that something of consequence is coming. Not only will this rabbi favor the poor and the religiously suspect among his own people, he will also reach out to the outcasts and the Gentiles, and he will fall into such serious disfavor with the Roman authorities and their surrogates that they will end up executing him for sedition. In fact, the very words the *magoi* blurt out to describe the infant they are seeking ("king of the Jews") are the ones Pilate, the Roman prefect, later inscribed over the cross on which Jesus was liquidated.

We had just discussed this passage in class when a student handed me a fascinating clipping from his hometown newspaper. It stated that a certain Father Giancarlo Sivieri had insisted he had only the best intentions in mind when, during the days before Christmas in 2001, he placed a small replica of Osama bin Laden in the Nativity crèche outside his church, the Basilica of the Sacred Heart in the Tuscan city of Grosseto in Italy. He had cut out a photo of bin Laden from a newspaper, mounted it on cardboard, and positioned it alongside the wise men, the animals, the shepherds, Mary, Joseph, and the child.

Father Sivieri's creative visual interpretation of the familiar story, however, did not go unnoticed. According to the Italian news agency ANSA, complaints poured in to the priest not only from the parishioners and the other people of Grosseto, but also from the bishop of the diocese, Giacomo Babini, and from the mayor of the town, Alessandro Antichi. Father Sivieri said he was saddened that these people did not understand the theological message he was trying to convey, namely "that Christ came to earth to redeem every sinner, man or woman, and bin Laden is one of them. The baby Jesus," he continued, "did not come for the poetry of Christmas but to take on himself the sins of the world." The article did not say how this unusual retelling of the Christmas story ended. But I suspect Father Sivieri removed the offending figure, which is too bad because he was making an interesting point. And he was also making the all-too-familiar strange and noteworthy, a hard thing to do.

In Matthew's story King Herod obviously represents both Rome and the Jewish quislings who were collaborating with their captors. This is why the interaction of the *magoi* with Herod is so important. As we will see later, it foreshadows the encounter Rabbi Jesus will have with a Roman centurion, but that story contains a surprising plot reversal. The passage immediately follows the Sermon on the Mount. Having taught Torah at the summit, the rabbi is pictured clambering down and immediately running into a leper. Lepers were by definition ritually unclean, so physical contact with them made other people ritually unclean as well. But without hesitation Jesus heals the sick man by touching him and sends him off to offer his gift in the Temple, "as Moses has commanded."

Then, as though touching a leper were not enough for one day, the centurion, an officer from the detested Roman occupation forces, approaches him. But this dreaded embodiment of Roman might does not try to kill him. Instead, he wants Jesus to heal his sick servant who is "lying at home, paralyzed and in great distress." Jesus offers to come with him but the centurion tells him he has confidence that this rabbi can accomplish the healing by merely "speaking the word." Then Jesus says to him, "I have not found so great faith, no, not in Israel . . . [M]any shall come from the east and the west and shall sit down with Abraham and Isaac and Jacob in the kingdom of heaven" (Matthew 8:5–10). The *magoi* had come from the east; the Romans from the west. The leper had come from outside the border of ritually clean society. The same symbolic cast of characters who had been present at his birth is in the picture again. But this time Jesus is drawing them all around the family table of the same patriarchs who are listed in his genealogy. There are numerous accounts throughout Jewish history and folklore of Gentiles who seek out the great Hebrew *zaddiks* and *maggids* to ask them for help. In this story it happens to Rabbi Jesus.

Here is boundary-breaking Rabbi Jesus at his most vivid: lepers, Romans, what next? Recently some biblical scholars have raised questions about whether the "real, historical" Jesus really evidenced such concern for Gentiles. They suggest that sayings such as this one must have been written back into the record retroactively after the early Jesus movement failed to win over anything like a majority of the Jews to his interpretation of Torah and turned to the Gentile world. We will never know for sure, of course. But I have not been persuaded by these arguments, in part because Jesus did not himself invent the strong, open-ended strain in Judaism. The prophets had taught it long before him. Isaiah wrote,

> I shall appoint you a light to the nations so that my salvation may reach earth's farthest bounds. (Isaiah 49:6)

During the two thousand years since the life of Jesus, Judaism has continued to live with a certain tension between its universalistic and its particularistic characteristics. Recent scholarship suggests that there was more universalism in the first three centuries of the Common Era than had previously been acknowledged. When Christians became arrogant and imperialistic, especially after the conversion of Constantine, Jews understandably emphasized their own particularity. But the universalistic current in Judaism never disappeared. It is said that the famous Rebbe of Kuznitz once prayed, "O Lord, I beg of you to redeem Israel. And if you do not do that, then redeem the Gentiles." It is true that Jesus' teaching put a particularly strong emphasis on this open strain in his tradition, but his remark to the centurion is in no sense anti-Judaistic, and it is just what Matthew presaged in the story of the *magoi*.

Today, at a time when many Christians still caricature Judaism as closed and clannish, and some Jews still see Rabbi Jesus as having overstepped the boundaries of his tradition, it is important to remind ourselves that a fervent desire to open the covenant to the

Gentiles began early in Jewish history and has continued throughout its many centuries, emphasized in some periods more than others. In fact some Jewish teachers agree that acting on this impulse
was precisely the genius of Jesus' approach. In 1901, to take just one
example, a young and then quite unknown German scholar and
rabbi named Leo Baeck wrote that there had been a moment nineteen hundred years before when the time was ripe for a "God-sent
personality." The time had come for the pagans to learn and absorb
Israel's values. Baeck believed that the Jewish people did respond to
this moment, and that the response was in the form of Jesus of
Nazareth. Christians, alas, have done much to poison the relationship between themselves and the Jews that Baeck hoped for. Still,
writing in 1966, the American Jewish scholar Will Herberg expressed virtually the same thought in different terms. In claiming
that it is only through being part of a covenant people, not individu-
ally, that any human being has any standing with God, he goes on to
say, "It is hard to avoid the conviction that Christianity emerges, in
God's plan of redemption, to open the covenant of Israel to the 'nations of the world.' " It is important to remember that when the
magoi came to the stable, Christianity did not yet exist. But the event
that took place below those pigeon-nested rafters suggests that a
new phase in God's unbroken covenant with his people was beginning, and that they too would become part of its enlarging scope.
Then, however, the birth story took an ominous and violent turn.

> When Herod realized that the astrologers had tricked him he flew
> into a rage, and gave orders for the massacre of all the boys aged
> two years or under, in Bethlehem and throughout the whole dis-
> trict, in accordance with the time he has ascertained from the as-
> trologers. So the words spoken through Jeremiah the prophet
> were fulfilled. "A voice was heard in Rama, sobbing in bitter grief;
> it was Rachel weeping for her children, and refusing to be com-
> forted, because they were no more." (Matthew 2:16–18)

Among the stories of the birth of Rabbi Jesus, this is one that is
never depicted in Sunday school Nativity productions. No wonder.

It is a vicious and ugly story, but one that has also returned all too frequently throughout the later history of the Jewish people, and of other peoples as well, even today. It is the story of Herod's massacre of the innocent children and the flight of Jesus' family into exile in Egypt. King Herod, the story says, foiled in his attempt to cozen the *magoi* into revealing the whereabouts of the child he suspected might be a threat to his teetering throne, decides on a strategy that has become all too familiar in the modern world. So as not to miss the one child in question, he orders all the male children in that area butchered. Brueghel's overpowering painting *The Slaughter of the Innocent* brings the story brutally to life. Soldiers wearing steel helmets and carrying pikes stride through a village after a new-fallen snow. Hysterical mothers clutch vainly at their children as the soldiers hack and stab them. Spatters of blood discolor the white drifts.

Herod's murderous mission fails, at least as far as the child Jesus is concerned. Warned in advance, Joseph and Mary hurriedly set out for Egypt, clutching the baby, before the troops arrive. But this is not quite a happy ending. One time a student asked me if I thought that, when he grew up, Jesus was told about all the children who had died so violently because the king was trying to kill him. If he had been told, how did he feel about it? We know that children often suffer agonizing mental torment because they think they have caused someone's death. In this case Jesus did, at least indirectly, cause the deaths of the children of Bethlehem. Ironically, although Christians often say of Jesus, "he died for us," in this case those children died for him. Another student once asked me if I thought he ever suffered from what is now known as survivor guilt. Of course, I had no satisfying answer for this question. But I told him that maybe Jesus did know, and that maybe it contributed to his unusual capacity for sympathizing with the suffering of others. But whether he did or not, the student's question illustrates again how a compelling narrative can evoke serious moral reflection.

The family of Jesus did not escape all the consequences of Herod's fear and malice. They fled, and they were neither the first nor the last family to be harried into exile by a tyrant. For centuries the expatriate life became the lot of generation upon generation of Jews, but in our time many millions of people have tasted the same kind of exilic existence. Diaspora has become all too normal, and Jewish history the pattern for Rwandans, Tibetans, Salvadorans, and many others. The twentieth century has been called the century of the refugee. There may be more displaced and uprooted human beings today than in any previous era. When I mentioned this in class one day some of the students — mainly Asians, Africans, and Latin Americans — told me this was one aspect of the Jesus story — and the Jewish story — that resonated with them. Either they themselves or their families had survived a Herod only by packing and getting out — fast. They knew from firsthand experience the shock and jarring sense of dislocation that comes with flight. One student, a West African, wrote an eloquent term paper, "Jesus as a Refugee," after reading the account of Joseph, Mary, and their child in the light of his own family's hasty and harrowing flight from a country shredded by civil war, dictatorship, and mayhem.

A few years ago I stopped at a tiny shrine by the roadside near Bethlehem where legend says a weary Mary paused to give her breast to the child Jesus. It is called the Milk Cave and mothers who are having problems with lactation visit it to this day to seek Mary's assistance. The day I was there both Christian and Muslim women were lighting candles and praying to the Virgin for help in fulfilling this most basic of all needs. Seeing these women together reminded me that Mary is mentioned with great respect in the Qur'an. But these women were fortunate. After their prayers most could return home. Nearly every day our TV screens and newspapers reveal a much bleaker picture of refugee life: Roadsides are choked with displaced and homeless families, and with weary mothers desperately trying to feed children when their breasts have run dry and there is nothing else to eat. For most of them there is no miraculous cave to turn to, and the following day they must shove on to the next way station. Becoming displaced persons pushes people onto a long and taxing road, one that often seems to have no end. The Holy Family, spared the lances of Herod's security elite, was not spared the dust and exhaustion of the flight, or the humiliation and disorientation of living as displaced persons.

What did this early exposure to dislocation mean to Jesus? Did he remember it when he grew up? When I give way momentarily to the respected rabbinic practice of *midrash,* of imagining what is not explicit, I visualize what this little family found when it got to Egypt. Historians tell us many thousands of Jews were living there during Jesus' lifetime. They were migrant workers, day laborers, and uprooted farmers looking for work and for the first-century equivalent of a green card so they could earn something like a living. A Jewish legend dating back to the second century holds that Jesus worked for many years in Egypt as a laborer before eventually returning to Palestine. Matthew says that the family returned only after Herod's death, but does not say how long after. In the next mention we have of Jesus, he is twelve years old and has accompanied his family to Jerusalem for the holidays. It is not clear how many years they stayed in Egypt. What is clear is that the first memories of the child who was to become the Nazareth rabbi were of life in exile.

But as hard as life in exile is, it can teach some valuable lessons. If Jesus did live some of his early life as a refugee, he was exposed every day to people with a different language and culture and religion. It is hard to believe that all his encounters with Egyptians were painful ones. Might this help explain his amazing openness to so many different kinds of people during his brief adult life? His childhood as a stranger in a strange land also makes his rabbinical vocation more plausible and appropriate. The rabbi is the spiritual leader and teacher of Israel par excellence in the situation of diaspora. There were of course rabbis for at least a few years before his birth. But they became the main vehicle of leadership in the Jewish community only after the destruction of the Temple in A.D. 70 ended the sacrificial rituals and there was no longer any role for priests.

Taken as a whole, the stories people told about the birth of the Galilean rabbi sketch the outlines of what his life would later fill in.

A teacher who lived his years at the heart of the tradition of his ancestors, Jesus also read the signs of the times with fierce accuracy. He saw, as Rabbi Baeck writes, that the "time was ripe" for the Gentiles, the "nations" to be welcomed around the table of the covenant. His heart was touched by those who were too poor or too sickly or too morally suspect to appreciate the love of Torah, and he had no patience for anyone who made their lot harder. He saw both the futility of armed opposition to the Roman behemoth and the disgrace of craven bootlicking. He enjoyed the camaraderie of social misfits and vagabonds. He discerned strength in what most people regarded as vulnerability. He did not avoid conflict with the tyrant. But he faced power with truth. And all these qualities are already present in the stories of his birth and boyhood. That, simply put, is the whole point of them.

8

Riffing on Simeon

There was at that time in Jerusalem a man called Simeon. This man was upright and devout, one who watched and waited for the restoration of Israel, and the Holy Spirit was upon him. It had been revealed to him by the Holy Spirit that he would not see death until he had seen the Lord's Messiah. Guided by the Spirit he came into the temple; and when the parents brought in the child Jesus to do for him what the law required, he took him in his arms, praised God, and said:

> "Now, Lord, you are releasing your servant in peace,
> according to your promise,
> For I have seen with my own eyes
> the deliverance you have made ready
> in full view of all nations:
> a light that will bring revelation to the Gentiles
> and glory to your people Israel."

The child's father and mother were full of wonder at what was being said about him. Simeon blessed them and said to Mary his mother, "This child is destined to be a sign that will be rejected: and you too will be pierced to the heart. Many in Israel will stand or fall because of him; and so the secret thoughts of many will be laid bare." — LUKE 2:21–35

THE RELIGIOUS IMAGINATION is like what jazz musicians call *riffing*. A jazz player starts with the theme or the chords of a tune, then without departing from the structure they provide, creates an embellishment that remains true to the original. It is a fine art. A good riff neither replicates the original nor leaves it completely behind. Just after the birth narratives, Luke tucks in a marvelous example of just such a riff. This is the religious imagination at work.

Joseph and Mary bring their newborn son to the Temple to be circumcised according to Jewish law. An elderly man, an inhabitant of Jerusalem named Simeon, is inspired by the Spirit to find them in the Temple so he can bless the child. God had promised him that he would not die until he laid eyes on his people's deliverer. The old man takes the tiny baby in his arms, but the blessing he bestows exceeds anything Joseph and Mary had expected. He declares that Jesus will not only be the liberator of Israel, he will also be "a light to lighten the Gentiles." His words surprise the parents (they "marveled at what was said about him"), even though the phrase is a quotation from the prophet Isaiah. But Simeon also warns Mary that this will not be an easy assignment, and that "a sword will pierce through your own soul also." The iconography of Mary for many centuries has pictured her with a sword through her heart.

The Simeon sequence is a perfect illustration of a religious riff, a creative extrapolation from a given theme. It is also typical of the kinds of stories that circulate about rabbis and other spiritual teachers. There are similar tales, for example, about an old man named Asita who foretells the destiny of the child Buddha. Some scholars identify Simeon as a first-century rabbi who was the son of Rabbi Hillel (after whom Jewish student associations on college campuses are still named today) and the father of Rabbi Gamaliel. The latter is especially important for more than one reason. He belonged to the Sanhedrin, the Jewish ruling council, during Jesus' lifetime, and some traditions say he was the teacher of St. Paul. He is known to have advocated a generous interpretation of the Law and, more famously, to have advised the Sanhedrin not to crack down on the emerging Jesus movement but to allow the future to determine whether or not it was blessed by God.

There is no doubt that Hillel and Gamaliel were historical figures. Beyond that, every one of these historical connections with Simeon and with Jesus is disputed. But most of my students were gratified to learn that it doesn't matter that much. They were happy not to have to plod through a ream of critical arguments and counterarguments. If Rabbi ben Israel, the Baal Shem Tov, who lived in the eighteenth century, can have attracted so many stories about himself, some during his own lifetime, it should come as no surprise that the same process was at work with Simeon and Jesus. The Simeon story is a classic case of what the Jewish tradition calls *midrash*.

The word itself derives from the Hebrew word *darash*, which means "to inquire." The possibility, indeed the necessity, of midrash arises because the commandments God gave to Moses, the foundation of all Jewish ethics, are mostly phrased in generalities, while actually applying them requires specifics. Yet the Bible itself often merely says one should do "as the Lord commanded Moses." It does not say exactly what that is. Midrash is a method invented by the rabbis to fill in the blanks, to span the gap between the general and the specific, and between then and now.

Midrashim (the plural) often take the form of stories. They are what *The Oxford Dictionary of the Jewish Religion* calls "imaginative expositions," and can deal with theology, ethics, and popular philosophy. They sometimes find expression in fables or allegories. They frequently rely on analogies, echoes of other texts, and the rhythms of the words. Their purpose, however, is clear. They are "an instrument for imparting contemporary relevance to biblical events." They are meant to "keep the ethics of the Torah fresh and meaningful" for subsequent generations and different situations. They are intended, as Jacob Neusner writes, to "show how the received Scriptures of ancient Israel in fact refer to, or are realized in, moments of our own day."

There are literally thousands of midrashim. What they have in common is their effort to read between the lines of the Bible and to use the power of narrative to bring the central point of old texts to the contemporary hearer. Take this parable, for example, from another Simeon, this one Rabbi Simeon ben Eleazar, which presents his midrash on the Adam and Eve story from an angle that seems much more sympathetic to Eve:

To what may the first Man be compared? He was like a man who married a proselyte, who sat and gave her instructions, saying to her, "My daughter, do not eat a piece of bread when your hands are cultically unclean, and do not eat produce that has not been tithed, and do not profane the Sabbath, and do not walk about with any other man. Now, if you violate any of these orders, you will be subject to the death penalty."

What did the Man himself do? He went and in her presence ate a piece of bread when his hands were cultically unclean, ate produce that had not been tithed, violated the Sabbath, went around making vows, and with his own hands placed before her [an example of what he himself had prohibited]. What did the proselyte say to herself? "All these orders my husband gave me to begin with were lies." So she went ahead and violated them.

No definite date has been established for this midrash, but it probably comes from the early medieval period. This explains why, although its fanciful extrapolation of the Garden of Eden story undercuts those Christian interpretations that blame the Fall mostly on Eve, it still appears antiquated in its ethical views. But this is not an insurmountable problem for rabbis or for the midrash process. Subsequent updatings will be equally authoritative, and then subject to even further reinterpretation and emendation. The story goes on and on. It develops a life of its own, but it is always tethered, albeit with a very long cord, to the biblical text itself. This is exactly what the old Simeon in Luke's Gospel is pictured as doing. The biblical texts he refers to are from the prophet Isaiah (40:5; 52:10; 42:6; 49:6, and 46:13), who had lived six hundred years before him, and the story depicts Simeon applying them to the current situation.

Sometimes the rabbis filled in missing scenes from the biblical account and then, having done so, went on to draw a moral from them. Like the conversation between Simeon and Mary, many portrayed conversations between the older and the younger generations. When we discussed the Simeon story in class, it reminded the students of exchanges they had had with old people, sometimes their grandparents, but also other elderly folks who had advised or scolded or encouraged them. Some students voiced their regrets that the older person they described had died before they got a chance to express their appreciation. I knew this was a common sentiment. But others said that, frankly, the old people they knew were often boring or distracted, that they had often craved the kind of wise counsel they had heard came from the gray heads, but they never got it. They thought the whole "wisdom of the elderly" business was overrated. Those discussions could have gone on for weeks.

One of my favorite examples in the midrashic literature of these intergenerational conversations is the discussion the rabbis invented between the aging patriarch Jacob and his sons. The sons had just returned from Egypt, where he had sent them in search of food during a famine. As the Bible itself tells it, they had met their brother Joseph, whom they had sold into slavery years before, albeit without recognizing him ("And Joseph knew his brethren but they knew him not"; Genesis 42:8). Joseph had helped them but had told them not to come back unless they brought their youngest brother, Benjamin, along with them. Old Jacob, having already lost — as he thought — his favorite son Joseph, was understandably reluctant to put young Benjamin in danger. His son Judah, however, tries to reassure him. He promises to bring the young boy back, so Jacob eventually concedes. But the intriguing question is: What made the old man change his mind?

The rabbis do not keep us in suspense long. Here is the "filled out" conversation as it is recounted in Louis Ginzberg's *Legends of the Bible*. It begins with Jacob reprimanding Judah for telling this powerful Egyptian that he had even had a younger brother. But notice that the rabbis do not hesitate to bring God himself into the argument:

> And Jacob said, "Wherefore dealt ye so ill with me as to tell the man ye had yet a brother?" . . . And God said, "I made it my business to raise his son to the position of ruler of Egypt, and he complains, and says, Wherefore dealt ye so ill with me?"

Now Judah, resenting the reproach, argues back to his father and claims he had little choice since the ruler seemed to know nearly everything about their family and their native land anyway.

> "Why he knew the very wood of which our baby coaches are made, Father!" He continued, "If Benjamin goes with us, he may indeed, be taken from us, but also he may not. This is a doubtful matter, but it is certain that if he does not go with us, we shall all die of hunger."

Now Judah drives the moral home to his father:

> It is better not to concern thyself about what is doubtful, and guide thy actions by what is certain.

This is a midrash with a clear lesson for the moral life: Base your decision on what you know rather than on what you guess. Not all midrashim are this explicit. Many are puzzling and even gnomic. They also sometimes seem to be making conflicting points. But in the rabbinical tradition contradictory readings, often appearing side by side in the same collections of midrashim, do not appear to have been a problem either. The rabbis believed that any verse, any story in the Bible was open to many possible interpretations, and they enjoyed pointing out that within those parts of the Bible that were written later, there are interpretations and expansions of earlier biblical passages. The writers of the Bible, it seems, were not themselves literalists.

This is a good corrective for those Christians, both the historical-critical scholars and the fundamentalists, who insist there must be one and only one "real meaning" to any given text. The critical scholars expend prodigious energy investigating the original context, the historical situation from which the text comes, and — if the verse is in the Greek in which the New Testament Gospels are written — what the Aramaic in which Jesus himself spoke might have been. Whole retranslations of the Gospels back into what someone thinks the Aramaic said have been published. But they involve an enormous amount of guesswork. More important, no one

will ever be able to recover the tone of voice in which Jesus spoke
his words, or his hand gestures, or the body language that accompanied it. This obsessive search for the *ipsissima verba,* which has
marked modern biblical scholarship, never quite reaches its goal. It
is at best a highly speculative enterprise.

The fundamentalists, on the other hand, solve the problem by insisting that every word was divinely inspired and that anyone with
common sense can see the plain meaning. But this has not solved
the problem either, since even the most accomplished linguists do
not know for sure what certain Greek and Hebrew words actually
mean. They often have to insert words or phrases just to make a
sentence complete or to fill in an obvious gap. In the classic King
James Version of the Bible, the editors signaled these additions by
putting them in italics. As for the "plain meaning," even the fundamentalists do not agree on what it is, which raises serious questions
about just how plain it is.

The later rabbis, of course, eventually came to disagree with the
midrash about Jesus attributed to Simeon. They did not accept his
claim that Jesus signified the beginning of the fulfillment of the
prophecy of Isaiah. Still, the midrash form remains a valid teaching
and interpretive device. Maybe the time has come to take a page
from the rabbis and decide that there need not be any one, final, and
definitive meaning to a biblical text. We have a good example of this
in Rabbi Jesus himself, both in the stories he told and in the ones
people told about him. A Christian cannot possibly read the rabbinical midrashim without thinking of the birth stories with their angels and shepherds and "wise men." Spinning midrashim, riffing on
the old themes, is just what the rabbi from Nazareth was doing.
Like rabbis before and after him, he was interpreting and applying
the Law and using — among other things — fabulous stories to do
so. I believe Jesus fully expected his words and his parables to grow
shoots and sprouts, to scatter seeds that would themselves bud and
blossom. The big mistake we have made is to suppose that his interpretations, directed to the daily problems of people who lived in
first-century Palestine, are not open to the imaginative enlargement

and updating so characteristic of rabbinical teaching. By doing this we are, in effect, wresting Jesus away from his own teaching and, ironically, negating one of the few things about him that the historical Jesus scholars agree on, that he was indeed a rabbi. This is precisely why taking the "rabbi-hood" of Jesus seriously is an essential key to understanding his ethical significance for today.

9

Beat the Devil

Jesus was then led by the Spirit into the wilderness to be tempted by the devil. For forty days and nights he fasted and at the end of them he was famished. The tempter approached him and said, "If you are the Son of God, tell these stones to become bread." Jesus answered, "Scripture says, 'Man is not to live on bread alone, but on every word that comes from the mouth of God.'"

The devil then took him to the Holy City and set him on the parapet of the temple. "If you are the Son of God," he said, "throw yourself down; for Scripture says, 'He will put his angels in charge of you, and they will support you in their arms, for fear you should strike your foot against a stone.'" Jesus answered him, "Scripture also says, 'You are not to put your Lord God to the test.'" The devil took him next to a very high mountain, and showed him all the kingdoms of the world in their glory. "All these," he said, "I will give you if you will only fall down and do me homage." But Jesus said, "Out of my sight, Satan! Scripture says, 'You shall do homage to the Lord your God, and worship him alone.'"

— MATTHEW 4:1–10

FOR MY STUDENTS, the word *temptation* exudes a steamy, seductive scent. Or it has to do with calorie-rich desserts. A campus restaurant carries a chocolate sundae on its menu labeled "The Tempter." But the "temptation scene" in Matthew is about something else. It is about the use and misuse of power. Dostoyevsky drew on it when he wrote his searing tale of the Grand Inquisitor in *The Brothers Karamazov,* a kind of Christian midrash. Christ's encounter with Satan in the wilderness has sparked endless debates among psychologists about the unusual mental states that can be induced by fasting. However, I don't think it is useful to argue about whether a devil figure actually confronted Jesus, as biblical literalists insist, or whether he imagined one, or whether this is a graphic way of describing a brutal struggle he fought with his own inner inclinations.

It is helpful to place this desert encounter in the full trajectory of Jesus' life. After the brief mention of his visiting the Temple with his parents at the age of twelve, Jesus reappears only when he joins a highly suspect movement led by a shabby wilderness rabble-rouser named John the Baptist. John's followers were all harshly critical of the religious leadership at the Jerusalem Temple, and John had seized on an ancient Jewish purification ritual of submersion in water, which is still used by Orthodox Jews today, and adapted it for his own purposes. To be baptized by John was an act of protest against the religious establishment. But the religious establishment was the vehicle by which the Romans ruled their disorderly province, so it should not be surprising that King Herod had John beheaded. His execution prompted Jesus to hurry to another area to escape the security forces, but there can be no doubt that he had accepted John's views. Later he deepened and sharpened them, but — unlike John — he took his own message into the towns and cities rather than expecting people to seek him out in the desert.

No one knows for sure, of course, what actually happened when, shortly after his baptism by John, Jesus retreated to the desert for forty days to fast and pray and to think things through. The psychological quibbles about it obscure the real thrust of the story, which is about what kind of life he would live and what options he would face. He knew by now that he was going to have to be a leader. That insight had come to him during his baptism, and is expressed in the story or the voice from heaven announcing his adoption as the Son of God. The question was: What kind of leader would he be?

But even when they hear this interpretation, the temptation scene is a hard one for present-day students to appreciate. The main obstacle is their mental image of the devil. It is usually that of a *grande*-sized Halloween goblin in horns and a red suit, brandishing a pitchfork. But it is important to get behind the imagery and see what this story provides: a typology of leadership styles. It suggests that early in their careers people inevitably develop a certain approach to decision making, what Aquinas called a *habitus*. Then they apply this way of making choices throughout their careers. The temptation story supplies a useful grid for examining some of the root postures from which people, including leaders, make their decisions.

There are three temptations, each vividly illustrating one of the most common root postures.

The first, changing stones into bread, is the all-too-human hankering to see and control the results of what we do, the inability to live with ambiguity.

The second, being borne up majestically by the angelic legions, is the human hope to garner the credit, to have one's achievements admiringly acknowledged. Today's equivalent might be to get hoisted onto the shoulders of the admiring crowd.

The third temptation is the most seductive. It is to surrender to the suspicion that, when all is said and done, "there is nothing you can do about it." The cards are stacked. Why fight city hall? But this simply allows evil to have its way. It "puts the devil in charge." Doing homage to Satan is not bowing one's knee to a Halloween imp. It is more like throwing up one's hands, giving in to the temptation to believe "that's the way it's done, and there's nothing much you can do about it." Lucifer wins again.

The temptation story shows Jesus at the outset of his public career struggling with the question of what leadership style he will choose. This may be why Matthew places the temptation scene just before his description of Jesus' selection of his first disciples — Peter, Andrew, James, and John. This was, after all, his first big decision as a leader, and the men he chose constituted the core of his staff, his inner cabinet, right to the end.

Jesus' choice of disciples — why these and not others? — was a decision that registered immediately with the students. Even at a young age they knew how important friends and colleagues are;

they recognized the importance of the other actors in the sopho-more play, their teammates on the soccer field, their laboratory partners. And in this class, as they grappled week after week with baffling choices, they knew they needed fellow travelers, trusted as-sociates with whom they felt safe in trying out new ideas. They were pleased to find out that Jesus did, too.

There is ample evidence in the Gospels that Jesus was not born with his life mission fully in mind. He did, after all, spend some time as a disciple of John the Baptist before John was arrested and killed. He often asked his disciples questions. Although a certain Christian view holds that these were just rhetorical teasers, meant to test the disciples, and that he already knew the answers, I do not accept that. Christians believe that Jesus was the *fully human* expression of God's love, so like any other human being, he felt the torment of uncer-tainty. He sweated drops of blood in the Garden of Gethsemane as he tried to decide whether to continue with his mission even when he had become aware that it would cost him his life. He was fully human, and human beings need other human beings, not just as disciples but also as friends, which is what Jesus told his own follow-ers at the Last Supper that he wanted them to be (John 15:15). The point is clear. Living a moral life is not a solo flight.

This may be one of the most important things my students picked up from the course, and it was not an easy lesson in a univer-sity that — like most other universities — places a high premium on individual achievement. Also, many approaches to moral decision making outside the classroom seem to imply a solitary chooser. In the "personal advice" columns in the daily newspaper, for example, the alleged expert on manners or ethics usually delivers a straight-forward answer to a questioner, but only rarely suggests that the in-quirer talk the matter through with other people. The transaction is a one-to-one affair. But even though the prolonged and intense dis-cussions in the ROTC building were sometimes painful, the stu-dents gradually realized that living a moral life is ultimately a shared enterprise.

Still, some students — and I am sure many adults — remain baffled by this devil figure. As several students kept asking me, even after I told them I had no answer: What if all this only happened in his imagination?

Well, suppose it did. I have already suggested that the human imagination is the underdeveloped organ of the moral life, and perhaps the spiritual life as well. Encouraged by the tradition of midrash and the rabbinical imagination, I had already become convinced of this. But then, after I had been teaching my course for a few years, I found a marvelous supporter at the heart of the Christian tradition itself, the famous *Spiritual Exercises* of St. Ignatius of Loyola (1491–1556). What I learned from them enabled me — and the students — to be less suspicious of the role of imagination in life.

Loyola began his life as a soldier, but changed course in his middle years when he barely escaped death after being seriously wounded. While recovering he read the Gospels and some of the lives of the saints and decided to become a soldier in the service of Jesus and to follow his commands. He then recruited several like-minded men and organized what he called the Society of Jesus, known more widely today as the Jesuits. But Loyola knew that the men he recruited faced a predicament. If they were to "follow Jesus," how were they to know what to do in situations that Jesus never faced? This is the same dilemma anyone trying to follow Jesus must face twenty centuries after his earthly life, and Loyola wrote the *Spiritual Exercises* in large part to answer this question.

The Spiritual Exercises bear a striking resemblance to midrashim. Like the rabbis, Loyola turned to the power of imagination to span the gap between then and now. He prescribed a specific form of meditation, which every Jesuit was obliged to practice on a regular basis. It required the reader to project himself back into the Gospel stories and into the presence of the living Jesus, and then to carry on an imagined conversation with him. First used almost exclusively by the Jesuits themselves, this potent combination of biblical study, prayer, and imagination has now deepened and enlarged the faith of thousands of men and women. But it is rarely applied directly to moral reasoning.

My own encounter with Loyola's *Spiritual Exercises* did not occur in a classroom. Classrooms do not often encourage much imagination. But the more I learned about the classes my colleagues were teaching in moral reasoning, and the more I struggled with the relevance of Jesus for decision making today, the more I saw the desperate need to reincorporate imaginative thinking into the moral life. I came to feel that we needed to encourage the students to step back from the texts of Kant or Hume or even the Gospels and use their capacity for fantasy and inventiveness, which I knew they had because they demonstrated it in so many other parts of their lives. Some of them acted in campus plays, so they knew how to be someone else and somewhere else on a stage. Some wrote stories, others crafted poems. But few had ever thought that their gift for creativity could be applied to moral reflection.

Still, my discovery of how to quicken both my own and my students' moral imaginations was something of an accident. For some years I had heard about people whose faith had been strengthened by working over a period of a time with a "spiritual director." After hesitating awhile, I decided to try it myself. Finally I found a spiritual director who was willing to take me on. A Jesuit, he worked at an institution called the Center for Religious Development, near Harvard Yard, where skilled practitioners train people of many different denominations to become spiritual counselors. I told him I did not want to become such a counselor, but he generously agreed to take me on anyway for regular weekly sessions over the course of a year.

That year marked a turning point not only in my teaching but in my personal faith as well. I knew that the Jesuits still use the rigorous four-week schedule of Spiritual Exercises, but I also knew that Jesuits are famously flexible. This proved to be true. My spiritual guide did not try to make a Jesuit out of me. Instead, he patiently took the time to discover the shape of my own spiritual background and to help me go on from there. Fortunately, I was raised in a faith in which the idea of "walking and talking with Jesus," the concept that Loyola had also made central to the Exercises, is not all that strange. Anyone familiar with gospel songs knows that those of us who grew up singing them were encouraged to imagine meeting him "In the Garden" or by the Sea of Galilee and to "Have a Little Talk with Jesus." It is also true that those of us who were taught these songs sometimes feel embarrassed about them as we grow older. They can seem childish, and they hardly match a Mozart mass or Bach chorale in musical distinction. Consequently, when I started my year with the spiritual director, I was a little self-conscious about my early background. But he soon put me at ease. Why, he asked, should anyone want to banish imaginary conversations from the spiritual or ethical life? Has our "just the facts"–obsessed society denigrated imagination so thoroughly that it must now skulk on the outskirts of human thought?

I was reassured. Within a few weeks I was carrying on regular imaginary conversations with Jesus. I had them while I jogged, while I walked in the park, while I sat in my study, or while I read passages from the Gospels. After a few months, however, I began to have some reservations. What if these conversations, instead of a creative form of prayer, were nothing but massive excursions in self-delusion? My spiritual director was not surprised when I told him about my doubts. He quietly suggested that the best test of whether I was merely projecting was to note whether Jesus ever gave me advice I did not want to hear or suggested I do something I did not want to do. When I told him he did, he smiled. I got the point. Now, years later, I still carry on imaginary conversations with the rabbi from Nazareth. It has become my principal form of meditation.

I had sought out a spiritual director for personal reasons. But then one day I made an important connection. I usually had an appointment with him on Monday afternoon. On Tuesday and Thursday I lectured to my class, and I met the discussion section on Wednesday. Slowly these two parts of my life began to merge. I began to see how vital it is to reinvigorate the power of imagination when we try to teach young people — and to learn ourselves — how to think about moral questions. But it was just at this point that I faced the most difficult dilemma. Religiously, my students were a very mixed crew. Was there any way I could adapt this powerful wedding of moral reflection and imagination for them?

I decided to start by reading Loyola's original *Spiritual Exercises* and some of the commentaries on them for myself. This was something my spiritual director had never suggested I do, and when I told him he shrugged his shoulders and looked doubtful. I could see why. I had hardly begun when I almost immediately gave up the effort. Both the *Exercises* and the commentaries, even in recent translations, are written in such baroque theological language that they lost me almost completely. I knew they would be no help at all to my students. Still, under the gaudy rhetoric, they seemed to be saying something important. But I knew that to make use of them I would need to "translate" not only the language but also the ideas into an idiom they — and I — could understand. I doubt that the result was something either Loyola or those who still live within his sixteenth-century religious worldview, would appreciate. But it made sense to me, and it made a big difference both in the way I understood Jesus and in the way I approached the course.

The Spiritual Exercises consist of a precise series of highly structured meditations on the earthly life of Christ as recounted in the Bible. The four weeks are divided into four separate but interconnected programs. Loyola insisted that the purpose of this contemplation was to discern, within Jesus' earthly life, the hidden life of God. I realized, however, that for many of my students, especially those who did not believe in the Incarnation, this was something I could hardly ask them to do. I decided I wanted to present this valuable practice in such a way that the students who believed in the Incarnation, those who did not, and those who had no idea what it was could all be included. I reasoned that the first people who encountered Jesus came to him because of his gifts as a healer and a teacher. The doctrine of the Incarnation, as one way of describing *how* the Spirit of God was present in Jesus, was developed many years after that. So, without knowing what would happen, I plunged ahead.

This was not, however, the last obstacle. The First Week of the

Exercises is taken up with a relentless self-examination, something for which the Jesuits subsequently became famous. Loyola believed that such an introspective beginning was necessary in order to prepare the ground for what was coming later. But students, like most people who contemplate moral choices, believe that although they must make a choice, the issue itself is "out there" not "in here." They want to weigh pros and cons, and ponder what principles might apply. They want to *do* the right thing, not waste valuable time contemplating their own navels.

Still, my own experience with the greatly simplified version of the Exercises had convinced me that this "in here, out there" gap is one of the problems with the way we think about moral issues today. We mistakenly sever the question of "Who am I" from the question of "What must I do?" The two belong together. I agree with something one of the commentators on the *Spiritual Exercises* wrote when he described what this method adds to the standard logical approach to ethical thought. It provides, he says, "that constancy of mind and heart which no intellectual reflection can devise, which no frenzied activity can wrest, and which no cultivated apathy can feign." Still, I wondered how the idea of starting to think about a moral question by looking into yourself and instead of directly at the question would sit with a crowd of hyperactive college students.

To my surprise, it sat quite well. The Jewish students knew about the self-examination required during the Days of Awe between Rosh Hashanah and Yom Kippur. The Christians knew about Lent. Other students had had experience in various twelve-step programs in which the whole effort begins with a self-administered "moral inventory." Others had dipped into one or another form of sitting discipline such as Zen or Vipassana, or had tried to meditate with a mantra. Socrates said that the key to living a truly human life is to "know thyself." I do not believe that is enough, but it is an indispensable start. As I read the *Exercises* I also remembered a conversation I once had with the Tibetan Buddhist teacher Chogyam Trungpa Rinpoche twenty-five years ago. He told me that what

Americans, and especially young Americans, needed more than any-thing else was just to sit still a couple hours every day and get to know their own thought processes. He believed, correctly I think, that we are all assaulted by so many messages battering us from the outside every hour of the day that our capacity for listening to our own inner voices is often drowned out. Loyola, it seems, was a kind of guru before his time.

But there were other elements of the First Week of the Exercises that puzzled me as well. For example, those engaged in the exercise were encouraged to begin their self-examination by reflecting on the "sin of the angels" before going on to think about the "sin of our first parents," and only then to examine our own personal con-sciences. Again I almost gave up. How could I, to say nothing of my students, make any sense out of this? Admittedly angels of a certain variety are once again popular in songs and on television. But they tend to be silly apparitions who fill largely comic roles. Nor did the sin of our mythical forebears Adam and Eve seem particularly relevant. Why not get right into the painful probing of my *own* conscience?

Once again, however, I found there was real wisdom in Loyola's formula, although I had to "translate" it. Biblical scholars and theo-logians today believe that when the ancients talked about good and bad angels, they were struggling — in their own idiom — with the mysterious origins of good and evil. And they were wrestling with the age-old question of why evil persists not just in individuals but also in cultural patterns and institutions. Angels are the spiritual de-scendants of the gods and demigods of the era of polytheism, each of whom had his own realm to rule over — the hearth, the fields, the furnace, the banquet table, the marriage bed — and all the other areas of human life. They predated and would outlast individual human beings. One ignored the gods to one's peril, as every page of the *Iliad* and the *Odyssey* demonstrates.

Angels and demons are mythical expressions of our awareness of powerful currents in our world that can pick us up and sweep us along. Marx and Freud both knew about these forces, even though they did not call them angels. Clearly, to think productively about oneself and the choices one faces, no one can ignore these forces. So I advised my students not to begin their self-examination with themselves (especially since that can be so discouraging that some people quit right away), but to get a little perspective. Better to begin calmly by giving some careful consideration to questions like, "Where did this issue come from?" and "How did it appear in my life?" Some things that are pressing issues today once were not. What are the institutional patterns that make it an issue, for me or for anyone? What this requires is an expedition into what might be called the social archaeology of moral issues. I did not use the term *angels,* and I hope, given the circumstances, Loyola would approve.

The "sin of our first parents" was not as hard to translate. People have been making good choices and bad choices for a very long time, and residues of those choices remain with us and in us. When the students thought about the decisions they had to make, they loved to talk about "where I am coming from." By that they often meant their extended family backgrounds, their ethnic heritage, their memories of the influence of their own parents. In large measure, although by no means completely, these factors had made them who they were and defined "where they were coming from." Recalling this background is valuable because it helps clarify what is often a blurry half-remembered set of factors. Also, by thinking about it systematically, we gain a certain distance from it. We can move beyond blaming the people who were responsible for "where we are coming from" and take some responsibility for our decisions ourselves.

By the time we had left "the angels" and "our first parents" behind, students were ready to take the next step Loyola prescribes — looking into their own personal conscience. The central motif for Loyola here is the Crucifixion. Again, some students could imagine themselves — as he recommends — having a conversation with Christ as he hangs on the cross. But I had to help others grasp what Loyola wanted to make graphically clear: that "doing the right thing" often exacts a high cost. It can be painful, both for the decision maker and for the people around him. The great paintings of the Crucifixion, such as Grünewald's *Isenheim Altarpiece,* show that it is not only Christ himself who suffers on the cross. His friends and family and followers suffer too, and he must have known that they were suffering because of the choices he had made. This was difficult for many of the students to accept. Many were looking for what I came to call a "regret-free decision." They wanted to be able to make choices that would neither hurt nor displease anyone, choices where — as some people like to put it — "everybody wins."

I wished them luck, but I told them there would not be many such decisions in their lives. Still, many of the students did not like this prospect at all. An American history major told me he had read that on the night he made the decision to drop the atomic bomb on Hiroshima, President Harry Truman said he went to bed and "slept like a baby." I told him I hoped that was not true. Putting aside the question of whether his decision was right or wrong (generals Douglas MacArthur and Dwight Eisenhower both thought that he was wrong), Truman knew that while he slept, his decision would cause tens of thousands of innocent women and children to be incinerated in a distant city. Even if we can be at peace with the choices we make, we have to realize that those choices often cause other people pain, sometimes even death.

The sheer agony of making decisions is left out of much discussion about moral reasoning. When one reads the great moral philosophers, their approach often sounds like a method for solving a complex logical quandary. They rarely convey any sense of anguish. There is no crucifixion. But making decisions in the real world is inevitably anguishing. Of course, there are people who have learned to live with this ache simply by growing a thick skin. Still, they pay a heavy price for their coarsened hide because they often lose the very capacity for appreciating someone else's pain that moral decision making requires.

Loyola, however, does not wallow in the Crucifixion scene. He asks us to imagine ourselves in the stable with the shepherds, and with Mary and Joseph and the Christ Child. During the prescribed weeks of the Exercises, he encourages us to put ourselves "in the synagogues, towns and villages" where Jesus preached and taught, to "walk the dusty roads" with him, to "smell and taste" the scene as though one were there oneself. It is impossible for anyone reading this not to think of the stated purpose of the Jewish Passover seder, which is to make every person present feel that he or she was there, with Moses in Egypt, when the exodus took place. All this has further convinced me that to exclude the imagination from moral reasoning is to mutilate and ultimately to neuter it.

The temptation story ends with a warning. When the devil had finished with Jesus, it says, he departed. But not for good. He only left "until an opportune time." Temptation, it seems, never leaves us once and for all. Wanting to control how it all turns out, yearning to get all the glory, just sitting it out: These are all impulses that constantly haunt us. Temptation is something we learn to live with. As for Jesus himself, after he returned from the desert he immediately launched his public ministry with a controversial visit to his hometown.

The Campaign Begins

Then Jesus, armed with the power of the Spirit, returned to Galilee; and reports about him spread through the whole countryside . . . He taught in their synagogues and everyone sang their praises.

He came to Nazareth, where he had been brought up, and went to the synagogue on the Sabbath day as he regularly did. He stood up to read the lesson and was handed the scroll of the prophet Isaiah. He opened the scroll and found the passage which says,

> "The spirit of the Lord is upon me
> because he has anointed me;
> he has sent me to announce good news to the poor,
> to proclaim release for prisoners
> and recovery of sight for the blind;
> to let the broken victims go free,
> to proclaim the year of the Lord's favour."

He rolled up the scroll, gave it back to the attendant, and sat down; and all eyes in the synagogue were fixed on him. — LUKE 4:14–20

THE ACCOUNT of Jesus' return to Nazareth, "where he had been brought up," belongs on the borderline between stories they told about him and stories he told, or in this case stories he retold. One year a student from the Kennedy School of Government observed that it also bears many of the marks of the launching of a political campaign. There is a custom in American presidential politics for candidates to begin their pursuit of the office by making a speech in their hometown. This practice tends to "locate" the candidate, to assure the public that he or she really is from somewhere. There is also a good chance the candidate will find a friendly audience. In addition, such a stopover gives the candidate an opportunity to spell out the basic principles of the campaign that will follow and to outline the platform. All these standard elements took place during Jesus' brief touchdown in Nazareth, but this kick-off visit did not turn out the way campaign managers like.

It is hard to know what Jesus anticipated when he went back to the town of Nazareth, where everyone knew him as "the carpenter's son," and to the local synagogue where he had attended services on Sabbath and on the important holidays with his parents. In any case, his visit seems to have started quite positively. The local populace purred with appreciation and applauded his eloquence. But then something went terribly wrong, and the mood changed spectacularly.

He began to address them: "'Today,' he said, 'in your hearing this text has come true." There was general approval; they were astonished that words of such grace should fall from his lips. "Is not this Joseph's son?" they asked. Then Jesus said, "No doubt you will quote to me the proverb, 'Physician, heal yourself!' and say, 'We have heard all of your doings at Capernaum; do the same here in your own home town.' Truly I tell you," he went on: "no prophet is recognized in his own country. There were indeed many widows in Israel in Elijah's time, when for three and a half years the skies never opened, and famine lay hard over the whole country; yet it was to none of these that Elijah was sent, but to a widow at Sarepta in the territory of Sidon. Again, in the time of the prophet Elisha there were many lepers in Israel, and not one of them was healed, but only Naaman, the Syrian." These words roused the whole congregation to fury; they leapt up, drove him out of the town, and took him to the brow of the hill on which it was built, meaning to hurl him over the edge. But he walked straight through the whole crowd, and went away. (Luke 4:21–30)

This dramatic change in the congregation's mood seems to have happened quite suddenly. It took place when Jesus turned from reading the text and offering a rather conventional comment on it, and began to recall stories from other parts of the scriptures to make what turned out to be a quite radical interpretation. The purring stopped abruptly, and the appreciative congregation was transformed into a surly mob. They did not stand at the door to shake his hand and tell him how much they had "enjoyed the sermon." Now they wanted to throw him off a cliff: all in all, not a successful homiletical outing, at least by conventional standards, and a very unpromising launch for any campaign. What happened?

This was the question I asked my students to ponder until the following week. As usual, there were many and varied responses, depending on what resources they had checked and — I suppose — which students who had taken the course the year before they had talked to. In general their answers echoed the positions within the ongoing scholarly debate. Some, for example, opted for the harshest of the historical-critical opinion. It holds that the entire scene was invented out of whole cloth by Luke, who was determined to defend the entrance of the Gentiles into the covenant by demonstrating that Jesus' "own people" had ejected him. Hence, so this theory goes, Luke picked out the texts from Isaiah he portrays Jesus as reading here, composed the comments he makes, and concocted the brow-of-the-hill climax as a fittingly spectacular denouement.

This was a somewhat too conjectural solution for other students. They preferred the idea of an actual visit by Jesus to Nazareth, which had become part of an oral tradition that Luke later elaborated and used to make his point. What texts Jesus had actually read, exactly what he said in his comments, and whether the rejection was as brutal as the one portrayed seemed to them to be questions that were out of reach.

Still others favored a reading that gave the explanation in the Gospel the benefit of the doubt. Even if Luke wasn't actually in Nazareth at the time, they argued, such a vivid event could hardly have been made up completely. Of course, the fundamentalists in the course had no problem accepting the whole account verbatim. If God had inspired it, he would not have allowed errors or exaggerations. However, none of these interpretations explained just what it was about Jesus' commentary — whether historical, extrapolated, or invented — that sparked the ruckus.

Two elements in Jesus' short commentary on the texts from Isaiah help answer this question. The first is his proclamation that "the acceptable year of the Lord" was now in effect. The second is his description of who was going to benefit.

Scholars now largely agree that the "year of the Lord's favor" refers to the Jewish legal provision for a "Jubilee Year," which was to be celebrated every fiftieth year. The provision first appears in Leviticus:

> You are to count off seven sabbaths of years, that is seven times seven years, forty-nine years, and in the seventh month on the tenth day of the month, on the Day of Atonement, you are to send the ram's horn throughout your land to sound a blast. Hallow the fiftieth year and proclaim liberation in the land for all its inhabitants. It is to be a jubilee year for you: each of you is to return to his holding, everyone to his family. The fiftieth year is to be a jubilee year for you: you are not to sow, and you are not to harvest the self-sown crop, or gather in the grapes from the unpruned vines, for it is a jubilee, to be kept holy by you. You are to eat the produce direct from the land. (Leviticus 25:8–12)

A further description of the law appears in the later book of Deuteronomy:

> At the end of every seventh year you must make a remission of debts. This is how it is to be made: everyone who holds a pledge shall return the pledge of the person indebted to him. He must not press a fellow-countryman for repayment, for the Lord's year of remission has been declared. You may press foreigners; but if it is a fellow-countryman that holds anything of yours, you must renounce all claim on it.
>
> There will never be any poor among you if only you obey the Lord your God by carefully keeping these commandments which I lay upon you this day; for the Lord your God will bless you with great prosperity in the land which he is giving you to occupy as your holding. (Deuteronomy 15:1–5)

Taken together, this legislation amounts to a program of sweeping economic redistribution. Slaves are to be set free; all debts and liabilities are to be canceled; loans are to be forgiven; mortgaged property is to be returned to its owner; even the land is to lie fallow for a whole year. The Jubilee Year recognizes the cumulative power of injustice, and mandates a radical solution. Since the rich and powerful tend to get richer and more powerful, what is needed periodically is a drastic "new deal," a chance to "go back to 'Go' " and start the game again. It was called the Jubilee Year because it was to be signaled at the end of the forty-ninth year by the blowing of a loud trumpet (*Yobhel* in Hebrew).

But there is a serious catch. Was this demanding provision of Torah ever really practiced or enforced? There is some evidence that there were at least sporadic efforts to do so. Landlords and lending institutions periodically devised ways to circumvent its effects by depositing assets in escrow accounts and finding other ways to avoid its impact. But by the time of Jesus, it seems the idea of the Jubilee Year was honored as an ideal, not as a policy. It stood there in the sacred writings pious people listened to and studied. But as far as an actual legally enforced procedure, it was a dead letter.

When Jesus informed the populace of Nazareth that he was proclaiming the actual application of the "acceptable year of the Lord," he was offending them on two levels. First, most of the people in the synagogue wanted it to remain an inoperative ideal. Jesus had already attracted many poor folks, impoverished landless peasants afflicted by unmanageable debts. They were obviously the ones who would benefit from the enforcement of the Jubilee provisions. But they were not among the respectable gentry who gathered in the synagogue. Rather, they were the people he met and spoke to on the streets and in the fields.

Also, who was he to be proclaiming a Jubilee Year? How did this wandering healer and maverick rabbi get the authority to do such a thing? In theory the high priesthood would have had the responsibility to keep count of the years and to send out the trumpeters on the forty-ninth one, the Sabbath of Sabbaths. Even the most obtuse listener must have sensed that Jesus was challenging the authority of the established religious elite. He was taking that responsibility into his own hands. It was a highly provocative move. He would hardly have gotten away with using such language in Jerusalem, and even there in the hinterlands of Galilee it was a risky and dangerous gambit.

According to Luke's description, however, even after Jesus made this daring assertion, the congregation was still purring, although some had begun to murmur. Then he took a turn they could not ignore. Presumably to demonstrate just who would benefit from the Jubilee Year, he reminded them of two stories from their own sacred texts.

The first story is about the prophet Elijah in I Kings 17:1–24. It tells of a drought and a famine in the land of Judah. The prophet is suffering from it, so God sends him to Zarephath in the land of Sidon, where God has prepared a widow to take care of his needs. Clearly this woman was a non-Israelite. Elijah makes the journey, and the widow cares for him. But then some tensions arise between them. The widow's son becomes deathly ill, and she blames Elijah for having brought this misfortune to her home. But Elijah goes into the boy's bedchamber and prays to God to heal him. The boy recovers, and Elijah and the widow are reconciled.

Next Jesus recalls the story of another prophet, Elisha, who chose to minister to another non-Jew, a Syrian named Naaman. This story is even more noteworthy. Naaman is not just a non-Israelite. He is in fact the commander of an army that has made war successfully against Israel, and he had once kidnapped an Israelite maiden on a raid and brought her back with him to work as his wife's servant — a clear violation of the "Lindbergh law," an alert Law School student slyly pointed out, which makes kidnapping across a state border a capital offense. It is hard to imagine a person who would be less popular with the Israelites.

Despite his high office, however, Naaman suffers from leprosy. The servant girl suggests he seek out Elisha. He does and after a curious little dispute between the two of them about which river the commander is to wash himself in, he is healed (by bathing in the Jordan), and he returns to his native land praising the God of Israel.

This was the moment: "When they heard it, all in the synagogue were filled with wrath." They leaped up and mobbed the hometown boy, pulled him out the door, and shoved him onto the "brow of a hill" so they might "throw him down headlong." But Jesus somehow escaped and made his way to the nearby city of Capernaum.

I sometimes wondered what the Jewish students, many of whom took the course, thought about this story. Very few ever seemed troubled by it. The ones who were more conversant with their tradition could see how "Jewish" it was. Here was a rabbi, in a synagogue, interpreting the prophets and getting criticized for his explanation by some members of the congregation. They saw nothing unusual about that (even though the critics seemed to have gone a bit far on this occasion). The Jews who were not so familiar thought it was entirely right that Jesus wanted to extend the Jewish passion for justice to the Gentiles. Retrieving a familiar distinction, they both said it was not the "religion *of* Jesus" they had a problem with, it was the "religion *about* him."

This is a distinction that has been in circulation for a long time, but I am not sure it is an entirely valid one. As we will see, Jesus did often make himself central to his message. Still, at one level, the way the Jewish students read the text seemed sensible to me. Whatever the admixture of fact and imaginative elaboration this story contains, it is true to everything we know about Rabbi Jesus from other sources. Once more he is pictured aligning himself with his own people's religious heritage. Here he not only positions himself in the lineage of the prophets, which Christians tend to prefer, he also evokes the Jubilee Year from the book of Leviticus, which Christians often view dismissively as being "too legalistic." And he also makes inventive use of stories from the book of Kings. But what he says is not ambiguous: that the vision of God's reign celebrated in these texts is no longer to be a distant utopia. It is something people can begin to live in now. Even when he insists that the blessings of this new order of things will also flow to the outsiders, the Gentiles, and even to the nations thought of as the enemies of God's people, this is not an idea foreign to the Jewish tradition.

The Nazareth story is a transition. It begins with a description of something Jesus did. It continues with an account of what he himself said. And it concludes with the trouble he got himself into for saying it. It is a kind of mini-Gospel, with all the elements in place. We are now ready for some of the stories Jesus himself told.

II

STORIES HE TOLD

Jesus Retells
His People's Story

Those who carry pianos
to the tenth floor wardrobes and coffins
an old man with a bundle of wood limps beyond the horizon
a woman with a hump of nettles
a madwoman pushing a pram
full of vodka bottles
they will all be lifted
like a gull's feather like a dry leaf
like an eggshell a scrap of newspaper

Blessed are those who carry
for they shall be lifted.
  — Anna Kamienska, "Those Who Carry"

Seeing the crowds, he went up on the mountain, and when he sat down
his disciples came to him. And he opened his mouth and taught them
saying . . . — Matthew 5:1–2

IT IS UNIVERSALLY KNOWN as the Sermon on the Mount, and it
is the longest single segment of Jesus' teaching in the New Testament. It runs for three full chapters in the Gospel according to
Matthew, and it will occupy us for this chapter and the two that follow. With few exceptions, even the most religiously illiterate of my
students had at least heard of the Sermon on the Mount before we
discussed it in class. Once when I asked them if they could remember any of the phrases from it, some did. They had heard "Turn the
other cheek" or "Love your enemies" or "Blessed are the poor." But

most did not know the context of these familiar phrases, and very few had any inkling of how the Sermon on the Mount relates to the rest of Jesus' life and teachings. Still, I could always feel a sense of anticipation when we came to it. I think it was because, although they often did not know what to make of some other parts of the Gospels, such as Jesus' walking on the waves or turning water into wine, they expected that now at last — with the Sermon on the Mount — they were going to get to the heart of Jesus' *moral* teaching, and wasn't that what the course was supposed to be about? Still, despite the students' great expectations, I sensed a certain disappointment in what they actually found. Was I presenting it wrong?

As the years passed, I came to see that what disappointed them was not the words of Jesus. They even used one of their own favorite words — *awesome* — to describe them. A Japanese student whose family administered a Buddhist temple in Tokyo told me it was the first time he had ever read the Sermon on the Mount, and he thought it was one of the most beautiful things he had ever seen. What bothered students was that Jesus' words seemed so out of reach. It was their suspicion that the world they lived in was not going to make it easy, or maybe even possible, for them to apply what he said in their lives. It was a particularly vivid reminder that there is a distance, and not just a temporal one, between Jesus and us. But I also recognized that this was a valuable insight. They sensed that the Sermon on the Mount is not a code of ethics for individuals. It is meant for a community. Nor can it be lifted from the rest of the Jesus story as a kind of handy moral guidebook. But then what is it?

In short, the Sermon on the Mount is a description of how people would live when the reign of God, which Jesus believed was dawning, had come in its fullness. But it was also, then and now, an invitation to his hearers not to wait, but to begin living as though that time had already come. It is Jesus' version of a vision hinted at earlier by the Hebrew prophets, and not in the sense of an idle pipe dream. He constantly insisted it did not just beckon from some distant future. It was appearing — albeit in bits and pieces — in the here and now. He wanted his hearers not just to wait and pray for it (although he taught them to do that too), but also to start living in it right away as best they could. It was the old story with a decidedly new accent.

For centuries the people of Israel told a story. They told it *to* themselves and they told it *about* themselves. They told it with twists and variations. They spiced it and colored it and embellished it. But it was essentially the same story. It said that God had created the world and all its peoples, and that he intended them to love and live in peace with each other, and to praise and serve him. But among all his many peoples, God had designated the Jewish people for a special assignment. He charged them to be a light to the nations, a herald of God's purpose, and a living illustration of what he wanted all peoples to be. God promised that when they fulfilled that responsibility, they would be showered with blessings and benefits. But when they did not, prophets would be sent to remind them of who they were and what they should be doing, and if they did not repent, and return to the task that had been set for them, they would suffer dire consequences. Then one day, in God's time, war and injustice would be banished and the world would take on the form that God had originally intended.

God knew — and the people of Israel learned — that the responsibility he had laid upon them would be a hard one to bear alone. But God also promised to be ready to assist them and, if they strayed, to receive them back and to help them start over. God also promised that in the end it would all turn out right, and that the day would eventually come when all the other peoples — the "nations" or the "Gentiles" — would become partners with the Israelites in the same covenant community.

It was a grand epic. It allowed room within itself for hundreds of adumbrations and applications. It provided a framework within which the Israelites could make some sense of the jostles and jolts of history, the massacres and exiles, and also the rare moments of serenity and security. The Israelites told the story in many different voices. They reenacted it in seasonal rituals and holidays, rehearsed through scriptures and folktales, and encoded it in their laws and customs. They all knew the plot. It was what bound them together as a people. Indeed, without it they would not have been a people at all, and they knew that, too. That is why one of their central commandments was — and still is — to tell the story, over and over.

Any narrative that carries this much weight, however, needs to be revised and renewed from time to time. Things change. New triumphs and new defeats occur, although for the Israelites the triumphs were often small and the defeats were frequently devastating. But each required a new enhancement of the story, a new layer of reinterpretation, a new spin. Maybe the best way to describe the Bible is to say that it is a vast compilation of the various versions of this one, underlying story, which like a *basso continuo* throbs through them all.

The rabbi from Nazareth knew the story as well as anyone ever has. He had been raised on it. And when he grew up he recognized that the time had come, as it had many times in the past, for another revised version. The moment demanded it. The relentless Roman occupation robbed his people of their dignity. The corruption of the priesthood infuriated them. The ugliness and desperation of the times were beginning to make the old story sound less credible. Instead of binding the people together, the story was becoming a source of conflict and animosity among them. They were also being inundated by other stories. Traders from the east carried tales of saviors with them in their sailing ships and camel caravans. The Roman legions bore on their standards the symbols of a divine emperor. Traveling teachers brought precepts about the cosmopolitan philosophy of Hellenism. The resulting cacophonous hodgepodge stirred confusion and despair. The people of Israel needed to hear the old story in a new way, one that was adequate to the bewildering times in which they lived.

Jesus took on this daunting assignment. The Gospel of Matthew in one of its most famous sections reports that one day he climbed to the top of a mountain, sat down (the traditional position for a rabbinical teaching), and taught. The words he spoke are what we now call the Sermon on the Mount. It is the most luminous, most quoted, most analyzed, most contested, and most influential moral and religious discourse in all of human history. This may sound like overstatement, but it is not. Jesus told the old story in his new way on many occasions. But on this mountain in Palestine, he gave it its most sequential and most systematic expression. It was his Fifth Symphony, his *Mona Lisa,* his masterpiece.

The Sermon on the Mount also reveals Rabbi Jesus at his most eloquent and most unnerving. The words are plain enough. But that has not prevented hundreds of contradictory interpreters from tumbling over each other as the centuries have gone by. Thomas Aquinas called it "counsels of perfection" intended only for the few. Immanuel Kant saw it as the encapsulation of the moral imperative. Ernst Renan, the nineteenth-century biographer of the earthly Jesus, dismissed it as an idyllic fantasy. Leo Tolstoy insisted it was the Law of Christ that one ought to follow to the letter. For Mahatma Gandhi it was the inspiration for his *satyagraha* (soul force). There will be more interpretations to come.

No Jew who read Matthew's account, or heard it read, could possibly have missed the parallelism the narrative obviously intends. The word *mountain* immediately recalls Moses and the divine revelation of the Ten Commandments on Mount Sinai. Indeed, in many different religious traditions, mountains provide the location for a teacher of wisdom to teach. The Aztecs designed their temples to echo the mountains that surrounded them. Mount Fuji is the most sacred spot in Japan. The Buddha gave one of his most memorable teachings on the Mount of Vultures.

When the rabbi from Nazareth reached the summit of the mountain, Matthew tells us he sat down and began his discourse. But he does not tell us something else most people would like to know. Who was there to hear it? Only his disciples, or was there a larger crowd of the landless and dispirited masses that had begun to trek after him wherever he went? Scholars differ about this. Legend says that when the Buddha taught on the Mount of Vultures, not only was everyone in the world there, but everyone who had ever lived or ever would. But knowing who was there to hear Jesus may not be all that important, because the words he spoke have reverberated through the centuries and reached every continent. With St. Francis, if another legend can be credited, they also reached the birds, the sun and moon, and at least one wolf.

The Sermon on the Mount begins with what are usually called the Beatitudes, Jesus' assurance to at least some of his hearers that they have found favor with God, not only that they *will* be blessed, but that they are already. For them there was good news.

> Blessed are the poor in spirit; the kingdom of Heaven is theirs. Blessed are the sorrowful; they shall find consolation. Blessed are the gentle; they shall have the earth for their possession. Blessed are those who hunger and thirst to see right prevail; they shall be satisfied. Blessed are those who show mercy; mercy shall be shown to them. Blessed are those whose hearts are pure; they shall see God. Blessed are the peacemakers; they shall be called God's children. Blessed are those who are persecuted in the cause of right; the kingdom of Heaven is theirs. (Matthew 5:3–10)

This is the good news. But there is also bad news. As the Gospel of Luke reports this same teaching, there are blessings, but there are also curses, or "woes."

> But alas for you who are rich; you have had your time of happiness. Alas for you who are well fed now; you will go hungry. Alas for you who laugh now; you will mourn and weep. Alas for you when all speak well of you; that is how their fathers treated the false prophets. (Luke 6:24–26)

When I was a child in Sunday school I had to memorize the Beatitudes for a Children's Day pageant. They were short and easy to memorize. I chirped them out, and my parents beamed. But somehow in Sunday school I never learned the "woes," the curses that go along with the blessings. Had I stood on the little stage next to the piano in my clean suit and declaimed, "Woe unto you who are rich," or "Woe unto you when all men speak well of you," my parents, and rest of the audience, might not have swelled with such approval. I doubt if they suspected that Jesus had ever said such things, and I am equally sure many Christians today still don't know it. The woes do not appear in church school materials and they are rarely the text for sermons. But after one becomes familiar with the Magnificat of Mary with its line about sending the rich away empty, or the manifesto Jesus airs in Nazareth with its emphasis on the liberation of the poor, the woes should not come as a surprise.

In the version of this teaching recorded in the Gospel of Luke, the words *poor in spirit* do not appear. Jesus says simply "blessed are the poor." Scholars have argued for ages about this apparent disparity. Was Matthew spiritualizing or even diluting Jesus' forthright promise of God's favor to those who were actually, physically destitute? If so, why would he do such a thing? Matthew wrote his Gospel thirty-five years after Jesus' death. Was he trying to make the growing Jesus movement sound less radical, less of a threat to the powers that be?

I have come to believe there is not that much difference between the two phrases. "Poor in spirit" does not mean resigned, patient, or acquiescent. It means dispirited, or even crushed. It refers to one of the cruelest aspects of real poverty, about trying to get through a day without the minimum means of survival: hopelessness. Poor people feel weak. They see themselves as subject to powerful forces beyond their control. They often begin to blame themselves for the wretched condition they find themselves in. When Simone Weil, a Jewish philosopher deeply sympathetic to Christianity, worked in a French automobile factory in the 1930s, she was shocked to discover that instead of blaming management for their hideous working environment — the unbearable noise, the numbingly long hours, the lack of safety precautions — the women workers tended to blame themselves or each other. The conditions were not arousing them to revolution, but crushing their spirits. Century after century the Jewish prophets had promised that God would vindicate those in dire need. Jesus was saying the same things, but with his characteristic twist: that the time had come to make that promise operational.

Jesus addresses his next words to the "sorrowful," or as the King James translation says,

Blessed are those who mourn, for they shall be comforted.

Using the word *mourn* helps clarify what the rabbi was saying. He is not primarily speaking about people who are grieving over their personal calamities. Again echoing the prophets, he tells his hearers that the national calamity that has overtaken them, corrupted many of their leaders, deprived them of their means of living, and robbed them of their dignity will not last forever. In the past his ancestors had mourned the affliction visited upon them by Egypt and Babylon. Now the Romans and their local puppets were doing the damage. But their rule was coming to an end. The arrogant legions, which fancied themselves invincible with their fluttering banners and gleaming standards, would collapse like the rest, taking their sycophantic supporters along with them.

Blessed are the meek, for they shall inherit the earth.

Standard English translations of the Sermon on the Mount still use the misleading word *meek* in rendering this fifth verse. But as one skilled commentator has pointed out, the word does not mean wimp or doormat or passive. It means one who endures with patience without becoming bitter and perpetuating the vicious circle of oppression. Maybe Rabbi Jesus is referring to Psalm 37:

Refrain from anger, and forsake wrath: Do not fret, it leads only to evil. For the wicked shall be cut off, . . . But the meek shall inherit the land, And delight themselves in abundant prosperity. (Psalm 37:8, 11)

But what is Jesus advising those who are being so cruelly treated to do? Warren Carter puts it well. "They are not to 'fret' or imitate the violent wicked. They are not to take justice into their own hands and inflict their own revenge. Though they are beaten down by unjust economic practices, their strategy is to live an alternative, righteous lifestyle and to look for God's response even when God seems slow to act. To be 'meek' here means to renounce retribution and to live faithfully and expectantly."

Jesus goes on to assure those who "hunger and thirst for righteousness" and "the merciful" and the "pure in heart" that they are already living in the nascent glow of the new reign. Then, however, he inserts a phrase that, despite the softness of the words, must have been heard as an insult to the suspicious authorities.

Blessed are the peacemakers, for they shall be called the children of God.

This is one of the parts of the Sermon on the Mount many people know, and most of the students in my class had heard it before the course. They had also heard that Jesus was often called the Prince of Peace, and they had undoubtedly sung or at least heard Christmas carols about "peace on earth, goodwill to men." But they did not know what to make of this curious blessing of the peacemakers. Whom, exactly, did Jesus mean? The slogan posted outside an Air Force base I once drove by proclaimed, "Peace Is Our Business." What kind of peace did Jesus have in mind? How does one go about being a peacemaker? It seemed like a nice idea, but quite vague.

Actually, at the time he said them, Jesus' words were anything but ambiguous. They were a direct challenge to the ruling Roman ideology. Like other words he uttered that might sound innocuous today, this blessing was a taunt hurled at the foreign rulers of his homeland and their domestic supporters. The empire's main claim to fame and legitimacy was that Rome and Rome alone was the peacemaker. It sustained the *pax Romana* under the magnanimous auspices of Caesar Augustus, a divine ruler. One of the imperial titles of the divine Augustus was that of "peace-bringer." The legions were the makers and guarantors of this peace, and it was something for which its subject peoples were expected to be supremely grateful — and happily cough up their exorbitant taxes. So, given such an ostensibly benevolent state of affairs, just who was this up-start rabbi from the outland who was going about the country suggesting that a new empire was about to be instituted in which God and not Caesar would be the ruler? And who was he to claim that his scruffy followers, not the armed forces of Rome, were the real peacemakers?

The Romans had mastered the art of talking about peace while waging almost constant war, always — of course — in the interest of preserving their *pax*. They littered the landscape with temples to peace and inscriptions about peace at the same moment their regiments were crushing rebellions and slashing their way to more and more conquests. But the peace Rabbi Jesus was talking about and demonstrating was *shalom*, not *pax*. It was not the peace that was brutally enforced in the emperor's name, but a peace nurtured by a loving God. It did not come from the top down but from the bottom up. It was not a peace marked by the jittery comfort of the gentry and the resentful passivity of those it dispossessed. It was the *shalom* of which the prophets had sung, in which every man would sit under his own fig tree and there would be no more poor in the land. It was peace among persons, between peoples, and between humankind and the natural world.

There can be little doubt that this is a demanding vision. No wonder interpreters for centuries have found different ways to dismiss it. One device, favored by Martin Luther, among others, was to teach that the Sermon on the Mount described how Christians should act in their personal relations with their families and friends and neighbors. But, the great reformer insisted, to try to apply it to the public realm was to defy the structures God had ordained to impose order on civic life. It was to undercut the responsibility of the magistrate who was not only permitted but was also commanded to wield the sword when necessary. The classic Catholic response was that those in "religious life" should be guided by these teachings, but they were not applicable to governance and certainly not to making war when war was called for. But, despite all the efforts to shrink the scope of their application, the Beatitudes (and the woes) continue to prick and trouble the consciences of millions of people. Still, Jesus did not leave these lofty ideas suspended in midair. In the next section of the Sermon on the Mount he goes on to sketch the proper relationship both between his movement and the rest of the Jewish community and between his movement and the world at large.

12

Salt and Lamps

You are salt to the world. And if salt becomes tasteless, how is its salti-
ness to be restored? It is good for nothing but to be thrown away and
trodden underfoot.

You are light for all the world. A town that stands on a hill cannot be
hidden.

When a lamp is lit, it is not put under the meal-tub, but on the lamp
stand, where it gives light to everyone in the house. Like the lamp, you
must shed light among your fellows, so that, when they see the good
you do, they may give praise to your Father in heaven.

— MATTHEW 5:13–16

DURING MY STUDENT DAYS in the 1950s it was widely believed that religion was in steep decline. I was in a disappearing field, suitable mainly for antiquarians. Some religion, it was said, might well survive the combined advance of
science, urbanization, and popular education, but only in family
rituals and ethnic enclaves with their folksy saints' days and picturesque festivals. Religion, it was predicted with unequivocal assurance, would never again play a significant role in the public policy
arena.

I was always skeptical about these forecasts, partly because as a
youngster growing up in a small town in Pennsylvania, I thought a
lot about "Big Questions" like the meaning of life and death, good
and evil, and whether the whole thing had any meaning. It was obvious to me, even then, that in most settings adults did not talk
about these matters much. But in church they did, sometimes. I also
began to think it was somehow not right that just outside of town

some people lived in sprawling mansions with expansive stables for their riding horses, while the people just across the tracks from us barely eked out a living. This was something the adults hardly ever talked about. But I knew these Big Questions would not go away.

Then there were the ministers. Since our tiny congregation could hardly afford a salary, the ones we had were usually fresh out of seminary, and because they could hardly survive on what we paid them, they usually left for greener pastures after a few years. Consequently, new preachers were continuously arriving in our provincial hamlet like emissaries from the outside world. In contrast to most of the other people in town, they did want to talk about the Big Questions. Besides, they always moved in with shelves of books on philosophy, religion, and theology, which — as I got older — they happily loaned me. There was a lot in those tomes I could not understand, but I tirelessly scoured them nevertheless. I loved the colorful maps of the ancient kingdoms of Judah and Israel, the charts of St. Paul's journeys, the interpretations of obscure biblical verses, and the accounts of what various philosophers had written.

In short, I was hooked. I could not imagine a more interesting way to spend my life than thinking and talking about these perennial subjects. By the age of fourteen I knew that I wanted to be either a minister or a teacher of philosophy and religion. A brief stint in the Merchant Marine just after high school exposed me to the post–World War II devastation in Germany and Poland. During our short stops in port, dirty, ragged children trooped after us through ruined streets, begging. Adolescent prostitutes in gaudy makeup and torn stockings waited for us at the foot of the gangway. It was a lot for a seventeen-year-old to digest, and it sharpened my questions about injustice and evil. Accordingly, when I arrived as a freshman at the University of Pennsylvania, I set out in a determined and systematic way to learn it *all* in four years. Dutifully I began in the fall term with ancient philosophy and ancient history. True, I enjoyed observing the drosophila fruit flies through the microscope in my required biology course, but that only intensified my curiosity about where life had come from and what it was about.

During those years Penn was flooded with returning veterans supported by the GI Bill. Many of them were enrolled in business courses and were not particularly fascinated by the pre-Socratic philosophers or by Plato's *Symposium*. But, largely because of their experiences in the war, they were asking the big questions too. Soon, like many undergraduates, I found a clique of like-minded students with whom I could study and sit up in the local all-night café arguing about politics and religion. I became a history major, but when the new Department of Religious Thought was introduced at Penn in my junior year, I immediately took a course in world religions. The combination of these pursuits taught me that the questions I had brooded over as a boy had always been there, and probably always would be.

When I published *The Secular City* in 1965, I argued that even though the institutional power of religions might well decline, the questions religions have grappled with would remain. One way or another we would have to address them. By the time I started teaching at Harvard the same year, it had become obvious to at least some people, though certainly not to everyone, that those confident predictions about the disappearance of religion were coming to naught. For good or ill, and usually for a little of each, religion was anything but dead. It was quickly becoming what it is now, the eight-hundred-pound gorilla plunked in the middle of the room. Sometimes the big simian is friendly, sometimes fierce. But he is always unpredictable; he is always *there;* and his looming presence makes everyone nervous.

The increasing visibility of religion, not just in charming fetes and folksy processions, but also in the public sector in many places in the world, impelled a growing number of students from the Kennedy School of Government to take my course on Jesus. They were curious about what role faith should or should not play in policy discourse. Their question was a venerable one. It had fascinated both Aristotle and Aquinas, and legions of other philosophers and theologians for millennia. It had received attention from Confu-

cius and Mohamet, and thinkers in every tradition have wrestled
with it in a variety of ways.

Jesus was fully aware of how tricky these issues can be. He de-
votes the second part of the Sermon on the Mount to the question
of the relationship between his neonate movement and the world.
The evidence suggests that by the time he told this "Story on the
Mountain," he had already attracted a sizable following. They constituted what historians today call the "Jesus movement." No one
knows for sure just how large the group was. But since the Gospels
repeatedly talk about Jesus trying to escape the crowds, they must
have included considerable numbers of people. He sometimes re-
paired to the desert or climbed into a boat to get away. So there
must have been enough people to jostle him, tire him, and make
him feel hemmed in occasionally. And if the crowds were that large,
they must have come to the attention of Herod, whose police had
already eliminated John the Baptist as a threat to public order (and
to Herod's power). Therefore, it is not surprising that Jesus should
turn the next part of his mountain discourse to the question of
what relationship his growing band of followers should have to the
public realm.

His key images are salt and a lighted lamp. However, it is important to recognize that this imagery makes sense only for a minority
movement, so it was not easy for government students to apply it to
the large current public issues they discussed in their seminars. The
Jesus movement constituted what its contemporaries undoubtedly
perceived as a marginal but troublesome sect, and possibly even a
dangerously subversive cabal. Jesus' metaphors suggest a strategy
for a tiny band of followers whose views were not supported by
most of their fellow countrymen and who were thought of by the
Romans as a bothersome burr under the saddle, albeit one that
might eventually cause real trouble. Jesus was fully aware of the
hazardous environment in which he lived. He chose his words carefully. He did once call King Herod a "fox," which at that time was a
nastier epithet than it is today. But he did not try to advise Herod or

Pilate. Even so, calling his followers the "light of the world" and "peacemakers" was also a calculated mockery of Rome. In his *In Catilinam*, Cicero describes Rome as "the light of the whole world." Jesus takes bold issue with that claim. Now there was to be another light.

Still, the Sermon on the Mount was anything but a strategy for "Christianizing the empire," or even making the Jesus movement into the majority among Israelites. A lamp serves no purpose when the sun is out and everything is bathed in its rays. A pinch of salt brings out the essential flavor of a fish stew, but put in too much salt and you spit it out at the first taste. After Constantine the Great converted in the fourth century c.e. and took the first steps toward "Christianizing" the Roman Empire, the salt and light metaphors became much less helpful. More and more people streamed into the churches, in part because it became the politically prudent move. How could you go wrong when you were joining the religion the emperor himself embraced, even if you were doing it with fingers crossed behind your back?

Now, however, things are changing again. In the twenty-first century we live in what has been called a "post-Christian" era. Even in those sections of America where a certain kind of "Christian politics" is politically correct, the people who practice it are constantly made aware not only that there are numerous ways of being Christian, but there are many other spiritual paths as well.

Although there are those who still claim that the United States is, and must continue to be, a "Christian nation," that is hardly the situation anymore. The United States has become perhaps the most religiously pluralistic country in a religiously diverse world. This means that for those who want to "follow Jesus," the salt and lamp metaphors make more sense now than they have for many hundreds of years. Today, the idea of "Christendom," the thousand-year-old theory of a benevolent fusion of throne and altar, is fading. True, there are some who would like to prop it up, but the truth is that although it was once a powerful theory, Christendom never really existed. Christians have almost always lived in the midst of other faiths, even when they ignored them or persecuted their followers or preached crusades against them. Still, since the political power was in the hands of Christians during the so-called Christian Middle Ages and during the early modern period when Christianity was theoretically the religion of Europe (and its American extension), to talk of Christians as light in obscurity made no sense at all.

Both the lamp and the salt metaphors also suggest a kind of humility, almost anonymity, and if the wisdom of the Sermon on the Mount is still to guide them, these are the qualities Christians should assume when they are in a position to contribute to public policy decisions. A lamp is not placed on a stand for people to gaze at, but to shed some light on something. There was a time, not many decades ago, when missionaries — inspired by the redoubtable founders of the Student Volunteer Movement — actually believed they could "win the world for Christ in our generation." But that was the last gasp of a kind of Christian imperialism, which sounds totally foreign to the spirit of the Sermon on the Mount. Far into the foreseeable future, Christians will live as a minority, maybe a large one or maybe a small one, but a minority nevertheless, in a world in which other religions and ideologies will play important roles. This means that in America, public policy should reflect the values shared by a variety of religious people, as well as their secular fellow citizens. But it also means that once again the idea of a lamp and a pinch of salt will come into new appreciation, and they will stand as a stark rebuke to Christian imperialists of whatever stripe.

Jesus did not ignore what we now call public life. But the circumstances he lived in did not permit him to influence it or shape it. He loved the law, and recognized how essential it is:

> Do not suppose that I have come to abolish the law and the prophets; I did not come to abolish, but to complete. Truly I tell you: so long as heaven and earth endure, not a letter, not a dot, will disappear from the law until all that must happen has happened. (Matthew 5:17–20)

This rabbi was not in the business of nullifying or circumventing Torah. He wanted it to guide Israel so that Israel could be a light to the nations. But he wanted to see its provisions honored in actuality, not just in the abstract. He exhorts his hearers to go beyond the letter of the law and apply its radical spirit. Do not just abstain from killing; avoid even expressing rage. Do not just avoid adultery; try not to fantasize it either. He tries to protect women from the whims of men who were permitted to divorce them virtually at will by making it much harder. He not only insists on the validity of the rule against swearing "in heaven's name"; he suggests forgoing swearing altogether: "Let your 'yes' be 'yes' and your 'no' 'no.' "

Toward the end of the Sermon on the Mount Jesus does, however, state a principle that, to the amazement of many, has informed the practice of some of the most admirable political figures of our time.

> You have heard that they were told, "An eye for an eye, a tooth for a tooth." But what I tell you is this: Do not resist those who wrong you. If anyone slaps you on the right cheek, turn and offer him the other also. If anyone wants to sue you and takes your shirt, let him have your cloak as well. If someone in authority presses you into service for one mile, go with him two. Give to anyone who asks; and do not turn your back on anyone who wants to borrow. (Matthew 5:38–42)

For centuries Jesus' exhortation not to retaliate or to return evil for evil has been reviled, ridiculed, explicitly rejected, admired in the abstract, or simply ignored. Occasionally some isolated saints have applied it on the individual level. But only in the twentieth century did someone take the core insight of this teaching and transform it into the actual strategy of a powerful social movement. That person was Mahatma Gandhi, and he was not a Christian. Still, I have always been struck by the similarities between Jesus and Gandhi, even though they lived nineteen hundred years and a thousand miles apart. Both grew up on the outskirts of an overtaxed and mistreated empire. Both drew on the classical sources of their own religious traditions — Jesus on the Torah, Gandhi on the Bhagavad Gita — but reinterpreted them in the light of current challenges. Both based their mission on a core conviction based on that faith. For Gandhi it was the power of truth, what he called *satyagraha*. For Jesus it was the ultimate power of God's love and justice. Both angered not just their imperial overlords but their coreligionists as well. Both were accused from the radical wings of their respective nations of being either an irresponsible rabble-rouser or a spineless compromiser. Both were more concerned with the practical results of faith than with correct doctrinal formulations. Both tried to model the kind of world they strove for in miniature, Gandhi by organizing his residential ashram, Jesus by appointing twelve disciples to accompany him. Both died violently in the attempt to fulfill their vision.

Gandhi was decisively influenced by Jesus, but especially by the Sermon on the Mount, and in particular by Jesus' teaching on non-violent resistance. He once wrote,

> Jesus put in a picturesque and telling manner the great doctrine of non-violent non-cooperation. Your non-cooperation with your opponent is violent when you give a blow for a blow, and is ineffective in the long run. Your non-cooperation is nonviolent when you give your opponent all in place of what he needs. You have disarmed him once and for all by your apparent cooperation, which in effect is complete non-cooperation.

Gandhi admired Jesus in large part because he saw him as a teacher who not only taught, but also put his teaching into action in his own life. When Gandhi's biographer Louis Fisher visited him in his tiny cottage at his ashram in 1942, he noticed there was only one picture on the wall. It was of Jesus, with the words "He Is Our Peace" (from Ephesians 2) underneath. But despite the efforts of several missionaries, Gandhi never became a Christian. He insisted that he loved Christ, but that Christianity had gone wrong when it became "the religion of kings."

For Gandhi, truth can never be vindicated by inflicting suffering on someone else, but by accepting suffering for oneself. The opponent must never be shamed or humiliated. In fact, the opponent should never be "defeated"; rather he must be "won over." Gandhi never claimed to have invented the principle of nonviolent resistance. His contribution was to take that principle and transform it into the ethos of a massive popular movement. It was a movement that eventually freed India from British rule and became a decisive influence in the program of Martin Luther King, Jr. In turn, King's example of nonviolent resistance inspired the liberation movements in East Germany and Czechoslovakia, which ultimately resulted in the collapse of another empire. According to King, we should be thankful that after twenty centuries, nonviolent resistance is no longer just a noble ideal, because in an age of nuclear weapons it is the only approach that oppressed people can now turn to. Maybe Jesus is not as irrelevant to public policy as some people think.

The Sermon on the Mount is full of difficult, but perhaps not impossible, tenets to follow, as even the limited success of nonviolence in our own era demonstrates. But Jesus goes one better. He concludes this section with the one teaching that will always be associated with his name, one that is never explicitly articulated in the Torah, but which he believed informed its deepest inner spirit:

> You have heard that they were told, "Love your neighbor and hate your enemy." But what I tell you is this: Love your enemies and pray for your persecutors; only so can you be children of your heavenly Father, who causes the sun to rise on good and bad alike, and sends the rain on the innocent and the wicked. If you love only those who love you, what reward can you expect? Even the tax-collectors do as much as that. If you greet only your brothers, what is there extraordinary about that? Even the heathen do as much. (Matthew 5:43–47)

For the first few years when the class got to these climactic verses, I discussed several different ways they had been interpreted. I mentioned, for example, the view of the Orthodox Jewish scholar Pincus Lapide, who says that "Love your enemy" represents an intensification of the Jewish exhortation (which occurs in the Passover seder) not to exalt in your enemy's tragedy (in that case the Egyptians who were being drowned in the Red Sea), because they too are human. I mentioned Martin Luther King's assurance that loving one's enemy does not require warm cozy feelings but a genuine desire for his well-being.

But after a few years I sensed that the students did not want to hear about different interpretations. So eventually, when I reached these verses in class, I simply paused after I read them. Invariably there was a profound silence in the room. Why offer a commentary on the *Mona Lisa*? If the Sermon on the Mount was Jesus' Fifth Symphony, this was its central theme. Why say more? Commenting on it, or even discussing it, seemed almost superfluous. It still does.

13

The Rabbi Teaches Torah

Beware of practicing your piety before men in order to be seen by them; for then you will have no reward from your Father who is in heaven. Thus, when you give alms, sound no trumpet before you as the hypocrites do in the synagogues and in the streets, that they may be praised by men. Truly, I say to you, they have their reward. But when you give alms, do not let your right hand know what your left hand is doing, so that your alms may be in secret; and your father who sees in secret will reward you. And when you pray, you must not be like the hypocrites; for they love to stand and pray in the synagogues and at the street corners, that they may be seen by men. Truly I say to you, they have received their reward. But when you pray, go into your room and shut the door and pray to your Father who is in secret; and your Father who is in secret will reward you. — MATTHEW 6:1–6

UNDOUBTEDLY THE MOST IMPORTANT CHANGE in the historical research about Jesus in the past few decades has been the recognition of how ensconced he was in the Jewish life of his times. This is a welcome change that has immeasurably deepened and improved the relations among Jews and Christians. The change took a long time and came about for a number of reasons. For centuries Jews who became interested in Jesus had to be wary of what they wrote. Since nearly all of them lived among Christian majorities, they were fully aware that church authorities would be reading and listening, and would expect what they said to conform to Christian doctrinal specifications. Therefore, rather than toe that line, the Jewish scholars simply avoided the subject, or kept their opinions to themselves. Even in more recent years, and in countries with no watchful inquisitors in the wings, most Jewish scholars —

with some important exceptions — steered clear of the rabbi from Nazareth.

All this changed dramatically after World War II, and especially with the establishment of the state of Israel. Shocked by what had happened at Auschwitz, many Christian scholars felt that the gap they had permitted to develop between themselves and their Jewish colleagues could well have helped poison the atmosphere that led to the Holocaust. Jews were soon joining theological and religious faculties that had previously been made up entirely of Christian or secular scholars. Harvard Divinity School created a permanent tenured chair in Jewish Religious Studies, the first in any non-Jewish theological faculty in the world. Some Jewish scholars chose to settle in Israel, where they could do their work without feeling that someone was looking over their shoulders. Further, these scholars were often working energetically on the history of that land, and could not help noticing that it was the very land where Jesus had lived. Thus, it became much easier to see historical connections they had not noticed before and to understand Jesus as a part of the Jewish story.

Among Christian and secular scholars, the new research on Jesus, sparked in part by the sensational discovery in 1947 of the Dead Sea Scrolls, also marked a turning point. The unearthing of these ancient documents, which were attributed to a Jewish ascetic group called the Essenes and had been preserved in a cave for two thousand years, revealed previously unknown facts about the religious and cultural context of Jesus' life. Another set of scrolls, found in Nag Hammadi in Egypt and coming from a somewhat later period, included the first extant copy of the Gospel of Thomas. Finding it prompted scholars to look more carefully at the apocryphal Gospels, those that were not included in the New Testament by the early church fathers. Together, these sets of scrolls presented historians with a treasure-trove. I can still remember the excitement I felt as a graduate student when, one by one, they were opened, unrolled, and laboriously pieced together. The more the historical picture was clarified, the more evident it became that there was more continuity than discontinuity between the movement Jesus launched and the other Jewish movements of the period.

Every year I offered Jesus and the Moral Life, large numbers of Jewish students enrolled. Although not many of them had read the scholars who were making these breakthroughs, they seemed quite able to see in the rabbi from Nazareth "one of their own." But they also knew that many Christians still insisted he belonged only to them. But now both wanted to explore what the proper relationship between Jews and Christians should be. I told them that in Jesus' day, of course, there were no "Christians" as yet, but that the Nazarene had in fact laid down some guidelines that might help illuminate this question even today. Those guidelines appear in the concluding portion of the Sermon on the Mount that we turn to in this chapter.

After his discussion of the moral dimensions of the kingdom of God, which he claimed was now dawning, and his teaching about the relationship between his tiny band and the civil society, Jesus took up this third subject. He turned to the role his followers, who were all Jews at the time, should play in the larger Jewish community they were part of. He did so by focusing on the religious obligations his audience was familiar with, such as giving alms and prayer. He did not dismiss these obligations as passé in the new era; instead, he gave them a new parsing.

But why did the rabbi from Nazareth find it necessary to say these things? Did some of his eager followers hope that since God's presence and rule would soon be everywhere, poverty and injustice would be abolished, and there would no longer be any need for prayer or almsgiving? That would seem logical. But Jesus took a different tack. Of course you pray, he said, but don't make a big deal of it. Of course you continue to give alms, but do it anonymously.

At first the passage quoted above is quite clear. But every year students, whether Jewish or Christian or another faith, asked why Jesus put this all in the language of "rewards." Do we really pray, or help the needy, in order to get a reward? What about praying to express gratitude or to give voice to some inner anguish? What about giving out of generosity or compassion? Doesn't the phrasing of these ideas appeal to a kind of selfishness, suggesting that we will reap a better reward than the other guy?

I did not know the answer to these questions and I continue to be puzzled. Some scholars have surmised that Jesus had to couch his unconventional message in the language of ordinary people, and that most of them must have been caught up in a rather primitive rewards-and-punishments conception of the moral life. But this explanation does not convince me. In most of the rest of his teaching he does not rein in the radical edge of his words.

Still, in thrashing through these verses with the young people of today, a problem arose that no one in Jesus' time could have anticipated. What the rabbi seems to be criticizing, even ridiculing here, is what might be called "spiritual ostentation." Do not parade your devoutness before men. Pray, but do it on the sly. Don't seek public acclaim and recognition for your piety. But the students I taught often had the opposite problem. In a secular culture they often felt they had to play down their religious practices. They dreaded being thought of as someone with a holier-than-thou attitude. They would not have been troubled by Jesus' suggestion that one should not sit in a prominent place in the synagogue (or church). They already felt more comfortable in the back row. John Updike once wrote that when he was living in Greenwich Village and woke on a Sunday morning with the impulse to attend church, he virtually sneaked across Washington Square with his collar turned up so that his fellow would-be bohemian intellectuals would not spot him.

This situation has been changing in the past couple of decades. Now students — and many other people — are more willing to identify themselves openly with a religious tradition. Jewish students wear skullcaps. Catholics and other Christians wear the smudge symbolizing their mortality on their foreheads all day on Ash Wednesday. Muslim women come to class wearing the *hijab* (headscarf). And yet students continue to feel suspicious of politicians and public officials who have their pictures taken going to church or solemnly intone the word *God* in their speeches. The spirit of Jesus' warning against religious ostentation still seems to be sharply relevant.

Jesus then goes on to teach his followers a simple prayer. It is the one most Christians learn almost before they are conscious, and if they know any prayer by heart, this is the one. It is still often repeated in the elegant English of the King James translation of the Bible:

> Our Father which art in heaven
> Hallowed be thy name.
> Thy kingdom come.
> Thy will be done on earth as it is in heaven.
> Give us this day our daily bread.
> And forgive us our debts, as we forgive our debtors.
> And lead us not into temptation,
> But deliver us from evil.
> (Matthew 6:7–13)

At this point Catholics usually stop, but Protestants continue:

> For thine is the kingdom and the power,
> And the glory forever. Amen

Why this strange denominational difference? The answer is interesting, since Protestants are usually the ones who say they want to go "back to the original," whatever that original is. In this case, however, it is the Catholic version that probably comes closer to the original. The lines now associated with the Protestant version were added in the early days of Christianity as a kind of response to the prayer itself. Further, Protestants usually call it the Lord's Prayer, while Catholics often refer to it as the Our Father. But what strikes any scholar about it is its singular Jewishness and its lack of any particularly Christian originality. As the New Testament commentator Sherman E. Johnson says, "The prayer is thoroughly Jewish and nearly every phrase is paralleled in the Kaddish and the Eighteen Benedictions; thus it is Jesus' inspired and original summary of his own people's piety at its best." On balance, I think the students got this part of the Sermon on the Mount about right. But the next part fired some heated arguments. Jesus says:

> Do not store up for yourselves treasure on earth, where moth and rust destroy, and thieves break in and steal; but store up treasure in heaven, where neither moth nor rust will destroy, nor thieves break in and steal. For where your treasure is, there will your heart be also.
>
> . . .
>
> No one can serve two masters; for either he will hate the first and love the second, or he will be devoted to the first and despise the second. You cannot serve God and Money.
>
> This is why I tell you not to be anxious about food and drink to keep you alive and about clothes to cover your body. Surely life is more than food, the body more than clothes. Look at the birds in the sky; they do not sow and reap and store in barns, yet your heavenly Father feeds them. Are you not worth more than the birds? Can anxious thought add a single day to your life? And why be anxious about clothes? Consider how the lilies grow in the fields; they do not work, they do not spin; yet I tell you even Solomon in all his splendor was not attired like one of them. If that is how God clothes the grass in the fields, which is there today and tomorrow is thrown on the stove, will he not all the more clothe you? How little faith you have! Do not ask anxiously, "What are we to eat? What are we to drink? What shall we wear?" These are things that occupy the minds of the heathen, but your heavenly Father knows that you need them all. Set your mind on God's kingdom and his justice before everything else, and all the rest will come to you as well. (Matthew 6:19–21, 24–34)

In this portion, Jesus is weaving together two much older narrative traditions. The first is the story of the Exodus, in which God delivers the Israelites from Egypt not simply so they can be free, but so they can serve him and not the pharaoh. Jews would have recognized this reference right away. But in addition, the radical rabbi is once again harking back to the Hebrew prophets and bringing their invective to bear against the wealthy elites, both of his own land and of the larger empire, who were so absorbed by the fancy clothes they sported and the pricey cuisine they imbibed.

When I was ready to begin discussing this famous passage with the class, I thought it best to warn them in advance that *Mammon,* which is used in the King James translation of the passage, "You cannot serve God and Money," is not the name of some silver-plated idol. It is the Greek form of an Aramaic word for wealth or possessions. Fortunately, the New English Bible translates it in an accurate and straightforward way as "money." Because what Jesus was saying here has a sharp edge, I expected a wave of skepticism: "Yeah, yeah. That *sounds* good, but look, we have to live in the real world . . ." They were, after all, preparing themselves for positions in life that would net some of them large salaries, and they knew it. I sometimes had students from the Business School in the class who would be taking jobs that paid them more in their first year after graduation than I was making after two decades of teaching. I expected some students to tell me that money was something they just did not want to talk about.

As it happened, however, I was mistaken about my students shying away from airing their attitudes toward dough, bread, shekels, and filthy lucre. (Why do we have so many names for it?) I had expected at least a few might skip the discussion section that week. I knew that they had little trouble talking about sex, or even about death. But money was rarely a topic of conversation. In an economics class they might discuss stocks and bonds, and even how to judge their relative values. But a student's feelings about his or her *own* money, or lack of it, almost never came up. Still, instead of avoiding the class when we got to "Mammon," they all streamed in. It was one of the best-attended discussion sections of the year. I quickly learned why they had not stayed away. They had apparently been looking for an opportunity to vent their feelings about money — whether they had it or did not — in a safe venue. To me this was another demonstration of the continuing relevance of Jesus. Somehow his words reached over the centuries and gave them a kind of permission to talk about a subject that was taboo elsewhere.

They seemed intrigued, even somewhat excited by the prospect of not living their lives pursuing something called "financial security." They were captivated by reading about St. Francis, whose highly prosperous father, an Italian cloth merchant, expected him to inherit the business, but who in effect told his father off and spent the rest of his days as a holy tramp, a traveling "troubadour for God." Others were deeply attracted by the life of Dorothy Day, the founder of the Catholic Worker Movement, who sought the presence of God among the homeless street people of the Lower East Side.

I should not have been surprised that the students wanted to discuss their mixed feelings about money. In every age there have been thoughtful people — with and without money — who realized that poverty was bad but who also became aware of the corrupting power of possessions. It was a complaint made at the time of Jesus by many sensitive Romans, who were sickened by what the obsession with opulence and consumption was doing to the moral fabric of what had once been a sturdy republic. The Roman poet Juvenal (first and second centuries A.D.) wrote in his *Satires* that the God his fellow Romans honored most, even though it did not have an altar of its own, was "Pecunia." Juvenal is noted for his biting attacks on the pomp and luxury of the privileged classes in the empire, and on the cruelty and corruption of the rulers.

It seems that both Jesus and Juvenal saw money as a god — a false and duplicitous one, but a god nevertheless. This agreement between the rabbi and the poet on the religious dimension of money-grubbing and the lust to accumulate gives us a valuable insight into the enormous attraction early Christianity had for many thoughtful Romans. The message of Jesus did not arrive in the Roman provinces, or in the capital itself, as something completely foreign. It resonated with some of the deepest inclinations of the most reflective people in the ancient world. Philosophers such as the Stoics and even the Epicureans taught that wealth is not necessary for the good life, and that it can even become an obstacle.

The subject of money has been a divisive issue throughout the history of Christianity. As soon as the early church began to attract wealthy people, squabbles arose about how much they should share with the less well off members of their congregations. This was already a cause for rancor in St. Paul's time, and he had to cope with the issue in some of his letters. Later, after the legal establishment of Christianity in the fourth century, whole groups of Christians, enraged by the wealth of the established churches, trooped off to live in shacks and caves in the desert in what came to be called the monastic movement. Throughout the medieval period, protesters periodically decried the worldly affluence of the church and even raised doubts about whether a rich church could really represent the message of the man who had so clearly warned about the spiritual dangers of possessions. One of Martin Luther's main complaints against the Catholic Church was that it was accumulating vast treasures by selling its services to the poor. The question has never gone away and remains a source of continuing discord today.

Money is a touchy subject, and I should not have been surprised that the students wanted a chance to talk about it. But there was a troubling catch. While many of them wanted to avoid the Golden Calf, they were not at all sure that the God whom St. Francis and Dorothy Day trusted would provide an adequate alternative. No one wants to step off the ladder of success into thin air. They admired the people who had chosen another way of life, but I sensed they resented them, too. How could St. Francis and Dorothy Day be so sure that "The Lord will provide"? Besides, neither of them had families to support (or huge college loans to repay). Instead of inspiring them to "go and do likewise," the obvious sense of joy and freedom that St. Francis exhibited seemed to mock them. Now I was the one who was troubled. Was exposing them to these radical ideas doing more harm than good? Is a guilt-ridden stockbroker any better than one who is not?

The answer to my question, or at least *an* answer, came when I invited a real live Franciscan to meet with the students. I had known Leonardo Boff, a Brazilian theologian, for a number of years. I had met him at conferences and had once visited him at the monastery he lived in just outside Rio de Janeiro, where he worked as the editor of an influential journal and served a tiny congregation in a nearby slum. Leonardo never wore the traditional Franciscan rough cloth robe tied at the waist with a knotted rope. He believed that although that had been appropriate garb when the first Franciscans rebelled against the emerging money-mad and clothing-conscious culture of early-thirteenth-century Italy, it was no longer suitable. It had now become a kind of religious uniform that, instead of signifying solidarity with the less privileged, set its wearers apart, the exact opposite of the effect St. Francis had desired. So instead he wore jeans and an open-collar shirt.

When he met with the students during his visit to America, Brother Leonardo listened thoughtfully to their ambivalence about the Gospel mandate to forswear Mammon, and detected their smoldering aversion toward those who seemed to have done so. Leonardo's answer to them was reassuring. First, he distinguished between the *voluntary poverty* St. Francis had chosen, which carries its own spiritual rewards, and *involuntary poverty,* which crushes and strangles millions of people in the world. The one is a blessing, the other a man-made curse. The purpose of the first kind of poverty is to relieve the misery of the second. St. Francis himself, Leonardo said, had never expected everyone, or even most people, to follow his example. He knew that, as St. Paul once wrote, "there is a variety of gifts." St. Francis and his band of friars believed they had a special task — to alleviate to some small extent the wretchedness of the sick and the poor. But they also wanted to live their own lives as a visible warning to those who had power and wealth that neither would buy them joy and freedom, and that the rich have an obligation to bring sustenance and healing to the destitute. Toward the end of his life St. Francis even created what was later called the Third Order, a league of ordinary laypeople who were inspired by his example, but because they were married or had families, or for other reasons, could not become friars. The saint himself realized that his way of following the difficult demands of Jesus was not everyone's.

Leonardo also explained that since St. Francis had lived nearly seven hundred years earlier, Franciscans in every generation were obliged to think through his mission in order to discern how best to witness against the enforced impoverishment that kills so many people early in life. St. Francis did it in ways appropriate to the early thirteenth century. But he lived before the advent of the sweatshops spawned by greedy corporations and the poisoning of the spirits of the poor by massive advertising. As a Franciscan, and *therefore* a liberation theologian, Leonardo said, he believed in using — indeed deploying — the talents and the education he had (he holds a doctorate from a prestigious German university) in the interest of the dispossessed classes and excluded groups. He believed that the biblical God reveals himself to be on the side of such people, and to encounter God we need to be with them in their struggle for life. He chuckled. Of course if anyone really wanted to join the Franciscans he would not turn them down. "We need a few good men . . . and women," he said, obviously familiar with the U.S. Army's recruiting slogan. "But the rest of you should get the best education you can; then use whatever power and money God allows you to have to subvert the social and economic structures that perpetuate misery and inequality." Nobody joined the Franciscans as a result of Leonardo Boff's visit, but the students appreciated his advice. He left wearing a crimson Harvard T-shirt.

After warning against serving Mammon, Jesus goes on to some of the most lyrical, most familiar, and most exasperating words he ever spoke: "Do not be anxious about your life, what you eat or what you shall drink, nor about your body, what you shall put on. Is not life more than food, and the body more than clothing?" He then encourages his listeners to "Consider the lilies of the field" who "neither toil nor spin, yet even Solomon in all his glory was not arrayed like one of these." He concludes: "Therefore do not be anxious about tomorrow, for tomorrow will be anxious for itself. Let the day's own trouble be sufficient for the day." The classical King James translation of the Bible has this as "Take no thought for the morrow" (Matthew 7:25, 28, 29, 34).

When we got to this passage the headshaking increased and the frustration level in the class rose several degrees. Now this was really too much. Turn the other cheek? Possible, maybe. Love your enemies? Within reason, perhaps. But to forget about tomorrow? Or next week? Or — especially — exam week? This can't be serious. What could anyone do with these pretty words except stitch them into a sampler, mount them in a frame, hang them on the wall — and then ignore them?

I found it hard to take the other side. Everything around these students seemed designed to shove them into thinking about the future. After all, weren't they getting an education to *prepare* them for something later? Hadn't that started when their parents tried as hard as possible to get them into the best nursery school, so they could have a better selection of grade schools and then high schools, so that they would have a better chance of being accepted into a good college, so that . . . ? And wasn't I part of the problem? After all, hadn't I assigned book reviews, a midterm and a final exam, and occasionally warned them about when these assignments were due, and even urged them to prepare?

Don't think about what you wear? Lilies may be magnificently arrayed. But they do not have to dress to impress for job interviews or be in touch with what is being worn this year (and what is not) when they go downtown with their friends. In fact, for American high school and college students today, the question of "what to put on" is doubly vexing. In their parents' days the problem was how to dress properly, not to appear unkempt or dowdy. But today's students tussle with a more complex challenge: how not to be *over*dressed, or appear snooty or simply "out of it." What you wear emits a signal about who you are, who you hang out with, what you think of yourself. Thinking about all this, it would seem, is a lot of work. The lilies in comparison have it easy.

Not thinking about what you are going to eat is also a very different question for privileged people who live in prosperous countries than it was for many in Jesus' day or than it is for the citizens of poor areas of the world today. The difference is a cruel one. Young mothers in some famine-stricken African countries can scarcely afford not to think about food for themselves and their babies. They think of little else, and we can hardly blame them for that. Young people in America, on the other hand, and many adults as well, worry constantly about whether what they are about to eat will add too many grams of flab to their silhouettes: "I told you I wanted a *Diet* Coke!" This is an especially niggling problem for women, young and old. Every "women's magazine" on the drugstore shelves features two things on the cover. The first is a touched-up picture of an always-smiling woman with perfect teeth and ample breasts but a slim waistline. The other is the most recent sure-fire and scientifically tested reducing diet. In short, not thinking about food or raiment seemed to my students to be one of Jesus' teachings for which the old medieval notion of a "counsel of perfection" — something required of monks and nuns but not of anyone else — seemed entirely appropriate. It was a nice idea, maybe, but not for them.

Again, however, I could discern a kind of yearning. How much they would *like* to live the carefree life Jesus seemed to be describing. Many of them spoke fondly about a high school friend or a distant relative who had "thrown it all over" and become a ski bum in Vermont or was hitchhiking through southern Europe — perhaps not exactly what Jesus had in mind. Some of them were also annoyed that in this case, the texts about not seeking after Mammon and forgetting tomorrow were a bit contradictory. One student told me acidly that the social dropouts he knew who did not worry about tomorrow — except possibly whether the slopes would have a nice cover — were able to be so nonchalant because their parents, or someone, *had* worried. Those people did, of course, think about what they were going to eat or wear. They wanted to wear the most with-it leisure togs and climbing boots. But they did not worry about the cost because they could pay with a credit card or draw on a trust fund. Another student introduced Immanuel Kant's well-known test of a moral action: What if everyone did this? What if everyone — grocery store managers, airline pilots, physicians . . . and yes, professors — "took no thought for the morrow"? Wouldn't the world grind to a halt? What would happen to datebooks, engagement calendars, and Palm Pilots?

Before I tried to answer these perfectly reasonable doubts, I had to admit that this passage, perhaps more than any other in the New Testament, underscores the truly radical nature of Jesus' message. He really did burn his bridges. He really did launch a new life in which he sometimes had "no place to lay his head." But he did so because he truly believed that God would indeed somehow provide for his necessities. And he was asking his followers, then and now, to try to live this way too, to seek an alternative to the kind of security — itself often very shaky — the world of money and accumulation seems to offer. "Seek first the Kingdom of God and his justice," he says as he concludes this section, "and all these things shall be yours as well."

But did Jesus expect everyone to live exactly as he did? It is true that he appointed one of the disciples to be the treasurer (although that particular appointment — Judas — does not indicate a very sagacious ability in personnel matters on his part), so his little band must have had something in the purse. He also seems to have had friends — Mary and Martha, Simon, and others — who were happy to welcome him into their homes and who obviously had not left everything to follow him. He was not an ascetic. He enjoyed eating and drinking, and provided the wine for the wedding at Cana. But the core of his wisdom here is found in his rhetorical question: "Is not life *more* than food, and the body *more* than clothing?" Food and clothing are essential, he is saying, but *then what?* The key to his attitude was not some reckless abandonment of material goods, but an unswerving confidence that life has more to offer than making a living, and that God would somehow supply what he really needed.

I do not always agree that modern translations of the Gospels are useful. But in this case I do. The words *be not anxious* in these passages are a more accurate rendering of the text than *take no thought*, which is truly sampler copy. Human beings by their nature are capable of thinking about the future. Indeed, we should and must. Thought can be constructive, but anxiety is paralyzing. Millions of members of Alcoholics Anonymous have discovered that practicing "One Day at a Time" helps them avoid the sickening worry about whether at some future time of stress they will resort to the bottle, a worry that can itself, paradoxically, drive them to drink. As Jesus says, tomorrow will bring its own worries (Matthew 6:34).

Jesus concludes the Sermon on the Mount with a rush of words. "Do not judge, so that you may not be judged." Don't worry so much about the speck in your neighbor's eye, he advises with a dose of raucous hyperbole, when you are carrying around a log in your own. "Do unto others as you would have others do unto you." "By their fruits you shall know them." He ends with these familiar sentences:

> So whoever hears these words of mine and acts on them is like a man who had the sense to build his house on a rock. The rain came down, the floods rose, the winds blew and beat upon that house; but it did not fall because its foundations were on rock. And whoever hears these words of mine and does not act on them is like a man who is foolish enough to build his house on sand. The rain came down, the floods rose, the winds blew and battered against that house; and it fell with a great crash. (Matthew 7:24–27)

Wrestling along with my students with the Sermon on the Mount year after year taught me a hard but important lesson. I was thankful that, centuries ago, someone took the trouble to write it down so that we can read it today. It is almost impossible to imagine what Western, or even world, history would have been like without it. Still, I was repeatedly frustrated to realize that I could never live up to it, even as I admired the people who came closer than I could to doing so. Consequently, each year when we were finally finished with the Sermon on the Mount, I sometimes felt that I had physically scaled a formidable peak myself. But I knew I could not stay at that altitude for long. I had to come down. I'm sure that at least some of the students felt the same way. I sometimes think Matthew had a similar reaction. In the next verse after the Sermon ends, he reports that the demanding crowds closed in on Jesus again, and among them there was another leper who wanted to be healed.

14

Parables and Zen Slaps

Wanting to justify his questions, he asked, "But who is my neighbor?" Jesus replied, "A man was on his way from Jerusalem down to Jericho when he was set upon by robbers, who stripped and beat him, and went off leaving him half dead. It so happened that a priest was going down by the same road, and when he saw him, he went past to the other side. So too a Levite came to the place, and when he saw him went past on the other side. But a Samaritan who was going that way came upon him, and when he saw him was moved to pity. He went up and bandaged his wounds, bathing them with oil and wine. Then he lifted him on to his own beast, brought him to an inn, and looked after him. Next day he produced two silver pieces and gave them to the innkeeper, and said, 'Look after him; and if you spend more, I will repay you on my way back.' Which of these three do you think was the neighbor to the man who fell into the hands of the robbers?" He answered, "The one who showed him kindness." Jesus said to him, "Go and do as he did." — LUKE 10:29–37

LIKE ALL RABBIS before and since, the Nazareth rabbi loved to spin tales. Nothing about him is more Jewish or more rabbinical. About sixty of these stories are recorded in the New Testament, and even the most skeptical of critics are inclined to believe he actually told them. As one scholar says, "They radiate a genuine Galilean flavor." The stories told in later centuries by subsequent generations of rabbis constitute a fabulous treasury of wisdom. Millions of people have heard them. But the ones Jesus told have reached many hundreds of millions. They have been passed on and retold so often that many of them have found their way into our everyday idiom, so much so that many people toss out phrases from them without knowing where they originated. I once tried a playful exercise on my students. How many of the following familiar phrases, I asked, were first spoken by Jesus? I listed them on the blackboard: "going the extra mile," "not hiding your light under a bushel," "killing the fatted calf," "casting your pearls before swine," "poor little sheep who have gone astray." The correct answer, of course, is all of the above, and most are phrases taken from his parables. If Jesus had gotten a copyright on his collected sayings, his estate would be worth a fortune.

Stories were Jesus' stock-in-trade, the main medium by which he conveyed his message. The parables occupy fully 35 percent of the first three Gospels. But one of their most surprising features is that they are *not about God*. They are about weddings and banquets, family tensions, muggings, farmers sowing and reaping, and shrewd business dealings. God is mentioned in only one or two. Like the great Hasidic rabbi the Baal Shem Tov, who lived fifteen hundred years later but who resembled him in so many ways, Rabbi Jesus obviously wanted us to look closely at *this* world, not some other one. It is here and now — all around us in the most ordinary things — that we find the divine presence.

The story of the mugging victim on the Jericho road is one of his most famous. In this one, three people, two of them stock characters, come along while the luckless traveler lies sprawled in the ditch bleeding and probably unconscious (the story says "half dead"), his wallet stolen and his head and body bruised. Of the three characters, two — the priest and the Levite — were totally predictable to Jesus' audience. They appeared in many other contemporary anecdotes, but in the standard cliché, the rescuer would have been an average Israelite. That was the formula, encompassing the three familiar ranks of society at the time, with the ordinary Israelite always trumping his higher-ups. But Rabbi Jesus throws in a surprise. Instead of the expected everyday Israelite, someone else happens along — a half-breed foreigner, a Samaritan (from whom it was commonly said that "nothing worthwhile could be expected"). Up to this point the actors are all cardboard cutouts, like today's gags that start, "An Italian, a Frenchman, and an American all walk into a bar . . ." But then comes another of the unexpected twists for which Rabbi Jesus was becoming notorious. The priest and the Levite, establishment figures in that world, all carefully cross to the other side so they can avoid the ill-fated traveler, and maybe make it appear that they did not even see him. The only one who stops and helps is the ne'er-do-well, the Samaritan who does not belong in the anecdote to begin with. He gives the first-century equivalent of first aid, pouring wine and oil onto the injured man's wounds. Then he puts him on his own donkey and takes him to an inn, where he makes arrangements to have him cared for. He even digs into his own purse to pay the innkeeper.

When the students read this parable their first response was to stifle a yawn. Not only was the story quite familiar, the moral seemed entirely obvious. If we should come across a mugging victim sprawled over a curb along Brattle Street, we should help him. So what else is new?

But Jesus was not trying to sketch a moral example. He had something else in mind. The story is an instance of his bait-and-switch technique. He wanted to lead his audience along what sounded like a familiar path and then, at the last minute, reverse the accepted social stereotypes and shake up the conventional worldviews of his hearers. His stories are like "changeup" pitches in baseball, which begin looking like one thing but turn out to be something so different they throw off the batter's timing.

When we compare Rabbi Jesus' parables with the stories other teachers of wisdom told, we can recognize both striking similarities and important differences. Telling stories is the favorite teaching method in many spiritual traditions. Like the rabbis, the ancient Christian "desert fathers" taught through stories. So did the Sufi masters and the Buddhist monks, and they still do.

The kind of stories told in these traditions is a particularly good clue to both what they have in common and where they differ. But I believe the stories of Jesus can be understood best by comparing them to the famous *koans* told by the Zen Buddhist masters. Like Jesus, these teachers wanted not so much to drive home a moral point but to snare the listener into a change of consciousness. Take, for example, the Zen tale about the day a young adept took leave of his own master, Su Feng, and went to visit another one named Ling Yun.

"What was it like in the world before the Buddha appeared?" the adept asked.

Ling Yun said nothing, but merely raised his *hossu* (the fanlike wand used to chase away flies during meditation).

Puzzled, the youthful seeker asked him, "Well then, how was it after the Buddha's appearance?"

This time Ling Yun raised his *hossu* exactly as he had done before. In considerable consternation the young monk returned to his master, Su Feng.

"Back so soon?" Su Feng said.

"Yes, alas," said the adept, "I have understood nothing at all."

"Well, why not ask me then?" his original master inquired.

So the adept put the same two questions. Then Su Feng raised his own *hossu* in answer to each of the two questions. This time the young monk bowed. Su Feng struck him on the head with his *hossu*. End of story.

A modern reader may be both charmed and infuriated by this *koan*. Did the adept ever get an answer to his questions? Are there any answers? Should he even be asking? Did he finally "understand" what the two masters were saying? Or did he understand that there was nothing to understand? And why does he get whacked on the head?

Like the famous Zen puzzler, "What is the sound of one hand clapping?" which can seem utterly silly or downright profound, or possibly both, the one thing we can safely say about the story of the adept's encounter with Su Feng and Ling Yun is that it is certainly not intended to convey a moral precept as one of Aesop's fables might. Zen tales are intended to rattle the way the hearer thinks and perceives the world. This was also Rabbi Jesus' style. Nearly all his stories end with a reverse loop. They leave the hearer not so much better informed as jolted.

In his classic book *Zen Buddhism,* the great Zen teacher D. T. Suzuki sets out to help the Western reader get a feel for what a *koan* is supposed to do. His explanation also helps us better grasp the intent of Rabbi Jesus' tales. The very essence of Zen Buddhism, Suzuki explains, consists in "acquiring a new viewpoint" from which one looks at life. But, he continues, acquiring this new perspective will require "the greatest mental cataclysm one can go through in life." It compares, he says, to storms and earthquakes and the breaking in pieces of rocks. This "unfolding of a new world hitherto unperceived" is what *satori* is. With this *satori,*

> our entire surroundings are viewed from quite an unexpected angle of perception . . . The world for those who have gained *satori* is no more the old world as it used to be . . . it is never the same again . . . [But] *satori* can be had only through our once experiencing it.

Suzuki goes on to compare the gaining of *satori* to the process of solving a difficult mathematical problem, or to what happens when someone makes a great discovery and shrieks "Eureka!" But, he warns, all this still refers only to the intellectual side of *satori,* which, to be complete, must include all aspects of life.

Jesus' stories have a similar intention, and this is exactly why I often resist calling them by their traditional name, *parables.* This word can too easily lead us to think of them as mere allegories. The Hebrew word *mashal,* which lies behind the word *parable,* is a more forceful one. It does mean "story," but it is also used at times to refer to taunts and ballads. Some scholars believe that its oldest meaning referred not to something spoken but to something acted out. In any case, just as Rabbi Jesus took the Jewish teaching of his day and, while being faithful to it, gave it a new and potent thrust, he also took the ancient form of the *mashal* and put it to a new use.

He used it to shake people up, to smack them on the head with a verbal *hossu*.

Also, Jesus was not satisfied with merely telling his stories. As with the earliest meaning of the *mashal,* he also acted them out in a kind of roving street theater. He did not stop with merely *recounting* his ideas about seating outsiders and misfits around the family table. When he went somewhere to teach he made it a point to *associate* with well-known characters of shady reputation, individuals with loathsome illnesses, and Gentiles, including the universally despised representatives of Caesar and their local Israelite lackeys. When upon entering Jericho he noticed Zacchaeus, a local tax collector, who had climbed a tree to get a better view of this notorious rabbi, Jesus called him down and then invited himself to dinner at the man's home. The *mashal,* spoken and enacted, was his natural *métier.* One could even say that the entire trajectory of his life, as the Gospels tell it, is a parable. It takes the form of a story with a surprise ending.

But Jesus' stories, though similar to Zen *koans* in some ways, were also different in important respects. While the Zen stories aim at changing one's *perception* of the world, Jesus wanted people to see that *the world itself was changing,* and that therefore, they had better change the way they looked at it. He invited them, in effect, to become part of the change. Time after time he said, "He that has eyes to see, let him see, and he that has ears to hear, let him hear." He simply wanted people to *pay attention* to what was going on around them and to discern a reality that was just under their noses. To describe this change he used a term that his listeners would have found familiar, though they might have been startled by the way he used it. He called it the coming of the "reign of God." What he meant was that something was happening, not just in the consciousness of the listener, but also in the world itself. Something new and unprecedented was happening, and they could be a part of it.

In one way or another this was the central point, made in many different ways, of all the stories Rabbi Jesus told. The melody, repeated over and over again, reminds us of the themes we heard in the stories people told about him in the genealogies and the legends of his birth. They are about the unbounded mercy of God to all people, whether or not they belong to the commonwealth of Israel. They crackle with plot reversals and unexpected denouements. They draw on all kinds of life situations. But this is the underlying thrust: Just look and listen, and you will see that hints of the dawning presence of God's shalom are appearing right here and right now. No one hearing Jesus' message could have thought that he meant you could do nothing and just wait for it to happen. The need to respond, one way or another, was integral to everything he said and did.

Obviously the responses to Jesus' note of urgency have varied widely, both then and now. Some, indeed most, people in his time simply ignored him. It was, after all, a disconcerting message that would have required some uncomfortable changes in the way they were living. Some took it very seriously. Many, over the centuries, have been somewhere in between. Most of the students fell into this middle category. But as a teacher I took some comfort in the metaphor Jesus used in one of his best-known parables about the grains of wheat falling on various kinds of soil — thorny, stony, or fertile. It takes a while for seeds to sprout and grow, and I knew it is often the fate of teachers not to see the full blossoming of what they have planted. But I was sure the students would never forget the shaking up they received from those changeup pitches.

15

The Crooked CEO
and the Spoiled Brat

He said to his disciples, "There was a rich man who had a steward, and
he received complaints that this man was squandering the property. So
he sent for him, and said, 'What is this that I hear about you? Produce
your accounts, for you cannot be steward any longer.' The steward said
to himself, 'What am I to do now that my master is going to dismiss me
from my post? I am not strong enough to dig, and I am too proud to
beg. I know what I must do, to make sure that, when I am dismissed,
there will be people who will take me into their homes.' He summoned his master's debtors one by one. To the first he said, 'How
much do you owe my master?' He replied, 'A hundred jars of olive oil.'
He said, 'Here is your account. Sit down and make it fifty, and be quick
about it.' Then he said to another, 'And you, how much do you owe?'
He said, 'A hundred measures of wheat.' And was told, 'Here is your
account, make it eighty.' And the master applauded the dishonest steward for acting so astutely. For in dealing with their own kind the children of this world are more astute than the children of light.

"So I say to you, use your worldly wealth to win friends for your-
selves, so that when money is a thing of the past you may be received
into an eternal home." — LUKE 16:1–9

Is THIS REALLY the Jesus we have come to know speaking?
He seems to be commending a greedy, corrupt — indeed
fraudulent — administrator who pads his own nest and guaran-
tees his future financial security by cheating his employer. What is
the rabbinical storyteller up to here?

When we got to Jesus' parables in class I had to be very selective.
With sixty-odd parables to choose from and only one short semester to find our way through the entire story of Jesus, I had to pick

the most representative ones, and I also had to decide which one to start with. I could have chosen The Rich Fool, The Mustard Seed, The Lost Sheep, or The Rich Man and Lazarus. But I wanted to start off with one that would most effectively upset the students' expectations. I tried different ones, but the parable above, which I call The Tale of the Crooked CEO, was the one I eventually settled on. The last thing I wanted was for them to think they had "done" the parables. I wanted to tease them into coming back to them for years to come. I picked this tale because it so clearly demonstrates the changeup style Jesus used to shock his hearers into a different way of looking at things.

The parable of the crooked CEO is not one that ministers preach on very often. Most of the students had never heard of it, and they were bewildered when they did. Some had a hard time believing Jesus really told it. It seemed so out of character. The newspapers were full of accounts of CEOs lining their own pockets at the expense of stockholders and employees. Yet here, Jesus seemed to be commending a sneaky, self-serving manager, a charlatan who sounded as though he might well have headed a division of Enron. What was going on?

Despite a lot of pressure from the class, I never gave in and "explained" to them "the real meaning" of this puzzler. First, I did not know for sure myself, despite having read half a dozen more or less credible interpretations of it. But mainly I wanted to be true to the spirit of the Nazareth rabbi and of this parable in particular. I wanted them to be perplexed and at a loss, to have to rearrange their own thinking, if not about the whole world, then at least some of their preconceptions about Jesus. The parable itself continues with what passes for an explanation:

Anyone who can be trusted in small matters can be trusted also in great; and anyone who is dishonest in small matters is dishonest also in great. If, then, you have not proved trustworthy with the wealth of this world, who will trust you with the wealth that is real? And if you have proved untrustworthy with what belongs to another, who will give you anything of your own?

No slave can serve two masters; for either he will hate the first and love the second, or he will be devoted to the first and despise the second. You cannot serve God and Money. (Luke 16:9–13)

But this internal explanation still leaves a lot unexplained, as it should. Maybe Jesus was emphasizing, as he often did in his parables, that every moral choice in light of the coming of God's reign is an urgent one: Better act fast! Maybe he was saying, as he also often did, that things are not necessarily what they seem. The people we think of as rogues and scoundrels may have something to teach us. Or maybe the story has no single meaning at all. Like a Zen fable, it may be designed to short-circuit one's neuron paths and open the mind to new possibilities. I had discovered over many years of teaching that one of the most seductive temptations in my profession is to explain too much too soon. Perplexity and confusion are not always obstacles to learning. They are sometimes allies. I am convinced that Jesus often left his hearers with their brows knitted and their heads shaking. It was basic to his teaching method.

Discussing the parables with my class often offered me a surprising learning moment too, if not about the text, about the youthful world I found myself in. Take the following story, often called "The Parable of the Prodigal Son":

Again he said: "There was once a man who had two sons; and the younger said to his father, 'Father, give me my share of the property.' So he divided his estate between them. A few days later the younger son turned the whole of his share into cash and left home for a distant country, where he squandered it in dissolute living. He had spent it all, when a severe famine fell upon that country and he began to be in need. So he went and attached himself to one of the local landowners, who sent him on to his farm to mind the pigs. He would have been glad to fill his belly with the pods that the pigs were eating, but no one gave him anything. Then he came to his senses: 'How many of my father's hired servants have more food than they can eat,' he said, 'and here am I, starving to death! I will go at once to my father, and say to him, "Father, I have sinned against God and against you; I am no longer fit to be called your son; treat me as one of your hired servants." ' So he set out for his father's house. But while he was still a long way off his father saw him, and his heart went out to him; he ran to meet him, flung his arms around him, and kissed him. The son said, 'Father, I have sinned against God and against you; I am no longer fit to be called your son.' But the father said to his servants, 'Quick! Fetch a robe, the best we have, and put it on him; put a ring on his finger and sandals on his feet. Bring the fatted calf and kill it, and let us celebrate with a feast. For this son of mine was dead and has come back to life; he was lost and is found.' And the festivities began.

"Now the elder son had been out on the farm; and on his way back, as he approached the house, he heard music and dancing. He called one of the servants and asked what it meant. The servant told him, 'Your brother has come home, and your father has killed the fatted calf because he has him back safe and sound.' But he was angry and refused to go in. His father came out and pleaded with him; but he retorted, 'You know how I have slaved for you all these years; I never once disobeyed your orders; yet you never gave me so much as a kid, to celebrate with my friends. But now that this son of yours turns up, after running through your money with his women, you kill the fatted calf for him.' 'My boy,' said the father, 'you are always with me and everything I have is yours. How could we fail to celebrate this happy day? Your brother here was dead and has come back to life; he was lost and has been found.' " (Luke 15:11–32)

Unlike the parable of the shady CEO, the moral of this one seems very straightforward. It celebrates the father's generosity and openheartedness, even for a son who would qualify in anyone's judgment as a spoiled and self-indulgent brat. The heir, it seems, just can't wait until the old man dies. He asks for, and receives, his inheritance. He then goes off and squanders it in riotous living, whatever that may be. Reduced to herding pigs, an especially disgusting job for a Jew, he is so hungry he begins to pick at the garbage he is dumping before the swine. Then he decides to go home, throw himself on his father's mercy, and offer to live as a hired servant. (One student astutely observed that the son probably surmised that his father would never permit him to engage in such a menial occupation and would probably eventually accept him back.)

On his way home the son mentally rehearses the touching little speech he will make to his father. Some scholars claim this is the first example of an interior monologue in Western literature. But even before he can declaim his well-practiced discourse, his father spots him approaching, runs out, embraces him, and welcomes him home. The father even orders that a banquet be prepared to celebrate the occasion.

The contretemps surfaces when the older son, trudging back from toiling in the fields, hears the uproar of the partying and understandably rails against his father for favoring this wastrel instead of him. Incidentally, it is instructive to notice that when this older son complains to the pater familias, he says that the younger son has been spending his money on whores, a tidbit that does not appear in the foregoing text and may well have been a product of the older son's angry fantasy. The father assures the older son that he loves him just as much but that "your brother here was dead and has come back to life; he was lost and has been found."

I thought discussing this text with my students would be easy after the crooked manager story. But I encountered an unexpected snag. When I emphasized how impressive the father's love was, especially for such an ungrateful little monster, they were puzzled. What was the big deal? "But he actually went out to meet him," I insisted; "he welcomed him even before he had heard any explanations. Wasn't that an unusually generous father?"

They disagreed. Isn't that what *any* father would do? Of course he would welcome him back home, kill the fatted calf, invite his friends, open the keg. That is what fathers *do*. They also admitted that they could understand the resentment of the older son. (The third of the class who were older siblings especially saw this point.)

But once the father explained the situation and the older brother had joined the celebration, they were sure he would feel better about the whole thing the next morning.

What this little conversation taught me was that changing family patterns will always mean that succeeding generations will read any story involving a family in their own way. The parable of the prodigal son surely evoked different responses in the first century than it did in the medieval period or than it does today. But the power of such a narrative is that it continues to speak from century to century.

Finally, here is a parable that always made my students both squirm and, I think, learn:

Jesus spoke to them again in parables: "The Kingdom of Heaven is like this. There was a king who arranged a banquet for his son's wedding; but when he sent his servants to summon the guests he had invited, they refused to come. Then he sent other servants, telling them to say to the guests, 'Look! I have prepared his banquet for you. My bullocks and fatted beasts have been slaughtered, and everything is ready. Come to the wedding.' But they took no notice; one went off to his farm, another to his business, and the others seized the servants, attacking them brutally, and killed them. The king was furious; he sent troops to put those murderers to death and set their town on fire. Then he said to his servants, 'The wedding banquet is ready; but the guests I invited did not deserve the honour. Go out therefore to the main thoroughfares, and invite everyone you can find to the wedding.' The servants went out into the streets, and collected everyone they could find, good and bad alike. So the hall was packed with guests.

"When the king came in to watch them feasting, he observed a man who was not dressed for a wedding. 'My friend,' said the king, 'how do you come to be here without wedding clothes?' But he had nothing to say. The king then said to his attendants, 'Bind him hand and foot; fling him out into the dark, the place of wailing and grinding of teeth.' For many are invited, but few are chosen." (Matthew 22:1–14)

For the first ten verses this is a pleasant enough tale, and even rather typical of what Jesus frequently taught. The privileged elite around the king, the wellborn grandees and maharanis, for some reason, do not show up for the wedding soiree. The table is set, the silverware in place, the wine uncorked. But where are the guests! The king is beside himself. Impetuously, he throws the gates open to the riffraff, anyone who happens to be wandering by on the street. He even sends his heralds out to collar passersby and conduct them to the manor.

So far this is a typical "great reversal" scenario, reminiscent of so many of Jesus' aphorisms: "The last shall be first and the first shall be last." So far, so good, and with a perfectly obvious point. But then comes the changeup. Surveying his newly recruited guests, who were probably blinking in astonishment that they had been yanked off the highway and were about to be treated to a fine spread, he spots one recruit who is not dressed properly. He reproaches him testily, but the confused man has nothing to say in reply. Why should he? How could he have known that on his way home from cleaning the stable or tilling his field a messenger from the king would conduct him immediately into the royal dining salon? Of course he had not had time to change into evening clothes. The wonder is that any of the other last-minute invitees had either. The king's fury swells. He has the poor man bound hand and foot and thrown out into the dark, "the place of wailing and grinding of teeth." It seems, at a minimum, like an extremely unjust punishment for a hapless bypasser who suddenly finds himself in an unexpected setting.

Again the students were baffled. Was Jesus actually *commending* this hotheaded king? What was the point? Why hadn't Jesus simply stopped the story when those fortunate wayfarers, and maybe even some homeless people, finally got to sit down to a solid meal? Why had he ruined it at the end with this blatant breach of common sense and equity? *What is the real point?*

Again I tactfully refused to minimize the offense or rationalize the illogic of the parable. Yes, if the reign of God is breaking in now and could confront you at any point, you better be ready. Many parables make this point. Yes, a certain kind of behavior is expected of those who respond to the call of God. We saw this in the Sermon on the Mount. But the sharpness of this story of the nasty monarch still left a sour taste for many students. Some even told me later they suspected I could not "explain the meaning" of some of the parables because I had not done my own homework. They were, after all, taking a course in moral *reasoning*. Was it too much to ask that the parables of Jesus communicate some reasonable moral points? They did not like to be served up riddles and conundrums.

But despite the students' discomfort, I never gave in to requests to elucidate, explicate, or "make clear." They were in the process of growing up, as we all are, as long as we live. And growing up means learning to live with unsatisfying and incomplete endings, with people whose lives are cut off before they should be, or spin out in unexpected directions and sometimes crash in flames. No matter how ordinary they are, all our lives end with a kind of question mark as we reach the threshold of the final mystery. This is why the truly great literature of our race, from Sophocles to Shakespeare to Dostoyevsky, does not soothe us with happy endings. The parables remain vivid because they refuse to cater to our craving for tidy completion. Even though here and there one or another of the Gospel writers gives way to the temptation to decode one of Jesus' parables, I think one stays closer to the rabbi's own pedagogy by refraining from doing so. He wanted to shake people up, and when the parables are taken straight, with no chaser, that is exactly what they still do.

Jesus told parables. But he also acted out parables. Nearly everything he did was designed to get his radical message across, to unnerve some people while comforting others, to leave hearers so unhinged they had to rethink themselves and the world from the bottom up. This parabolic style of life also colored Jesus' work as a healer, to which we turn in the next chapter.

16

Why the Crowds Came

HOW HIS HEALINGS TOLD HIS STORY

And when Jesus had crossed again in the boat to the other side, a great crowd gathered about him; and he was beside the sea. Then came one of the rulers of the synagogue, Jairus by name, and seeing him, he fell at his feet, and besought him, saying, "My little daughter is at the point of death. Come and lay your hands on her, so that she may be made well, and live." And he went with him.

And a great crowd followed him and thronged about him.

— MARK 5:21–24

IT IS PERFECTLY CLEAR that the mobs of people who thronged Jesus did *not* seek him out to hear his message. They came because he had gained a reputation as a healer. This is something those who focus on his moral teachings and example often forget. It is also not something that is so easy to interpret at a modern university where just down the street the most advanced research in the treatment of everything from AIDS to bone cancer to manic-depressive syndrome is racing ahead on a daily basis. What connection could there possibly be between the healing stories we find both in the Bible and in other religious literature, and the latest research in stem cell therapies and microscopic brain surgery?

This is a hard gap to close. But in teaching the course I also found Jesus' healing a sensitive topic to deal with for another reason. At least one or two students always arrived for the lectures in wheelchairs. Every couple of years there were also some who came accompanied by guide dogs. Still, during the first years of the course I said virtually nothing about the many stories of Jesus healing sick people. When, occasionally, students asked about such an obvious omission, I lamely told them, "Well, you can't possibly cover *everything* when there is so much material." But I knew that was not the real reason for such an obvious omission. The truth was that I did not know what to say about the "healing miracles." I was particularly reluctant to discuss them in a class including science majors who were studying anatomy and epidemiology, dozens of premedical students, and some auditors from the School of Public Health. I expected that they would be skeptical of these accounts, and I was not prepared to defend their literal accuracy. But the main reason I skipped over the healing stories was the students in wheelchairs and those assisted by dogs. What could I say about the descriptions of Jesus restoring sight to the blind or making the lame walk without raising false hopes? So I said nothing at all.

My preparation in seminary had not been much help. When I studied the New Testament there many years earlier, my liberal professors, applying the historical-critical method then in vogue, lumped the healing stories along with other "miracles," such as Jesus' walking on the Sea of Galilee or changing water into wine at the marriage in Cana. They suggested that these were legends from a prescientific age, which his followers and succeeding generations attributed to Jesus in an effort to certify his authority in a period of history in which such miracles were expected if a prophet was to be taken seriously. My teachers also urged us to look below the surface of the miracle stories for their symbolic significance and their echoes of Old Testament narratives. They did not seem to entertain the possibility that Jesus had actually healed sick people. They left that to Christian Scientists, Pentecostals, and the gullible Catholics who visited Lourdes and Fatima. As years went by I was less and less content with these interpretations, but I found nothing to take their place.

There was another reason I steered away from the subject. It was the TV evangelists. Once in a while if I cannot get to sleep I wander downstairs and flick on the living room TV while I sip warm milk and munch graham crackers. But once I noticed something odd about my nocturnal channel surfing. As I flipped past old movies, talk shows, and diet ads, whenever I happened upon an evangelist prowling the stage with tie askew and open Bible in hand I paused and watched, at least for a while. I did not know what to make of it when they claimed their prayers could actually heal diseases, and streams of people crowded to the microphone to testify that they had indeed been healed. Some, like Jimmy Swaggart, even assured viewers that if they merely placed their hands on the screen God would heal them in response to his prayers. One woman evangelist claimed she could tell there was someone in the TV audience who suffered from a liver ailment or lower back pains, and that God was healing them at that very minute.

I was strangely fascinated by these programs, but I was also highly skeptical. I couldn't help wondering about the people who attended those services and fervently prayed for healing but then had to stagger out on the same crutches. But I also wondered why in the midst of my channel-hopping I always stopped and watched. I was both repelled and mesmerized. Despite the hype, something important, indeed something real, seemed to be going on. Still, I did not know what to say about Jesus as a healer.

This began to change when I got a phone call one day from a professor I had never met from Harvard Medical School. He said his name was Herbert Benson, he was a cardiologist, and he wanted to chat with me about something. Naturally I was curious, so we arranged a coffee date. When he arrived a couple of days later we sat in the snack bar and he told me he thought he was onto something very important but that he was afraid his colleagues in the Medical School might not appreciate it, and might even disparage or ridicule him. He said that for some time now he had been experimenting with an alternative treatment for patients who had suffered heart attacks. Like a good researcher, he had divided his patients into two groups. To one group he administered standard medications to prevent a second attack. With the other he used a completely different approach. He taught them how to meditate on a daily basis using a mantra method that had recently been introduced by a teacher from India. He gave this second group no medicines at all.

To his surprise, Benson said, there were significantly fewer heart attacks among the second group — the mantra meditators — than among the first. The problem was, he said, that the patients who used the mantra often found it boring or strange. So he asked one patient if there was something in his own religion he could substitute for the mantra. The patient thought, and then told him that there was, after all, the Lord's Prayer, which he remembered from childhood. Benson suggested he say it very slowly several times over for the twenty-five minutes he advised his patients to meditate each day for several weeks. When this approach also worked, Benson began wondering about other prayers, and then about other possible healing resources in spiritual traditions. He had come to me to ask for advice on what to read on the subject.

I did not have many suggestions to make, but — with the help of some very solicitous librarians — I quickly remedied the situation. I read reams of articles I would not have read if Benson and I had not met, then recommended some of them to him. We began to meet for lunch to discuss what had become a mutual learning project. An enormously inquisitive man, he was then going on to investigate a range of non-Western healing systems, including Tibetan and Indian Vedic practices. He looked into how Buddhist monks in deep meditation could sit for hours in freezing temperatures without appearing to feel the cold and (especially interesting for him) show no signs of frostbite. He invited the personal physician of the Dalai Lama to accompany him on grand rounds through Massachusetts General Hospital. The wizened old man, he told me, relied heavily on smelling urine samples, but — allowing for translation difficulties — got most of the diagnoses right. When he invited me to visit his laboratory at the Medical School, I gladly accepted.

Benson's spotless lab was crammed with shiny stainless steel apparatus replete with mystifying dials, knobs, and levers. As soon as he showed me his equipment I knew he was not interested in anecdotal or impressionistic evidence. He was nearly obsessive about measuring things, and measuring them accurately. He carefully calculated the skin temperature, heart rate, brain activity, and myriad other characteristics of the patients he examined. And he had the tools to do it. He obviously wanted to make his case for alternative ways of healing not to drowsy insomniacs perusing late-night TV, but to hard-nosed, skeptical scientists. He told me that to convince them he had to be a skeptic himself. When I told him about a student of mine who was going to engage in "fire walking" and asked if he would like to come with me to witness it, he eagerly accepted.

Fire walking was something of a craze at that time among young professionals. It was touted as a way to overcome one's fears and build self-confidence. The organizers met with the potential fire walkers, who had paid a handsome fee for the privilege, in a hotel function room, where they talked about fear and shouted slogans for a couple hours. Then they gathered in the hotel parking lot around a pit of coals about ten feet long and three feet wide, the smoldering residue of a roaring wood fire the sponsors had stoked earlier. One by one they took off their shoes, walked quickly over the coals (it required three or four strides), then had their feet sprayed with cold hose water by one of the organizers. The evening we were there thirty-five people walked across the coals.

I was impressed, even astonished. Benson was neither. He had subtly positioned a clinical thermometer on the coals, and pointed out to me in the car as we drove home that although the coals were hot, it would take at least a couple seconds of exposure to do any damage to the tissue. He reminded me that at the rate the walkers strode across the coals, with each step requiring hardly more than a second, there was little chance of anyone being burned. He dismissed the whole thing as a scam, though allowing that it might bring some psychological benefit to the people who did it. Our little field trip increased my appreciation of Benson. He could be open to unusual things, but he was not easily fooled.

Benson also had a very conventional — some might say Western —

understanding of what "healing" means. For him, healing meant that people who are sick get better. Once I introduced him to a colleague from the anthropology department who studied healing rituals among nonliterate central African peoples. I thought they might enjoy knowing each other. But I was wrong. When the anthropologist told Benson that among some of the people he studied a healing could be considered successful even if the patient died, because the tribe had been healed of some squabble or division in the process, Benson just shook his head. For the physicians to whom he was trying, with his tubes and gauges, to demonstrate that there was actually something to spiritual healing, a patient who dies can never count as a successful healing. The anthropologist, for his part, told me later he found Benson to be impossibly stuck in a "Western" model of healing.

Soon Benson and a handful of other researchers who shared his passion for healing and powerful curiosity persuaded a growing number of their colleagues that all this was something worth taking seriously. After all, he had the numbers to prove it. Within a few years of his groundbreaking work, the federal government organized the Office for Alternative Medicine in the National Institutes of Health. Its first director, Dr. Joseph J. Jacobs, initially confessed that he felt "like a flea trying to wag an elephant," but his office boldly set out to assess several therapies that had previously been viewed with suspicion or hostility by the medical establishment. His staff began evaluating the results of treatment by acupuncture (using needles to stimulate spots on the body with neural connections to various organs) and chiropractic (manipulating the spinal vertebrae). These approaches had already been granted a measure of approval because they did seem to produce demonstrable benefits. Other treatments — like biofeedback, hypnosis, bee pollen, a wide variety of herbal remedies, and shark cartilage — would clearly not be recognized so quickly. The therapy on Jacobs's agenda that intrigued me the most was "antineoplaston therapy." It involved the use of compounds from human urine that seemed to be able to halt division in some cancer cells. I was relieved to find, however, that these compounds can now be produced synthetically. Still, with all of this under way, it was obviously a new world in which established ideas about healing would now have to be thoroughly reexamined.

Indeed, within a few years the Harvard Medical School itself was doing something that would have been unimaginable even a decade earlier. It was sponsoring huge conferences on faith, spirituality, and healing. Benson invited me to speak at one of them. It was held at a big downtown hotel in Boston. When I arrived I had to elbow my way through hundreds of people crowding the corridors. The costumes — robes, turbans, clerical collars, business suits — and variety of skin colors of the guests and speakers suggested a vivid polyglot of cultures. The Medical School, at Benson's urging, had invited everyone from Native American shamans, Mexican *curanderas,* and Christian Scientists to Pentecostal preachers. I was especially intrigued by some registered nurses who spoke convincingly about how much merely touching patients hastened their recovery. Everyone with anything to contribute to healing seemed to be present at this extraordinary gathering. I would not have been surprised to see Jimmy Swaggart himself walk in. But he did not attend.

The massive rediscovery of alternative modes of healing in America, sparked in part by the pioneering work of Herbert Benson, changed my way of teaching. It convinced me that I could no longer merely skip over the many accounts of Jesus healing people that leap out at the reader from nearly every page of the Gospels. I had to talk about them. Not only was it now entirely respectable to do so, it was irresponsible not to. But it also presented me with a theological challenge. I did not want merely to subsume Jesus' healing into the fuzzy category of what is now called "alternative and complementary medicine." On the other hand, I have always resisted interpreting them as spectacular suspensions of the natural laws God created in the universe. I was also aware that Jesus was not the only spiritual healer to appear in history. Healings are attributed to the Baal Shem Tov and to many of the rabbis in the Hasidic movement he founded. Indian holy men, Buddhist monks, and

Christian saints are all believed to have healing powers. In short, spiritual healing — often to the discomfort of fundamentalists — is not restricted to Jesus. It is something that transcends the borders of religious traditions. Was there, however, something distinctive about Jesus' healings? I decided to look again, this time with a more open mind, at the healing stories in the Gospels.

As I reread these sections I found accents I had not noticed before. I had already realized that what first made most people seek out Jesus was not his teaching, least of all his ideas on "moral reasoning," but his healing. Still, I had not appreciated the passion and sometimes desperation of their quest for the restorative touch of the Galilean rabbi. People climbed trees, shoved their way through crowds, lowered their friends on ropes through holes in the ceiling, and tried to snatch at his robe — not in the first instance to hear his inventive interpretations of Torah or even his perplexing parables. They came because they or someone they cared for was sick and wanted to be healed.

But the most important element I had failed to grasp earlier was that, as far as Jesus was concerned, there was no distinction between his healing and his teaching. They were all of a piece. Those who collected and handed on the stories of Jesus' acts of healing did not present them as eye-popping wonders. They interpreted them as part of his larger message. They were "signs" (the Greek word is *semeion*) of the dawning of the new order God was initiating. Consequently, the Gospel writers almost always packaged the healing accounts within webs of engaging plots and memorable characters, which — like the parables — pointed beyond themselves to the big picture. The healing accounts are, like the parables, stories that contain an unexpected twist. There are dozens of such stories in the Gospels. One in particular, however, captures the essence of the whole genre. It is found in Mark 5:21–42. The first verses are quoted at the head of this chapter. I incorporate the rest in this part of the book because it is a good example of how Jesus' actions, including his healings, are also parables, integral to the way he communicated his total vision. They are among the "stories he told."

And there was a woman who had had a flow of blood for twelve years, and who had suffered much under many physicians, and had spent all that she had, and was no better but rather grew worse. She had heard reports about Jesus, and came up behind him in the crowd and touched his garment. For she said, "If I touch his garments I shall be made well."

And immediately the hemorrhage ceased; and she felt in her body that she had been healed of her disease. And Jesus, perceiving in himself that power had gone forth from him, immediately turned about in the crowd, and said, "Who touched my garments?" And his disciples said to him, "You see the crowd pressing around you, and yet you say, 'Who touched me?' "

And he looked around to see who had done it. But the woman, knowing what had been done to her, came in fear and trembling and fell down before him, and told him the whole truth. And he said to her, "Daughter, your faith has made you whole; go in peace, and be healed of your disease." (Mark 5:24–42)

In the verses here and at the start of this chapter, the Nazareth rabbi finds himself in a typical situation. A crowd of people is pursuing him, pushing and shoving, trying to attract his attention. They have clearly "heard the reports" that he is a healer, and that is why they have come. Then an important personage named Jairus, a "ruler of the synagogue," approaches Jesus. How did he get through the crowd? Probably he was well known in the area, and powerful enough that the others stepped aside. Then he prostrates himself before Jesus, itself a somewhat bizarre act. Jesus, the maverick rabbi and roadside healer, was already at odds with the political and religious rulers. They would eventually conspire with the Romans to kill him. But Jairus is evidently frantic. His daughter is deathly ill. He seems almost beside himself, so desperate that he throws himself at Jesus' feet, a position of deference not customarily granted to rabbis, let alone loose cannons like Jesus. It was like the servile scraping that oriental despots expected from those who were seeking favors.

For whatever reason, Jesus chooses to listen to this man among the many jostling each other and contending for his attention. I have never been quite sure why he did. He did not customarily respond with deference to those in power. But this time he not only takes interest in the synagogue ruler's pleas, he even sets out to accompany him to his home. Undeterred, the crowd comes trooping along behind.

Then, however, comes the first plot twist. A woman with a nasty hemorrhage pushes up behind Jesus and clutches at his cloak. How did she get so close when there was a mob surrounding him? My guess is that if she had indeed been bleeding for twelve years, and given the strong taboos against any contact with blood in her society at the time, the other people may well have stepped back to avoid being brushed by her. Her odor might even have been decidedly unpleasant. She was also, of course, ritually impure according to Levitical law. By rights she should have been segregated. If the others in the crowd had even inadvertently been touched by her, it could have required a ritual purification, which was inconvenient and expensive. In any case, the woman makes her way to Jesus and takes hold of his garment, saying (to herself, or anyone nearby who could hear her?) that if she can just touch those garments she will be made well. Finally she tugs at his hem and immediately feels healed.

Then Jesus reacts to the woman. Contrary to those who contend that he was omniscient throughout his whole life, he does not know what has happened. He turns around to the crowd trudging behind him and asks who touched his garments. His disciples reply, somewhat testily, that with so many bodies swarming around him, how could anyone say who touched his cloak? It was a mob scene. But the woman herself quickly takes the responsibility, and paradoxically falls to the same prone position that Jairus had, and admits it was she. The story says she did so "with fear and trembling." Why? She clearly knew that she had broken more than one taboo. With blood seeping out of her she was ritually polluting everyone near her. As a woman she was failing to observe the don't-speak-until-spoken-to status assigned her by the custom of the day. In a strange but creative reversal of the behavior of Jairus, who had come down off his high perch because he needed Jesus' help, she had pushed her way up from the gutter, a clear case of "not knowing your place."

Jesus tells her that her faith (not he himself, not even God) has healed her (even though she seems to have sensed it before he says so). But the delay caused by his unsought interaction with this brazen woman has a consequence. Messengers come from Jairus' house and inform him that his daughter has died, so why bother the rabbi anymore? But Jesus tells Jairus not to fear and, taking Peter and James and John, continues to make his way to the synagogue ruler's house. There they find that the neighbors and the professional mourners have already started their wailing and keening. Jesus tells them the girl is not dead but in a coma ("sleeping"). They ridicule him, but he tells them to leave, takes the girl's parents, and goes into the bedroom where the child is laid out. He takes her hand and speaks to her. Although the Gospel of Mark, like all the others, is written in Greek, it retains the Aramaic words he spoke, *Talitha cumi* ("Little girl I say to you, arise.") She gets up, and Jesus then gives two instructions. First, they should not tell anyone about this incident. Second, they should give the girl something to eat.

As a typical healing story of Jesus, this one is loaded with messages. Jesus is constantly reminding anyone who comes within earshot that in the new order he is announcing, "The last shall be first, and the first shall be last." Here he demonstrates that teaching by endangering the daughter of a privileged family in order to lavish his attention on a destitute woman who is a ritual pariah, a social outcaste, and an obstreperous nuisance as well. In the twentieth century a movement called liberation theology arose among poor people, mainly Catholics, in Latin America. It was sparked at the beginning by the work of a Peruvian priest named Gustavo Gutierrez. One of its principal champions, Bishop Oscar Romero of El Salvador, was killed, as were many dozens of other priests, nuns, and laypeople. The basic teaching of liberation theology is that the Bible shows a consistent "preferential option for the poor," and that idea has now spread throughout the Christian world. But the liberation theologians always insisted that what they were saying was not new.

They were right. In this account of the bleeding woman Jesus is seen demonstrating a preferential option without the fancy language, nineteen centuries earlier.

This woman is obviously poor. The story says she has spent all that she had on physicians, but was no better. Jesus not only treats her "preferentially," he even refers to her as his daughter. Still, it should be noted that the other daughter, the scion of privilege lying at death's door in the synagogue ruler's ample house, is not neglected either. Jesus heals her, too. But only after he has healed his own "daughter," the intruder from the dust.

It is also important to notice that both these healings, one at the top and one at the bottom of the social hierarchy, involve women. In the Gospel accounts, Jesus, of course, healed men as well. But in this story he seems to indicate that wherever women find themselves on the social hierarchy, they still bear the burden of the "second sex." In reading it, the echoes of a statement he made to the religious leaders of his time seems to reverberate: "Behold, tax collectors and prostitutes are entering the kingdom of God before you" (Matthew 21:31). The pairing of taxmen and hookers in this saying is significant. Both were bottom feeders who were forced into their repugnant lines of work by the poverty of their families. The tax collectors ("publicans") endured the ire of their fellow countrymen to do the dirty work of the Romans. Prostitutes, as current historical research has shown, were mostly daughters of the poorest Jewish families who were pushed into the brothels that served the Roman legions to help their households escape starvation. Jesus' frequently demonstrated favoritism for women does not spring from some awe he felt for the eternally feminine. He favored them because they, like the tax collectors, were despised and detested by everyone else.

There are dozens of stories of Jesus' healing in the Gospels. But this one of the ruler of the synagogue and the woman with the hemorrhage crystallizes the essence of most of them. They all suggest that Jesus practiced a strict nondiscrimination policy in his healing. You did not have to be Jewish or a respectable citizen (or an outsider or dissolute) to be healed. In some instances Jesus suggests that faith is a necessary prerequisite, but at other times he does not. The word *healing* is derived from the word *whole*. Jesus is demonstrating that God's whole-making was for all, beginning with the down-and-out, but including everyone. Also, Jesus never once suggests that the pain and distress caused by illness are good for the character. At times they may be, but in Jesus' view, disease was something bad that cried out for healing.

Jesus also had a view of what might be called the ontology of disease different from both the one prevailing at his time and the one predominant today. In antiquity there was a widespread belief that disease was the result of divine punishment, and that one should try to discover what offense one had committed in order to gain relief. This idea can even be found in some sections of the Old Testament. It persists in our own day. It drew the eloquent wrath of Susan Sontag who, when she contracted cancer, became furious when she heard from friends and read in books that cancer was the outward expression of some inward flaw. Jesus completely rejected this sickness-as-punishment idea.

However, Jesus' understanding of disease does not comport with our modern credo either. He made it clear that sick people were not responsible for their diseases, but at the same time taught that sickness was not part of God's intention for the natural order. He saw it as the result of a kind of structural disarray in the cosmos. Using the language of the day, he linked disease to demons or Satan or the power of evil. In other words, there was a flaw, a malevolent energy at work in the universe itself. St. Paul later referred to the same idea when he spoke of the creation as "subject to decay." These toxic forces manifested themselves in illness, injustice, and oppression. But Jesus saw himself as the emissary of a Benevolent Power who was engaged in a struggle with this antihuman nemesis, and would eventually triumph over it. Jesus' healings were not attention-grabbing dazzlers. They were an integral part of his message, signs of the dawning of God's eventual victory, an enticing apéritif of the banquet to come.

For the modern mentality, the idea that disease is not simply a "part of nature" is just as hard to accept as the idea of sickness as divine punishment. Diseases are demonstrably "caused" by pathogens, some of which can be observed under a microscope or detected by x-rays and CAT scans. Remedies exist for most of these pathogens. And if they are not available now they will be one day, if enough money and talent can be deployed in the research. Disease is not a mystery. It is just there. But little by little, thoughtful people are beginning to question this modern orthodoxy. Despite successive "wars" against polio and osteomyelitis and smallpox and diabetes, AIDS and SARS now appear. As soon as one disease is eradicated, new ones seem to take its place. The assumption that such campaigns might eventually stamp out all disease appears more and more illusory. Measles and tuberculosis may be almost a thing of the past, but now maladies brought on by stress, crowding, bad diets, atmospheric pollution, and the contamination of water and soil are affecting more and more people. These new ailments remind us time and again that we are part of nature, not separate from it. When we misuse it, it strikes back. Who could have predicted a hundred years ago that obesity would become a serious public health problem in America? Acquired immune deficiency syndrome only made its appearance within the last decades, but threatens to kill more people than the Black Death.

In short, our modern confidence in scientific medicine as the ultimate victor over all forms of illness now seems naive. New plagues constantly spring up to mock our presumptuousness. They grow out of the way we are coerced and cajoled into living our corporate lives by powers that seem unfathomable, or at least to lie beyond our control or even our understanding. Individuals should not be blamed for their illnesses. But it does seem to be true that injustice and oppression are linked with disease. What we need is a more modest and realistic view of what modern medicine can do (which is a lot) and what it cannot do (which is also a lot). Modern medicine can do many of the things Jesus did, such as make it possible for at least some of the blind to see (through lens implants and laser surgery) and the lame to walk (with prostheses and plastic joints). We should be grateful for the arduous work and imagination that made these and many other modern therapies possible. But scientific medicine is not the messiah that will deliver us from suffering and death. The utopian hopes and fantasies with which we have endowed it are misplaced.

Jesus' approach to illness was the right one. He did not refuse anyone who needed help. His motive was compassion, not publicity. In fact, he often instructed the people he healed not to tell anyone (as he did the woman with the flow of blood). He did not scold those who came to him for the lifestyle that might have contributed to their disorder. He did not charge anything. Apparently he realized that social isolation is one of the worst things about being sick, so part of his healing technique was to reintegrate the person back into society. He recognized that disease was not a legitimate part of the natural order, but a larger disorder that affected the individual. Still, he did not speculate about it. He just went ahead and healed. But he did not interpret his healings as isolated "miracles." He saw them rather as preliminary hints of a whole new order of things, one that lies beyond human grasping but can be discerned by those with eyes to see and ears to hear.

Once I began presenting the healing stories in class and talking about them in sections, I was surprised by the response. The premedical and public health students often turned out to be more eager to discuss these stories than those who had not yet been exposed to both the promise and the limitations of conventional medicine. But all the students were more receptive than I thought they would be. Many, apparently relieved that this was not a taboo subject to talk about at college, began recounting their own stories of sickness and healing. Even the students with the wheelchairs and the guide dogs joined in. Some said this was their first chance to talk about something quite personal to them, but which many of their friends avoided bringing up because they were afraid it might seem awkward. All in all, I came to see that trying to understand what Jesus was stating and doing without paying attention to the healing that played such a central role in his work short-circuits the meaning of his life.

As in Jesus' time, some people today still cling to the belief that a sickness is somehow a punishment for something we have done. Others nurture the illusory hope that someday science will "conquer" all known diseases. I don't think Jesus would accept either theory. He categorically rejected the punishment premise. As for the scientific utopians, there were plenty of sorcerers and snake oil charlatans in his world who, like them, promised a magical end to all illness. But he contested them as well. Like the parables he told, the healing stories told about Jesus not only defied the ideas about health and healing that circulated in his day, they defy ours as well.

17

The Armageddon Syndrome

As he was leaving the temple, one of his disciples exclaimed, "Look, Teacher, what huge stones! What fine buildings!" Jesus said to him, "You see these great buildings? Not one stone will be left upon another; they will all be thrown down."

As he sat on the Mount of Olives opposite the temple he was questioned privately by Peter, James, John, and Andrew. "Tell us," they said, "when will this happen? What will be the sign that all these things are about to be fulfilled?" — MARK 13:1–7

THROUGHOUT ITS HISTORY as a book, some people have insisted on scrutinizing the Bible for delphic predictions and secret coded messages. Rather than simply reading the contents as they are written, tireless textual sleuths have struggled to ferret out esoteric ciphers hidden behind the words and phrases printed on the page. There have been rabbinical kabalists who have taught that the spaces between the letters are just as fraught with meaning as the letters themselves, and both Jews and Christians who tenaciously believed that only a numerological deciphering of the verses would crack open their true import. Nowhere is this occult impulse more evident than when these cryptologists try to read the Bible like the book of the prophecies of Nostradamus, the early-sixteenth-century French astrologer, to squeeze out hints, forecasts, or even sure-fire prognoses of what the future holds.

I was never seriously tempted to look at the Bible this way. The ministers I knew as a boy taught me to hold it in high esteem and to respect its authority in spiritual matters, but they always warned against expecting it to disclose the arcane mysteries of the future.

From an early age I remember how they frequently quoted the following words of Jesus:

> Be on your guard; let no one mislead you. Many will come claiming my name, and saying, "I am he"; and many will be misled by them. When you hear of wars and rumours of wars, do not be alarmed. Such things are bound to happen; but the end is still to come . . . But about that day or hour no one knows, not the angels in heaven, nor the Son, but only the Father. (Mark 13:5–7, 32)

Since this had always been my view, I was a little puzzled that so many of the students in the course, including some who knew virtually nothing about the Bible, still believed that it was laced with concealed messages. Some of them thought these hidden clues were about the future, and some even expected me, as a scholar in this field, to reveal these veiled communications, and were disappointed when I did not.

At first I could not imagine why so many students who were skeptical about so many things could still harbor remnants of this superstitious attitude toward the Bible. Maybe they were influenced by TV programs or books such as *The Bible Code* that purport to uncover these fugitive gems. Still, they seemed disappointed when we discussed how Jesus had discouraged this kind of speculation whenever his disciples pressed him for predictions, as they do in the verses quoted at the head of this chapter. Why were they disappointed?

It gradually became clear to me that students today — like many other people — often fret and worry about the future, and they wanted to find out for sure whether the Bible might hold some key to what they could expect. Although few knew the word, these students were drawn to *eschatology* (from the Greek *eschata*), a technical term in theology that refers to teachings about the "last things." In recent years the word has come to mean any theory of the future, whether religious or secular, that responds to our hopes and fears about what is to come. Apocalypse (which technically means "uncovering") is a particularly violent and spectacular variant of escha-

tology. This colorful idiom existed when Jesus lived, and he sometimes drew upon it when he spoke. He did so, however, not to prog-
nosticate about the future, but to underline the urgency of the
present.

Jesus explicitly dismissed any claim to be a clairvoyant. But unfortunately his reticence is not something everyone emulates today.
The world today is awash with competing eschatologies and, like
older people, the students knew it, even though they were not familiar with the technical terms. Some of these future scenarios are
sanguine to the point of blandness: Thus Francis Fukuyama's sunny
assurance that with the global triumph of capitalism and democracy, we have already reached the "end of history," and nothing of
interest will happen until the Milky Way cools. Some are tenebrous,
like the meteorologists' dire warnings that at the present rate of
heat increase our planet will be 10 degrees warmer by the end of
this century, rekindling plagues we had thought were banished
forever. Radical jihadists envision a world purged and purified by
blood and flame. Walt Disney World allows visitors to Orlando to
sample the vinyl bliss of a technological Tomorrow Land ruled by
benevolent corporations. We are left to puzzle over whether we are
headed for an earthly Beulah Land or the vengeful return of the
Four Horsemen.

The eschatology that has recently captured America's attention
more than any other is the one elaborated in an immensely popular
sequence of novels called the *Left Behind* series. By 2004 an astonish-
ing 45 million copies of these books had been sold, a spectacular publishing feat. The writers — and presumably many of their
readers — confidently believe it is the *only* truly biblical vision of the
future, and in fact it has all but preempted the field from any rivals.
In addition to the *Left Behind* books, this same eschatology also
inundates religious TV programs, talk shows, chat rooms, and Christian bookstores. It suffuses American popular religious culture. Its
fervent support for right-wing Israeli politicians sways American
foreign policy. It laughs in the face of the postmodernists who contend that "all master narratives are dead." It supplies millions of

people with an illustrated eschatological Baedeker's in which they can trace the hand of the Almighty in the midst of the bewildering events on the evening news.

The *Left Behind* series is not significant for its literary merits, which are few, but because it is the latest example of "end-time" eschatology, the belief that we are living out the final pages of history. It may seem like trivial pulp to sophisticated readers, but the sheer enormity of its sales and influence demands serious attention from scholars, attention that has not yet been forthcoming. End-time eschatology is a narrative with roots sunk far back, even before Christianity. It appeared in America in its present form over a century ago under the aegis of fundamentalist "Bible prophecy" conferences and spawned a plethora of colorful charts depicting God's "Plan for the Ages," whose trajectory from Creation to Judgment neatly frames all history.

This is a "dispensational" theology, which teaches that history is divided into seven phases, or "dispensations," in each of which God deals with the world in a sharply different way. It is also a "millenarian" theology (from the word *millennium,* the thousand-year reign of Christ on earth), which some believe the Bible foresees. Consequently it holds that we are now living in the final dispensation, and that the millennium is about to begin. We are in the "end-time." This is clearly an ambitious theology of history, a poor man's Toynbee or Spengler. But though end-time theology's scanning of the past may be long, its view of the future is very short: "The end is at hand." For those who cling to a belief in this divine blueprint, its spiritual fruit is a sense of comfort and even a kind of smug fatalism. It is also a breathtaking trivialization of Jesus' vision of the reign of God.

Popular novels based on end-time themes are not new in English-speaking countries. Crawford Gribben, a scholar of literature in Trinity College, Dublin, traces the genre back ninety years to a British writer named Sydney Watson who published a trilogy of fictional apocalypses between 1913 and 1916. They bore titles like *Scarlet and Purple, The Mark of the Beast,* and *In the Twinkling of an Eye.*

Watson was worried about the dangers of spiritualism and the dire influence of "ritualism and Romish practices" in the Church of England. But Gribben believes he established the pattern for such eschatological thrillers. Even though the surface details of the plots differ from age to age, they all cope with contemporary anxieties.

It is sometimes said that the Protestant Reformation required not only Martin Luther but also Johann Gutenberg and Albrecht Dürer to produce the words and pictures — by means of movable type and woodcuts — that reached the masses and created a popular movement. Likewise, for end-time eschatology, paperback books, TV, and now the Internet with its chatrooms and Web sites are serving a similar purpose. It is not just another theology. It is now a movement.

The immediate predecessor of the current wave of what publishers call "apocalyptic thrillers" is Hal Lindsey's bestseller *The Late Great Planet Earth,* which appeared in 1969. The title is based on a pseudoscientific secular eschatology of that decade called *The Last Days of the Late Great State of California,* which had predicted that the Golden State would soon slip into the warm waves of the Pacific. But *The Late Great Planet Earth* caused more than just a small ripple. It has now sold 34 million copies in fifty-four languages. Its predictions are based on the same dispensational fundamentalist approach, and use Isaiah, Ezekiel, and Revelation — inventively decoded, of course, by Lindsey — to sketch a scenario of what is hurtling toward us from the future. Here is the schedule of end-time events.

First, the Jews return to their homeland. Then a Jewish state is reestablished with Jerusalem as its capital. (Remember, this was part of the timetable decades before Zionism or the establishment of the state of Israel.) Then the ruined Temple will be rebuilt, the moribund Jewish priesthood reconstituted, and animal sacrifices, which were interrupted when the Romans razed the city in 70 C.E., will be reinstituted. Naturally, dispensationalists were delighted by the establishment of Israel in 1948, but for reasons very different from those that thrilled those Jews who were longing for a homeland. End-time writers saw it as a proof that their theology had gotten it right, and that we were at the threshold of the last act. But what comes next?

Now dispensationalists are impatiently waiting to see the Temple rebuilt and sacrifices resumed. They work closely with some marginal Jewish groups who share the same goal. I once visited a workshop in Jerusalem where some ultra-Orthodox Jews were preparing the priestly garments and ceremonial implements to be used when the great day comes. None of this remains safely in the realm of futuristic fantasy. On one August day in 1969, a young Australian tourist named Denis Michael Rohan climbed to the mosque on the Temple Mount and set fire to it with gasoline-soaked rags. At his trial it became clear that he was a Christian who had been listening to dispensationalist preachers on the radio. He wanted to expedite the rebuilding of the Temple on the site to hasten the last days.

At this point in the scenario, however, Jewish and Christian end-time theologies part company drastically. The Christians predict that wars and earthquakes and other ominous signs will multiply. Then will come the spectacular grand finale: a massive attack on the newly reconstituted Jewish state by a godless coalition led by the Antichrist. The beast will desecrate the recently rebuilt Temple in Jerusalem, tear it down, and slaughter myriads of the city's ill-fated citizens. The warfare will culminate at Armageddon in the mother of all battles, and at first the forces of the Antichrist will appear to be winning. Then, just as things look most bleak, Jesus Christ himself will intervene, this time not as the humble carpenter or the rabbinic sage, but as a mighty warrior. The beast and his minions will be defeated, and the grateful Jews will recognize their true messiah. The millennium and the final judgment follow. The end of the endtime will have come.

The natural question for anyone to ask is, "But where do they *get* all this?" The answer is not an easy one. The scenario is a collage of scattered biblical fragments, lifted out of context and awkwardly cobbled together. One of its most curious features is that sometime before the end — no one claims to know exactly when — all true Christian believers will be snatched away from this troubled earth into the Savior's arms. This is called "the rapture," a concept popularized by the nineteenth-century British preacher John Darby who, for reasons of his own, rejected the idea that believers would have to wait for Christ's second coming to be taken to be with him. It is a theory that bears a remarkable similarity to the Roman Catholic doctrine of the Assumption of Mary, who is said to have been taken to heaven without going through the portal of death. "Rapture" describes the unspeakable joy those fortunate few will feel as they zoom toward heaven like crew members of the starship *Enterprise* in their dematerializing "transporter." The rest of us will be left behind on spaceship Earth to undergo the terror and tumult of the last days, called "the Great Tribulation."

It is this idea of the rapture that provides the fulcrum for the eleven epics of the *Left Behind* novels. The phrase *left behind* refers, of course, to the unhappy losers who are marooned when the true believers are raptured. The appeal of the series is only in part its peculiar theology. It has a long, titillating plot that packages the theology and follows its key characters through so many hundreds of pages that the series is approaching the dimensions of an epic.

It is a mistake to assume that end-time thinking represents only a marginal cult in American, or even world, evangelical Protestantism. And its immense popularity demonstrates something else: that the critics who review books are often out of touch with the fears and fantasies of the vast throngs of ordinary people. When the first of the *Left Behind* novels climbed near the top of the *New York Times* bestseller list, someone called the book review staff to ask what it was about, but no one there knew. None had read it, and they had only heard of it when the staggering sales figures began to pour in. Academic theologians have the same blind spot. Those who have even heard of the book dismiss its theology as nonsensical, but that does not make it any less influential. Ignoring it has allowed it to sweep the field in American popular religion. The sheer bulk and technical wizardry of the end-time advocates have all but drowned out alternative Christian views of the future.

When one compares the current end-time eschatology with

Jesus' message of the coming reign of God, the contrast is dramatic. First, Jesus believed the message he taught was good news for his own people and for all humanity. But this recent end-time theology is bad news for nearly everyone, and especially for Jews. End-time preachers continuously proclaim their love of "Israel and the Jewish people." Many refer to themselves as "Christian Zionists" and are indeed, for their own peculiar theological reasons, staunch supporters of the most conservative Israeli parties and politicians. They are avid hawks, and adamantly opposed to any thought of a peace settlement with a Palestinian state, since no such thing appears on their charts. But the role they assign to the Jews in their books is at once grim and all too familiar.

In this theology Jews are, first, the people who have stubbornly misunderstood their own scriptures, and must be corrected by Christians. Second, the Jews are fulfilling the scriptures in spite of themselves by establishing a homeland and soon, it is fervently hoped, by rebuilding the Temple and resuming animal sacrifice so that the desecration, the attack, the Second Coming, the conversion of the Jews, and the rest of the cosmic denouement — including the deaths of hundreds of thousands — can unfold as they foresee it in their diagrams. An element of *Schadenfreude* surfaces when Lindsey, for example, sighs his regret that those luckless Jews in Israel do not know what horrors they will suffer once the final confrontation begins since, according to his reading of the prophet Zechariah, half the inhabitants of Jerusalem will perish. Too bad, but it's in the scenario, and nothing can be done to avoid it.

In the *Left Behind* series the most prominent Jewish character is an Israeli rabbi named Tsion Ben-Judah. He accepts Jesus as the Messiah, so is threatened by Jewish zealots who murder his family. Fortunately, he is smuggled out of Israel and hides in a survivalist shelter near Chicago. Once there, the born-again rabbi, who has now learned the true meaning of his own prophets from the Christians, goes on the Internet to preach end-time theology. Again we are assured that Christians know better than Jews who Jews are and what God wants them to do. End-time theology is the latest edition of the age-old fable in which, once again, Jews are forced to play a role created for them by a fevered Christian imagination. But in this cosmic drama, other actors are also needed. Most important, who will play the villain? Who is the Antichrist?

In the halcyon days of the Cold War, it was easy to identify the beast of the Apocalypse and the other actors in the coming galactic shootout. Lindsey creatively translated the Hebrew word *rosh* in one of the prophetic passages as "Russia." (The word really means "head" or "chief.") His exegetical insight was confirmed by his delighted discovery that Moscow lies due north of Jerusalem, and that Jeremiah refers to a "King of the North" who will attack God's chosen people. Besides, weren't the Russians anti-Christian? Did we need any more collateral proof of what the Bible plainly says? It is reported, incidentally, that whoever wrote Ronald Reagan's famous "evil empire" speech was influenced by this ingenious school of interpretation.

With the collapse of the Berlin Wall, this prophecy also tottered. But, like any action-adventure film, end-time theology requires a heavy. In past generations, Napoleon, several popes, Hitler, and Stalin had all been cast as Antichrist. But all died before the last reel could be shot. A few years ago one particularly inventive exegete multiplied the numerical equivalents of the letters in "Henry A. Kissinger" and found they came to 666, the mark of the beast, according to Revelation 13:16, but the former secretary of state seems no longer to be in the running.

With the ending of the Cold War, the end-time theologians had to scramble for a new candidate to fill the role of the Antichrist. At first some seized upon liberation theology since they believed it was anti-Christian but had cloaked its diabolical visage in a religious disguise. Another was the Israeli peace movement, since achieving accord with the Palestinians would drastically derail the Armageddon story line. But these are mere subplots. The burning question remains: Who is the real Son of Belial?

For some end-time theologians, although not for the *Left Behind* authors, the answer is now becoming all too clear. It is Islam, or more often, "The Sword of Islam." After September 11, 2001, this contender threatened to trump all the others. It was a central casting dream come true, a perfect fit for the role. Islam is religious; it includes a coalition of nations; and — according to this view — it had already begun to "desecrate" the site of the Temple centuries ago with the construction of the al-Aqsa mosque. For fifteen hundred years, some Christians have viewed Islam as a nemesis, so this casting draws on a large backlog of negative images. It does not seem to matter that in the Middle East today, groups of Jews and Muslims, often along with Christians, are working together to build a civil infrastructure that can support a just peace. End-time zealots continue to derogate the very possibility of either peace — since Armageddon is in the screenplay — or interfaith cooperation by decreeing, in advance, that Islam is the scripturally designated Lucifer.

The *Left Behind* series is more subtle. The name of the Antichrist has already been revealed. It is one Nicolae Jetty Carpathia. The charming and charismatic former president of Romania, he becomes secretary-general of the UN and the "potentate" of something called the "Global Community." A perfect villain in the eyes of right-wing Christians, he supports the UN, encourages disarmament, wants a single world currency, and encourages ecumenical and interfaith organization. He experiences a slight setback when, in a later novel, he is assassinated in Jerusalem. But he is then resurrected in the Palace of the Global Community in a rebuilt city called New Babylon. There is a whiff of suspicion of Islam, however, in the name of his chief of security, Suhail Akbar.

The *Left Behind* series, like the Harry Potter books and Disney movies, has generated an avalanche of byproducts: clubs, games, discussion guides, a newsletter, and Internet links to other biblical prophecy sites. A new shelf of books for youngsters, spun off from the *Left Behind* novels, has now reached its thirtieth volume. But the themes in this youth series are the same as in the adult versions, and by casting international organizations in the villainous roles they follow an old tradition. Watson had worried about threats to British sovereignty ninety years ago. These current end-time novels appeal to those Americans who fear that our country may be losing its independence in some new world order. Like other pieces of popular literature, one can read this series more as a reflection of contemporary preoccupations than as actual attempts to foresee what is coming.

Curiously, end-time theology has little to do with Jesus. One of its most peculiar characteristics is that it declares that the life and teaching of Jesus belong to the *previous dispensation,* the one that ended with his crucifixion. Therefore, they are not relevant for us today. Truly faithful end-timers do not preach on these texts. They concentrate on different parts of the Bible, especially the prophets and the book of Revelation. But this principle of exclusion mangles the New Testament beyond recognition. Among other things, it leaves out the Magnificat, the birth narratives, the whole Sermon on the Mount, and all the parables, to say nothing of any of the passages in which Jesus turns aside his followers' persistent curiosity about when the end will come and warns them explicitly against false prophets and predictors.

End-time theology also undercuts purposeful moral choice. It is patently fatalistic. The interpretive foundation is that — to aficionados who are in the know — the Bible divulges the details of what the future holds. But this premise cuts the nerve of human freedom and responsibility. Human beings become puppets, or at best walk-ons with bit parts in the movie. Those who are "raptured" become an audience of voyeurs who watch the story unfold on the screen from their cushioned seats in heaven, while those who have been left behind suffer the torments of tribulation and judgment. The deck is stacked and the game is fixed. Only suckers think they can change the outcome. All we can do is hurry what has already been decreed. History is no longer the arena of free give-and-take between God and human beings. It becomes an unwinding scroll on which the letters are already indelibly written. This leaves historic Christianity behind. It postulates a modern form of deism. However, instead of fashioning an intricate clock and then walking away, as the absentee deity of the old deists did, this time God has constructed a time bomb with an inaccessible fuse.

Why are so many people, including some of my students, so intrigued by such a confused and implausible theology? Puzzled, I eventually asked the class why they thought this topic, and this end-time scenario, sparked such keen interest. They were largely a cheerful lot. They wanted both to do good and to do well. What was it then? Was it because of the underlying sense of resignation I had already sensed in many students?

It was that old third temptation: quiescent fatalism. The feeling that the real levers of power, like the fuse on the end-time bomb, were out of their reach haunted even those headed for positions of leadership in government and business. One year, in an attempt to remedy this situation, I decided to try a different approach. Instead of pointing out the ethical defects and logical flaws in the end-time books, I told the students that what we really needed was not a refutation (which academics do all too readily), but an alternative. For the next week I asked them to write the outline of a paperback book that would reach the same audience of nonspecialists the *Left Behind* books do, but sketch a different scenario for our common future.

I have rarely been so disappointed in a set of papers. I knew they could write engaging stories, because I had seen some of their other productions. But on this assignment most of them went limp. Most of their outlines were simply projections of medical wizardry and technological change. There were TVs with wraparound screens and five hundred channels; silent low-fuel cars humming along safe highways; pills that extended your life to 180; learning helmets that would teach you Chinese as you slept; safe excursions to remote galaxies. Of course, everyone in the world would be well fed and housed and would receive excellent health care and education. All known diseases would be eradicated. Grades would be abolished.

When they read excerpts from their outlines to each other in class, even the students admitted they would probably not sell. When I pressed about why they had done so poorly, one student thoughtfully suggested that virtually all the projections of the future they ever saw were either relentlessly bleak dystopias or shiny technological cloud nines. They were pinioned somewhere between *Brave New World* and Disney's Tomorrow Land. If their alternatives lacked inspiration, it was probably because there was little to inspire them.

My disappointment led me to think again about the *Left Behind* series and its source of appeal. On reflection, I had to admit its authors had hit on something. In its own distorted and self-serving way, the series skillfully draws on biblical themes familiar to our culture. It teaches that both Christians and Jews have vital roles to play in the fulfillment of God's will for the Creation. But in so doing, it casts the Jews in a humiliating role, demonizes Islam, and eviscerates Christianity. Can we imagine an eschatology that celebrates an equal partnership?

Also to its credit, and unlike some other quasi-Christian eschatologies, end-time theology is not just a heaven-when-you die scheme. It has its own political and social dimension, though a bizarre and dangerous one. It projects a connection between the times we live in and the ultimate goal of history. But it is disastrously narrow. It completely leaves out the wretched of the earth for whom Jesus was so concerned. Its eccentric notion of the rapture of true Christians, which historians have traced to a pious, excitable nineteenth-century Scottish girl, has become a handy escape hatch for people who would just rather not contend with the suffering and calamity that are part of human history.

Finally, in its own lurid way, end-time eschatology rightly questions the benign and avuncular deity of American consumer spirituality, the user-friendly buddy in the sky who regularly puts the whole Simpson family to sleep in church. It appropriately sees that what is good news for some will be bad news for others. But it gets both recipients wrong, and its most dangerous feature is its fascination with the catastrophic imagery of apocalypse. It is easy to understand why at various times in the past sorely oppressed people who had lost all other hope turned to fantasies of some fiery divine intervention that would save them from despair and obliterate their tormentors. Such apocalyptic imagery may once have been relatively harmless, and might even have given downcast peoples something to hope for when all else had failed. But today, after the advent of weapons of mass destruction, when the threat of a blazing man-made apocalypse is all too real, the human race must discard this imagery, whether it be secular or religious, once and for all. The danger of such language is that those who long for the apocalypse sometimes tire of waiting for the divine to act. Like Denis Michael Rohan, who set fire to the mosque, they themselves take on the task of saving by destroying. Apocalyptic purification, whether by human or divine means, has become too dangerous a language, and too real. Jesus himself suggested far better ways of thinking about the future in his repeated use of organic metaphors like mustard seeds and vines, images that suggest growth and gradual maturation.

The tactic I finally settled on with my students for thinking about eschatology was this: Follow the advice of Jesus. Avoid speculating on the "when" or "how." In the meantime, it is probably best to follow the counsel of the Hasidic rabbi who was interrupted by one of his followers while he was tending his garden. "What would you do, rabbi," the student asked, "if you knew the messiah was coming today?" Stroking his beard and pursing his lips, the rabbi replied, "Well, I would continue to water my garden."

III

MORE STORIES THEY TOLD ABOUT HIM

A choir of angels glorified the hour,
the vault of heaven was dissolved in fire,
"Father, why hast thou forsaken me?
Mother, I beg you, do not weep for me."

Mary Magdalene beat her breasts and sobbed,
His dear disciples, stone-faced, stared.
His mother stood apart. No one looked
into her eyes. Nobody dared.
— Anna Akhmatova, "Crucifixion"

18

The Transfiguration and
the Prophet's Night Journey

After six days Jesus took with him Peter and James and John his brother, and led them up a high mountain apart. And he was transfigured before them, and his face shone like the sun, and his garments became white as light. And behold there appeared to them Moses and Elijah, talking with him. And Peter said to Jesus, "Lord, it is well that we are here; if you wish I will make three booths here, one for you and one for Moses and one for Elijah." He was still speaking when a bright cloud overshadowed them, and a voice from the cloud said, "This is my beloved son in whom I am well pleased; listen to him." When the disciples heard this they fell on their faces and were filled with awe. But Jesus came and touched them, saying, "Rise, and have no fear." And when they lifted up their eyes, they saw no one but Jesus only.

— MATTHEW 17:1–8

THE LARGEST CHANGE in my approach to the study of religion in recent years has come about because of the challenge of global religious pluralism and the increasing religious diversity of America. In the small town where I grew up we had our own kind of diversity. There were eight churches (for about fifteen hundred people), of which all but one represented different varieties of Protestantism. The single exception was St. Patrick's Roman Catholic Church, which served a much wider geographic area and therefore had more cars in its parking lot on Sunday morning than the other churches did. There was one Jewish family in town, the doctor's, but no synagogue. One day I found a map in the encyclopedia at my junior high school that showed "the religions of the world," color-coded. Most of the Far East was pink, for Buddhism and Confucianism. The Middle East was a swath of yellow for what the editors then called "Mohammedanism" (which we now call Islam). All of India was dyed deep red for Hinduism. Europe, North and South America, and Russia were shown in light blue for Christianity. I assume the compilers thought that Sikhs and Jains and Jews were either too minuscule numerically or too dispersed to indicate on a world map. Nowadays that map would be quite misleading. With Buddhist pagodas appearing in London and Los Angeles, mosques in Rome and New York, a Hindu temple in West Virginia, and Christian churches nearly everywhere, it has become much harder to localize religions. Nonetheless, that multihued chart fired my curiosity, and as I grew older I read what I could find about these other faiths. But it was not easy at that time to learn much about them. Religion was ignored in public school (except for mumbling the Lord's Prayer each morning), and in church those red and yellow and pink areas were viewed as places to which missionaries should be dispatched with all possible speed. I remained curious even though it was still hard to get much information. In college I took the one single course offered in world religions, and even in seminary any study of theologies other than Protestant ones was rare and strictly optional.

Since the late 1960s, however, changes have taken place that have required alterations in my teaching. After John F. Kennedy's reforms changed the patterns of U.S. immigration policy, more Asian and Middle Eastern people started arriving. The pagodas, mosques, and temples began to appear on the main streets of America. Then, especially after the fall of communism, the other world religions became increasingly visible actors on the world stage. A Hindu nationalist party took power in India. The Dalai Lama's nonviolent campaign for the freedom of Tibet and his books on spirituality brought Buddhism to the attention of a wide audience. The spectacular revival of Islam seized the whole world's attention. But most importantly for me, the classes I taught in Harvard College and in the Divinity School began to reflect the new religious heterogeneity. I hardly ever taught a class that did not have students from the "other" religions enrolled. I had to work hard to make up for what I had missed in my earlier training.

As I did, it soon became evident to me that one of the best ways to gain new insights into one's own tradition is to compare and contrast it with others. My colleagues and my students gave me many opportunities to do so. Some of the most valuable occasions for this kind of comparison took place in a course I began offering on Jerusalem. It was a kind of spinoff from the course on Jesus, in which I had naturally become fascinated with the history of Jerusalem in the first century C.E. Then my interest in the Holy City began to extend back to the years before David made it his capital, and forward through its multiple sackings, plunderings, and regime changes. Both appalled and enthralled by the long, bloody saga of the city, I did what many professors do who want to learn about a subject: I offered a course on it.

Jerusalem: An Interdisciplinary Inquiry soon became one of my favorites. The main reason I enjoyed it was that it attracted Jewish, Catholic, Muslim, and Protestant students, understandable since Jerusalem is holy — though in different ways — to all three traditions. In addition to the lectures, I placed the students in small independent work groups in which I always tried to have representatives from each of these traditions. I was surprised and gratified at how well they worked together, producing jointly prepared reports on a variety of topics. One group, which included a Palestinian Muslim whose family had once lived in west Jerusalem and a veteran of the Israeli Defense Force, even produced a sensible proposal for a final status agreement on the Jerusalem issue.

I mention this at the beginning of a discussion of the New Testament account of the Transfiguration of Christ because in a curious way this story, which on its surface has little to do with Jerusalem, provided one of the most memorable sessions of the class. The story came up one day when we were going over the complex geography of Israel/Palestine and the often-conflicting claims about the sacred sites. But it was memorable because it illustrated again how invaluable stories are, both in moral reasoning and in interfaith conversation. The Transfiguration story was one that students from all of the traditions represented in the class could respond to.

At first sight this story seems misplaced, a peculiar interruption of the flow of the Gospel narrative. Jesus has been telling parables, teaching, healing, and conversing with his disciples. Then comes this curious hiatus, but a few verses later he is back doing the same thing. The story of his transfiguration on the "mountain apart" erupts like a glistening marlin breaking the otherwise smooth surface of the sea. It seems so out of place that some scholars suggest it really belongs with the Resurrection appearances, which come at the end of the Gospels, and has been inserted here by some earlier editor. Others insist this is where it belongs.

To me the debate seems pointless. This story, like many others told about Jesus, is redolent with overtones of his Jewish lineage and the faith of Israel. Any hearer at the time would have recognized them. Jesus here is being depicted as the new Moses. The allusions begin with the first line, "after six days." Why six? Why not seven or nine or forty? Because when Moses climbed Mount Sinai to meet God, it took six days. Moses also took his three favorite helpers — Aaron, Nadab, and Abihu — along with him, at least for the first part of his ascent. Jesus took Peter, James, and John. When Moses reached the summit, a cloud descended on him and a bright light shone (Exodus 24:9–18) as it does here on Jesus. In the genealogies, prophets and charismatic leaders are frequently identified with their distinguished predecessors. Here Jesus is seen with Elijah the prophet and Moses the lawgiver.

I was aware before the class began that this passage would be especially interesting to the Jewish and Christian students because it symbolically links Jesus to the earlier prophets of Israel. What I had not expected, however, was how quickly the Muslim students chimed in. Muslims sometimes compare Mohamet's daring trek through the wilderness from Mecca to Medina with the exodus of the Israelites from Egypt, and they identify Mohamet with Moses. Mormons think of Brigham Young, who led them through another wilderness to their Zion in Utah, as their Moses. Martin Luther King, preaching in Mason Memorial Temple in Memphis on the last night of his life, told the congregation that he had glimpsed the Promised Land — as Moses had from Mount Nebo — but "I may not make it there with you." The story of the Transfiguration is like another genealogy. It positions Jesus in the succession of Moses.

There are some other arguments about this story. Most scholars agree that the "high mountain apart" spoken of in this text is Mount Hermon in present-day Syria (*hermon* means "apart"). There is, however, an old monastery on top of Mount Tabor in Israel whose monks emphatically insist that it was there, not in Syria, that the Transfiguration took place. This is not the only dispute in the Holy Land about the actual venue where events in the life of Jesus occurred. There are two scenes of the burial and Resurrection of Jesus in Jerusalem. One is inside the Church of the Holy Sepulcher. The other (the "garden Tomb") is just outside the Damascus gate, next to a parking lot and a bustling Arab market. I myself have visited four different "authentic" locations of the baptism of Jesus, each staunchly defended by the different guides — each of them having mastered a smattering of archaeology — who showed them to me. Even Pope John Paul II tactfully prayed at two of these baptismal sites — one in Israel and one in Jordan — when he visited the Middle East in 2000.

But the spat over the location hardly matters. For a story like this one, and many others, almost any mountain will do. Mountain air seems to spawn stories. Mountains are simultaneously foreboding and inviting. They beckon and threaten. A towering expanse of rock, sometimes laced with snow and capped by clouds, evokes awe and fascination. If we manage to clamber to the summit we allow ourselves to savor pride and satisfaction, and we can see places we could not see below. No wonder mountains are associated with so many legends and folktales. No wonder they have such a central place in religion.

Prophets have a natural affinity for mountains. So it is hardly surprising that the story of the Transfiguration is placed on a mountain, like the Sermon on the Mount. Moses painfully hoisted his aging frame up Mount Sinai, not once but twice, to receive the Torah from God. One of the Buddha's most important teachings took place on the Mount of Eagles. There are many parallels. But it was the Muslims in the class who were eager to recount their parallel. They told about the famous passage in the Qur'an that occurs on a mountain, in this case Mount Zion, and is highly reminiscent of the Gospel accounts of the Transfiguration. It tells of what Muslims call the prophet's *isra*, his famous "night journey" to Jerusalem. The actual passage in the Qur'an is a short one, but it has been elaborated by many layers of tradition.

> Glorified be He Who carried his servant [i.e., the Prophet] by night from the Masjid al-haram [in Mecca] to Masjid al-Aqsa [the furthest place of worship]. (Sura 17:1)

Shortly after the Qur'an was completed, commentators began to identify the "furthest place of worship" with the Temple Mount in Jerusalem. They knew that Mohamet had started out by instructing his people to pray facing Jerusalem, which he believed was the site of the true primordial religion taught by Abraham ("Ibrahim" in Arabic) before there were either Jews or Christians, and the location of Solomon's ancient Temple. Only later did Muslims begin to face toward Mecca when they prayed.

The verse itself does not say much. But in the earliest biography of the Prophet, one Muhammad ibn Ishaq ibn Yassar, using a kind of Muslim midrash, filled in the details that have since become the standard version of the Night Journey. He claimed to have heard the Prophet himself tell crowds of people that while he was sleeping next to the sacred black stone in the Ka'ba, the temple in Mecca, the angel Gabriel came and prodded him with his foot. He did not wake up. Again the angel prodded him, to no effect. On the third poke the Prophet woke up, and Gabriel led him out the door and mounted him on a fabulous steed. It was pure white, half donkey and half mule. The creature's name was Buraq. An illuminated manuscript of the Night Journey from the fifteenth century shows the animal with the head of a woman. Buraq and the Prophet soared through the air and, in the wink of an eye, covered the distance between Mecca and Jerusalem. They even had time for a brief stop on Mount Sinai.

When the Prophet touched down on the Temple Mount, which Muslims call the Noble Sanctuary ("Haram al-Sharif"), a welcoming committee awaited him. It was made up of all the previous prophets. Adam was there, also Joseph, Enoch, John the Baptist, Jesus, Moses, and of course, Mohamet's favorite prophet, Abraham. Yassar, the biographer, even tells us that Mohamet described their physical features. Moses was "ruddy-faced, tall, fleshy, curly-haired with a hooked nose. Jesus, Son of Mary, was a reddish man of medium height with many freckles on his face and lank hair as though he had just come out of a bath." This sprinkling of details is consistent with the way stories are always told. Postbiblical stories have informed us that John the Baptist appeared scrawny from his exclusive diet of locusts and wild honey, and that Joseph — whose brothers sold him into slavery — was a pretty boy who wore eye makeup (a description that appeared in Jewish stories).

According to the story of the *isra*, after this highly ecumenical prayer meeting with his predecessors, the Prophet climbed the huge rock over which the magnificent, golden-canopied Dome of the Rock now towers. Then Gabriel, like an angelic Virgil or Beatrice, escorted Mohamet up through the various levels of heaven, climbing the rungs of a ladder of light. Another picturesque detail informs us that at first the rock itself wanted to go along. But Gabriel pulled it down and ordered it to remain on earth. Earnest guides will show you the marks left by Gabriel's fingers on the sides of the rock. Still, it must have been a big step to the first rung for the Prophet because he had to push himself up, and his footmark can be clearly seen on top of the rock, as the same guides reverently point out.

When, after exploring several of the inner courtyards of heaven, Gabriel and the Prophet finally came into the presence of God, the Holy One told Mohamet that he should instruct his followers to pray fifty times a day. Fifty seemed a lot, so on the way back down the Prophet stopped to speak again with Moses and told the patriarch about the prayer assignment. Moses warned him that prayer is a difficult thing, and that he should go back and ask God for a less onerous regime. Mohamet did, and God reduced the required daily prayers to forty. Again the Prophet reported the divine command to Moses, who told him to try for yet another reduction. Several times the Prophet went back and forth between God and Moses, until the number of prayers had been reduced to five. Moses urged Mohamet to try again, but this time the Prophet declined. He was too embarrassed, he said, to go on with this bargaining with the Almighty. Consequently the Muslim rule now calls for prayer five times a day (while Jews are told to pray only twice).

The *isra* story is a captivating one, but it is silly to ask whether it is "true." Mohamet's own wife said it occurred in a dream. It is a splendid example of what might be called "the prophetic imagination." It serves a variety of religious purposes within Islam. It makes Mohamet not just a messenger of God, but a visionary and a mystic, a tradition that millions of Islamic Sufis have followed for centuries. It echoes the story of Jacob who, in a dream, also saw a ladder to heaven with angels descending. Its inclusion of Jesus and the Jewish prophets demonstrates how much Mohamet wanted the faith he was teaching to build on the faith of Jews and Christians. It explains to Muslims why they are required to pray five times a day. It makes Jerusalem (along with Mecca and Medina) one of the Holy Cities of Islam.

One of the most valuable insights I gained from the students who took the course on Jerusalem is that the notorious "Jerusalem Question" *can* be solved. The solution is both extremely simple and terribly difficult: Eventually the city must be shared. If religiously committed students from all the traditions that consider it holy can think of ways to share it, the future of a city with a distressing past looks somewhat brighter. What is needed is the political and moral will, and a recognition that sacred spaces can be shared. It has happened in the past; it could happen again in the future. It is not too much to hope that one day Jerusalem might no longer be a center of rancor and hatred. It could become the primary place in the whole world where men and women of faith gather to study and to pray, but mainly to tell their stories to each other.

The most important thing from my venture into the comparative study of religion has taught me is that the multiplicity of faith traditions in the world does not make a common moral approach impossible. At the theological level these traditions often vary widely. But they also nurture a host of overlapping and common ethical values. Christians need to hear the Buddhist teaching about the worth of all sentient life, not just human life. And Buddhists have already begun to accept some of the Christian concern for justice. Jews and Muslims share the insight that God's law should suffuse every aspect of life.

In 1994 I attended a large gathering in Chicago called the Parliament of the World's Religions. In one of the sections representatives from virtually every tradition on the globe met under the leadership of the Catholic theologian Hans Kung to try to work out the basis of what we called a "global ethic." Of course, there were some disagreements, but as the work went on it became increasingly evident that there were more than enough shared virtues among the religions to forge the foundation, maybe for the first time in human history, of a truly global ethic.

The Dalai Lama, replete in saffron robes, addressed the huge closing session of the conference, assembled on a sparkling evening at the shore of Lake Michigan. His talk reminded the delegates again of how much we have in common, something that I had heard Pope John Paul II say on television when he brought together leaders of several faiths at Assisi, the home of St. Francis, to pray together. But after I left Chicago, I also realized that the religions have more than values in common. They also have stories that link them to each other, like the Transfiguration and the Night Journey. This is important to remember, because values do not float in the air. They are conveyed from generation to generation by rituals and narratives. Without them, the values quickly evaporate. No wonder the sages and prophets of these traditions did not just produce lists of moral principles. They also told stories, and we are their beneficiaries.

❧ 19 ❧

Bridge Burning
and Street Theater

They were approaching Jerusalem, and when they reached Bethphage at the Mount of Olives Jesus sent off two disciples, and told them: "Go into the village opposite, where you will at once find a donkey tethered with her foal beside her. Unite them, and bring them to me. If anyone says anything to you, answer, 'The Master needs them'; and he will let you have them at once." This was to fulfill the prophecy which says, "Tell the daughter of Zion, 'Here is your king, who comes to you in gentleness, riding on a donkey, on a foal of a beast of burden.' "

The disciples went and did as Jesus had directed, and brought the donkey and her foal; they laid their cloaks on them and Jesus mounted. Crowds of people carpeted the road with their cloaks, and some cut branches from the trees to spread in his path. Then the crowds in front and behind raised the shout: "Hosanna to the Son of David! Blessed is he who comes in the name of the Lord! Hosanna in the heavens!"

— MATTHEW 21:1–9

ONE OF THE CHURCH HOLIDAYS I remember most vividly from my childhood is Palm Sunday. It always came in the spring, of course, just a week before Easter, and was therefore sometimes melded into a seasonal ritual. The music was decidedly upbeat, and one of the songs that was always sung was: "Flowers and palms in varied beauty vie / dressed in the fragrant robes of spring to greet him." When I was a small child I was sometimes jealous of the Catholic children in the neighborhood who were given palm fronds to wave, but that inequity was corrected a few years later. As Protestant churches began to become more liturgical, often adding robed choirs and altar candles, palm branches also made their appearance in our church, despite the quiet grumbling of some of the older members who thought it seemed too Catholic. In churches today congregations still sing about the "hosannas" that people shouted, and now everyone seems to have palm fronds. But most Christians do not realize that Jesus' entry into Jerusalem was not really a religious event. It was political, a brazen display of non-violent rebellion.

Usually Passover and Holy Week, the days between Palm Sunday and Easter, do not occur on the same week. That is because Christians, at least in the Western churches, decided at one point to use the solar rather than the lunar calendar that Jews (and Eastern Orthodox Christians) still use. But once every few years Passover and Holy Week do coincide. I like it when they do, and if I had the power to change the Western church calendar, I would always have them on the same week. Having both celebrations together is a vivid reminder that when Jesus came from Galilee to Jerusalem with his disciples and apparently something of an entourage, he came to celebrate Passover. This in turn is a further confirmation of Jesus' attachment to his own tradition and of his rabbinical calling.

Most of the students who took my course were aware, although some of them only vaguely, of Jesus' entry into Jerusalem, riding a donkey, and that Christians mark this event on Palm Sunday. But like most other people, few were cognizant of what a huge risk he was running, or that this was one of the most decisive moments in his life. The truth is, however, that this event compares with an airplane's "point of no return," when it is racing down a runway for takeoff so fast it cannot possibly turn back. His bold public entry into the seat of authority of the elite Temple establishment and the administrative hub for the occupying Roman militia was comparable to Caesar's crossing of the Rubicon in 49 b.c. It meant he was courting a confrontation, and after it happened, there was indeed no turning back.

With this audacious public demonstration, Rabbi Jesus was propelled from relative obscurity in the isolated northern province of

Galilee, where it might have been possible for the authorities to overlook his subversive mission, to a place where they could not possibly ignore him. Arriving in Jerusalem the way he did was not just a "bridge burning" event, it was a provocation and a taunt, and after he enacted it, he lived for less than a week.

The entry into Jerusalem was also a parable. It was a drama staged as street theater, and the message was clear for anyone to see. With consummate cheekiness Jesus was announcing that the reign of God was beginning, and the clear implication was that the reign of Caesar would be drawing to a close. He did it by seizing upon a well-known Roman custom, the triumphal entry into a conquered city, adding some elements of a familiar messianic scenario, and then giving the whole thing his characteristic twist.

The Romans had perfected the art of putting on dazzling and intimidating triumphal processions. The formula was carefully planned. First the new ruler of a vanquished city would march in on horseback accompanied by his troops, wagons loaded with booty and prisoners in chains. The parade would be welcomed by cheering crowds who were often routed out of their houses and herded to the street by Roman soldiers. There would then be speeches by the local elites, perhaps written by the Romans, welcoming the conquerors. Finally the new ruler and his entourage would proceed to the local temple to offer a cultic sacrifice to whatever gods were honored there, and to the Roman deities who had made the conquest possible.

Seen in the light of such a typical Roman military extravaganza, Jesus' entry was both a mockery and an insult, and it is impossible to believe that anyone misunderstood it. He was lampooning imperial authority by bouncing into town, not on a prancing horse — the symbol of the warrior — but on a donkey, the peasant's plodding beast of burden. He was not surrounded by armed legions, but by unarmed civilians, most of them pilgrims from his home province. He was welcomed, but not by crowds rousted out by the legions. The people who greeted him shouted an unambiguous political title. They called him Son of David, and therefore the legitimate heir to the throne that had been established in that city five hundred years before. They waved royal palms, the equivalent of "Jesus for King" placards. He did then follow the established formula and proceed to the Temple, but it was to throw out the racketeers who had commandeered the animal sales and currency-exchange business.

In addition to ridiculing a Roman triumphal entry, Jesus was also acting out a familiar Jewish scenario for the coming of God's deliverer. Matthew makes note of this in his Gospel. But with this flamboyant gesture Jesus also did something else. He rewrote the messianic script. The standard expectation envisioned a Jewish liberator who would deliver his people from all foreign yokes, then live to enjoy the fruits of his and his people's victory. Jesus, however, refused to use force, and knew by the time he rode into town that he was a dead man. Despite the royal palms, Jesus did not want to be king. He was announcing that God's kingship was beginning. But he also knew that neither the Romans nor their Jewish collaborators could close their eyes to this jeering barefaced threat to their dignity and their power. He was right, of course. His enemies were waiting for their moment.

> Jesus went into the temple and drove out all who were buying and selling in the temple precincts; he upset the tables of the money-changers and the seats of the dealers in pigeons, and said to them, "Scripture says, 'My house shall be called a house of prayer'; but you are making it a bandit's cave."
>
> In the temple the blind and the crippled came to him, and he healed them. When the chief priests and scribes saw the wonderful things he did, and heard the boys in the temple shouting, "Hosanna to the Son of David!" they were indignant and asked him, "Do you hear what they are saying?" Jesus answered, "I do. Have you never read the text, 'You have made children and babes at the breast sound your praise aloud'?" Then he left them and went out of the city to Bethany, where he spent the night. (Matthew 21:12–17)

After his sensational entry Jesus, still satirizing the Roman script, continued on to the Temple. We can grasp the full import of what he did there, however, only if we understand that the Temple was a number of things. First, it was the symbolic center of ancient Israel. It was the Statue of Liberty, the Capitol dome, the Stars and Stripes, the Washington Monument, and the Lincoln Memorial all rolled into one. It was the totem of the tribe, the icon of its identity.

It was also, of course, the religious hub of the nation, a sacred precinct. There priests carried on animal sacrifices all day. It was an abattoir in which blood flowed like water. But it is misleading to separate this ritual function of the Temple from its symbolic significance. It was a symbol because that is where the sacrifices brought human beings close to God, and where God bent down to draw near to them. Therefore, since there was only one real God, the Temple was also the center of the whole cosmos, the navel of the world.

The Temple also served some important secular functions. Since it was the principal depository of funds, it was where one would go to negotiate a mortgage, purchase the equivalent of travelers' checks, or take out a loan. Historians believe it was the most important banking center in the eastern Mediterranean. It was also what might today be called a boondoggle. King Herod had been rebuilding it for decades when Jesus arrived in town, and it provided the livelihood for nearly one thousand blacksmiths, carpenters, and stonemasons, employing over 50 percent of the city's adult male population. Finally, it was not only a pilgrimage site; it was also a tourist attraction. It was admired as one of the most beautiful buildings in the ancient world, and those who could afford it traveled many miles to gaze at it.

The Temple covered a thirty-five-acre site and was divided into three main sections. There was an outer court, where Gentiles and women were welcomed. The inner court was open only to male Jews who were ritually clean. The innermost section was the epicenter, with its "Holy of Holies," which only the high priest could enter, and that on only one day of the year — Yom Kippur, the Day of Atonement.

The part of the Temple Jesus entered was the outer court. There he was in full public view, and there he came closer than at any time in his life to an act of violence. Seeing the merchants who sold pigeons and sheep for ritual sacrifice and demanded payment in the local currency, which they sold at excessively high exchange rates, he took direct action. He braided a whip of cords and upset the swindlers' pens and tables and drove them from the area. One can well imagine the ruckus, the noise and confusion that ensued. It was an obvious threat to public order. Even if the officials had somehow managed to overlook the donkey affair, they could not fail to respond to this episode if they hoped to maintain their credibility.

This is another incident in Jesus' life that has often been misunderstood. Though like many Jews of his time he despised the craven collaborators who were running the Temple, he was certainly not objecting to Temple worship as such. For example, he had instructed the people he healed to offer the traditional thanksgiving sacrifice in the Temple. Some of his parables featured people who were praying or sacrificing in the Temple. In his Sermon on the Mount he had said, "If you are on your way to make a gift at the altar [a sacrifice], and remember something you have against your brother, first make it right with him, *then go and make the sacrifice.*" Clearly this dedicated teacher of the Law was not questioning his people's way of worship. Rather, he was banishing the currency sharks who were robbing the poor. "Scripture says," he declared " 'My house shall be called a house of prayer' but you are making it a bandit's cave."

Class discussions about these well-known passages were always lively, and there was frequently considerable disagreement. There were usually some students who, despite the transparent clarity of the texts, clung to the idea that Jesus was not "mixing politics with religion." There were others who felt these accounts proved once and for all that when the Romans and the Jewish quislings decided Jesus was a threat to their power, they were surely right. There were others who said they would never be able to participate in a Palm Sunday service in the same way. Some liked this, but it made others uncomfortable.

The Temple event underscores Jesus' rewriting of the standard messianic scenario. He had said, by word and deed, that he was in fact God's messenger, his "anointed one" (which is what the word *messiah* means), and that the new day was dawning. But he also said that he would be humiliated and killed, and these two ideas simply did not mesh. If the messianic liberator failed and was murdered, then obviously he was not "the one." If he were the one, he would not be defeated and put to death. Now, however, Jesus was turning this scenario inside out. Yes, he was announcing the first gray daybreak of a divine reign — but one that would come quietly and unobtrusively, not with a military victory. And yes, he was going to die in dishonor, defeat, and failure. This was a startling assertion to make, and there is little wonder that few people got it. But what Jesus did was to force millions of people for centuries thereafter to ponder the meaning of "failure."

I once had a memorable discussion about the meaning of Jesus and of failure with Rabbi Irving "Yitz" Greenberg, an Orthodox scholar who is one of the most knowledgeable and sympathetic Jewish observers of Christianity. We were both on a panel when the sensitive question of Jesus' affirmation of his messianic role came up. For centuries this has been a central matter of disagreement between Jews and Christians. Jews have traditionally claimed that they cannot accept Jesus' claim because he clearly did not accomplish what someone who made such a claim should have achieved. Look around you: There are still wars and injustice and hatred in the world. Sometimes, therefore, Jews have grouped Jesus with the other "false messiahs" who have cropped up here and there in Jewish history, including the most famous one, Sabbatai Zwi, who eventually converted to Islam.

In the last two centuries Jewish thinkers have introduced a number of different ideas of what exactly a "messiah" is or what a "messianic era" would be like. Some have contended that the long-awaited one will come only when we no longer need him. Others have surmised that perhaps the entire Jewish people must be a "messianic people." Some followers of the late Rebbe Schneerson, the leader of the Chabad Lubavitch, who lived and taught in Crown Heights, Brooklyn, believed he was in fact a messiah and is still in some sense alive among his followers.

Still, the depiction of Jesus as a false messiah has persisted among many Jews. Rabbi Greenberg, however, did not believe it was an appropriate designation for the rabbi from Nazareth. It would be much better, he said, to consider him a "failed messiah," one who earnestly tried to fulfill the messianic dream, but just did not succeed. He should therefore not be despised or considered a counterfeit, but respected for at least having made the effort.

To Rabbi Greenberg's surprise, I told him I could agree with him, at least in part. If to be thought of as "anointed of God" required that Jesus had to fulfill the messianic script as it existed in his time, then he had indeed failed. But if what he was doing was rewriting the script, then we had to think of his "failure" in a different light. What if, for example, Jesus was demonstrating that we as human beings should not expect a divine intercessor to rescue us from our own cruelty and folly? Perhaps that is the underlying significance of his "failure." Jesus was, in one sense, a colossal failure, but his "failure" forces us, even today, in a culture intoxicated by "success," to reexamine what we mean by that word.

Nobody wants to talk much about failure today, especially at an elite university, where it is not easy to get students to talk about it candidly. They are where they are in large measure not because they have failed, but because they have succeeded, some even spectacularly, at whatever it takes to be admitted to such an institution. But once the students got started, it was clear that, at least at a certain level, they had all tasted failure. Some of these failures — not making the soccer team, for instance, or being passed over for the college production of *Macbeth* or for a choral group — may seem petty to them as they grow older. Others were obviously much more painful. For example, they had not won the desired response from someone whose affection they longed for. They had also felt the bite of real loss and failure in their families and among their friends in the form of death, crippling illness, loss of employment, or divorce. But this discussion gave them an opportunity to reflect on their own standards of success and their own definition of failure. Were these standards really their own, or had they merely absorbed them uncritically from the people around them? How does one, ultimately, judge success and failure? Jesus had plodded into Jerusalem and then met a disgraceful death, yet we were still studying him two thousand years later. How long will it take to decide for sure whether he was ultimately a failure?

One of the most powerful elements of the Jesus story is that even after two millennia, retelling it plunges any honest hearer into confronting some issues we normally avoid. The Palm Sunday narrative should do this in a particularly poignant way. It is not a festival of sweet-smelling flowers. It is about an ominous incident. It is about a man who could have remained out of public view, but thrust himself into it even though he certainly foresaw what it would cost. It is about how ephemeral success can be. Jesus may have been cheered, but a few days later he was being ridiculed and derided. And then he was murdered.

It is the custom in some churches to gather the leftover fronds from Palm Sunday and to burn them so that the ashes can be used to mark foreheads on Ash Wednesday as a sign of our recognition that we are all mortal, that as the Bible says, "We are dust, and to dust we shall return." It is a somber symbol, but an appropriate one for what is sometimes ironically called "the triumphal entry."

～ 20 ～

Trial and Retrial

They opened the case against him by saying, "We found this man subverting our nation, opposing the payment of taxes to Caesar, and claiming to be Messiah, a king." Pilate asked him, "Are you the king of the Jews?" He replied, "The words are yours." Pilate then said to the chief priest and the crowd, "I find no case for this man to answer." But they insisted: "His teaching is causing unrest among the people all over Judea. It started from Galilee and now has spread here." — LUKE 23:2–5

A S WE APPROACHED the arrest and trial of Jesus, no one looked forward to the class more than the law students. Despite the exacting demands of their Law School schedules, there were always a few in the class. Some told me they took it because they felt that even an excellent legal education today does not provide enough opportunities to explore the moral and religious dimensions of the practice of law. They needed a supplement. In the discussion sections I could see what they meant. The analytic skills they were developing often enabled them to run circles around the hapless undergraduates and the more philosophically oriented divinity students. Still, they often seemed just as puzzled and inarticulate about the moral conundrums as anyone else. Consequently, when we approached the trial of Jesus, they perked up. They thought they would be on familiar turf.

They were inevitably disappointed. But so were the other students, if for different reasons. The accounts of the trial in the four Gospels are confusing and contradictory. They are in no sense court transcriptions or eyewitness accounts. By the time the different hearings and interrogations that make up the trial of Jesus began, the disciples had all fled. The narratives are at best secondhand and are woven together with biblical prophecies and psalms by later compilers who intended to supply a frame of meaning. Furthermore, even on the evidence of the inconsistent reports in the Gospels, at the "trial" of Jesus there were no oaths, no defense counsel, no cross-examination of witnesses, no rules of evidence, no due process. It was no trial at all. It was a charade, a transparent ploy by the Romans and the Jerusalem elite to rid the land of a troublesome upstart under color of law. No wonder the law students were disappointed. One told me that if there had been any appeals mechanism for Jesus, she would have relished taking the case because she had spotted at least six flagrant procedural violations, even if one went by the Roman law code in operation at the time.

Piecing together the accounts in the four Gospels, here is what seems to have happened. After the disruption in the outer court of the Temple, the pace of events in Jesus' life sped up. He continued to teach in the Temple court every day. He assembled his closest friends for a Passover seder in the rented upper room of an inn. He shared bread and wine, prayers and a song with them. Then he took along three of his closest companions and climbed the nearby Mount of Olives to pray and prepare himself for what he knew must be coming. The friends fell asleep. But soon a posse arrived on the wooded hillside carrying weapons and torches. During a brief scuffle Peter wounded one of the members of the posse with his sword. (The fact he was even carrying one suggests there was still a lot of confusion on the part of the disciples about the nature of Jesus' mission.) Finally Jesus was taken into custody, but his friends fled and went into hiding. Jesus himself was then subjected to one of the most illicit kangaroo court trials in history.

The characters who play roles in this final drama have become archetypes. They include Judas the traitor; Peter the cowardly denier; Mary Magdalene, the titian-haired repentant prostitute; Pontius Pilate, the pusillanimous politician, and his superstitious wife; Herod, the effete sycophant; the two brigands on the crosses beside Jesus;

Mary, the grieving mother; plus many other bit parts and cameos. Each one of these figures has spawned reams of stories, fantasies, and the Christian equivalent of the Jewish midrashim. Their stories have been painted, sculpted, filmed, and set to some of the world's greatest music. The tragic plot they enacted has raised an endless series of urgent moral questions. Engulfed by this ocean of material, and with the semester drawing to a close, I made a tactical decision. I would not focus on the entire Passion story, but on the so-called trial of Jesus itself.

I did, however, tell the students to read all four Gospel accounts of the entire Passion, and then to listen carefully to one of Bach's musical settings, such as his *St. Matthew Passion.* This way I hoped they would somehow grasp at least some dimension of the poetry and drama of that last week. But then I asked them to concentrate on the four different accounts of the trial itself and to compare them carefully. I reminded them of some of the other great trials of history, such as those of Socrates and Galileo, and pointed out that at a trial many things come to the surface that had previously lurked underneath. In a real trial, there must be explicit charges, arguments pro and con, and evidence for and against.

In the case of Rome versus Jesus of Nazareth, however, hardly any of this happened. There were certainly charges, all based on rumors: He had said he would tear the Temple down; the Jews should not pay Caesar's taxes; he wanted to make himself king. As mentioned earlier, there were no defense witnesses, no counsel for the defendant, no right of cross-examination. This makes the trial — or what we can know about it — little more than a farce. The Romans proudly presented themselves as sticklers for the law. Their law was codified and administered by trained jurists. It was the instrument by which the *pax Romana* was enforced. It was supposed to be even-handed and equitable. But that vaunted impartiality was, of course, for Roman citizens, not colonial subjects. In their colonies, the Romans usually allowed the local legal system to function as long as the emperor's taxes rolled in and sedition was stifled. They reserved the right of capital punishment, however, for themselves. Colonial rulers were not permitted to impose the death penalty without Rome's approval. And the Roman legions carried it out. Crucifixion was the most common form, and they did not apply it sparingly. They used it all the time, abundantly and without hesitation. But they reserved it for slaves and foreigners guilty of crimes they judged to be threats to their imperial rule. It was thought to be a punishment so degrading it was inappropriate for a Roman citizen. By and large, the Romans were not interested in the internal squabbles of their subject peoples. They let the provincial magistrates deal with such bothersome infractions. They had larger matters to attend to.

Despite this neat division of legal labor, however, jurisdictional disputes sometimes arose. This was clearly the case with Jesus of Nazareth. Behind the blurry picture the Gospels present, the careful reader can detect a bizarre juristic Ping-Pong game among the three judges: Caiphas, the high priest; Herod, the "King of the Jews" the Romans had installed; and Pilate, the Roman prefect of the province, who held the ultimate power. Beyond this, one can also detect how these accounts were doctored and tailored to cast blame, cover tracks, and generally obfuscate the picture. By far the most horrendous disfiguring of the trial story are the verses in the Gospels that attribute the culpability to "the Jews." This blatant perversion of what had really taken place happened later, when the Gospels were written down, decades after the event. This blame-the-Jews ploy served a polemic purpose at a time of high tensions between most of the Jewish religious leaders and the emerging Christian movement. It was also a kind of realpolitik, an attempt by the early Christians to exculpate the Romans, in part because the Christians were trying to stay alive amid growing Roman persecution. But the damage this caricature has done over the centuries in fomenting anti-Jewish sentiment among Christians can hardly be overestimated. This is an important example of how a story becomes toxic when it is so palpably severed from history. This is why, in a time such as ours, when information is constantly hyped and cooked to serve political ends, sorting through the Gospels can be a valuable, if frustrating, learning experience. Besides, all the smudging over in the world does not obscure the basic brutal facts: Jesus of Nazareth, a Jew and a popular but unconventional rabbi from Galilee who was gathering a growing following, was lynched by the Roman tyrants and their local puppets.

Once in a casual conversation I mentioned to my colleague Alan Dershowitz, who teaches at Harvard Law School, what a hard time my students, especially the law students, had understanding the trial of Jesus. He listened with interest, then told me he had long believed that if Jesus had only had a good lawyer, things might have turned out quite differently. Dershowitz, of course, is famous for his well-honed skills as a defense counsel, so a few days later I called and asked him if he would be willing to serve — pro bono of course — in that capacity at a reenactment of the trial. He said yes immediately, so I proceeded to organize it. I asked Allen Callahan, who was then teaching New Testament on the Divinity School faculty, to serve as prosecuting attorney. He also agreed, though he confessed his reluctance to cross swords with Dershowitz in a courtroom arena. Since there was no question of a jury, I told the class they would play the role of an advisory council to Pontius Pilate. This was a fictional construction since it is clear that the prefect was a severe autocrat who kept his own counsel and made his own decisions. But it would force the students to weigh the arguments, and to imagine themselves in the crossfire the Gospels describe. I decided to play Pontius Pilate myself.

At his request, I had sent Dershowitz the latest scholarship on the trial. I was not surprised when he admitted he did not find it all that useful. Callahan knew his case as prosecutor was inherently shaky, but he also knew that, shaky case or not, he had the actual outcome, as recorded in the Gospels, on his side, for whatever that was worth.

I prepared for my role in part by reading Ann Wroe's fascinating biography–cum–historical novel, *Pontius Pilate*. In that book Wroe ransacks the historical sources about Pilate, but also delves into the centuries-long afterlife of this much-mythologized and caricatured minor Roman official who, except for the fact that he presided over the most famous trial in history, would long since have been completely forgotten. Her book enabled me to find my way into Pilate's world, and to understand why he has been so variously interpreted. "The Pontius Pilate we think we know," she writes,

> is a mixture of dozens of invented men, each symbolic of something: the State facing the individual, the pagan world opposing the Christian one, skepticism versus truth, ourselves facing God. He represents either man's free will, or his helplessness before fate, or his struggle to distinguish from evil, or the tyranny of hard choices.

At first I thought I was beginning to understand Pilate. But then, the more I read, the less I grasped what kind of man he really was. Was he the heartless and intractable tyrant we have grown to hate? Or was he the craven opportunist, constantly glancing over his shoulder at Rome and his next appointment, as he decided life-and-death issues? Or was he a bored provincial bureaucrat who saw Jesus more as a bother than as a human being? Given this latitude of possible interpretations. I decided to play Pilate as an official who felt unjustly put upon by being forced to make this decision, and angry at the Jews — all of them — who had put him in such an uncomfortable position. Of all the different ways one might play Pilate, I thought this one had the most immediate moral implications for our times. How many grave injustices are perpetrated just because the policymakers involved are bored, distracted, inattentive, or don't want to be bothered? Inaction can be the source of as much damage as action.

There were many visitors in the classroom on the day the "trial" convened. They included some students who drifted over from the Law School, faculty members from other parts of the university who had come to see the fun, and representatives of the local press who smelled a story brewing. I convened the assembly, then quickly got into my role as Pontius Pilate. Despite my adolescent son's suggestion, I did not wear a toga. I started by complaining to the "council" that I did not understand why after years of faithful service to the emperor, I had been consigned to this godforsaken and nettlesome province. Why not Crete, where the local wines were finer, or Egypt, where the living was sumptuous? The occasion afforded me a rare opportunity to exercise the repressed thespian impulses most professors strive, not always successfully, to hold in check.

Dershowitz and Callahan also warmed to their roles. As defense counsel, Dershowitz turned to Jewish law, with which he was familiar from his earlier years as a Yeshiva student in Brooklyn and his continuing study of the Talmud. He argued, correctly, that neither claiming to be a messiah nor being called a messiah by others was a violation of Jewish law. He insisted that the Jewish judges had been remiss in remanding this defendant to a Roman court, and that Pilate should refuse to hear a case that lay outside his authority. It was a tightly presented and persuasive case, possibly even a shrewd strategy. But it avoided the main reason why Pilate had any interest in the case — the accusation that this loose cannon from the north country was a dangerous pretender who claimed to be "King of the Jews." If true, that was an accusation Pilate could not ignore. The Romans had already made Herod King of the Jews, so if this upstart rabbi had royal pretensions, and since he seemed to be gathering a popular following, this was a clear and present danger to Roman rule.

As prosecuting attorney, Callahan immediately picked up on the fatal flaw in Dershowitz's case. This man Jesus, he contended, had indeed made claims to the throne established by the Romans and held by Herod. This was not just another superstitious squabble boiling up in this simmering Jewish cauldron. It was indeed a genuine threat to Rome, and — in the interest not just of Rome but also of Roman justice and civil peace — should be dealt with summarily. His argument openly hinted that if Pilate did not perform his clear prefectural duty in this case, it would surely not escape the attention of Rome.

As Pilate, I played the part of a worried, petulant, and self-serving minor official. I wanted this whole thing to be over quickly, and with as little damage to my dossier as possible. I asked both the prosecutor and the defense counsel some questions. They stuck to their arguments. Callahan, who spends much of his time analyzing ancient texts and translating Coptic documents, seemed surprised and pleased that he had done so well in his first bout as a trial lawyer against one of the best in the business. Or maybe he was smiling because, knowing how the original trial had turned out, he felt sure there would be no reversal in this most unlikely appeals court.

When the arguments were finished, I asked my "advisory council," including the students and guests in the lecture hall, what I should do. I gave them a few minutes to consult with each other in small groups. What began as a quiet buzz became louder as they wrangled and debated. The verdict was very close, with the decision to condemn Jesus winning out by a few votes. The "council" members had apparently warmed to their role as well. As a body appointed to advise Pilate, they understandably wanted to keep on his good side by doing what they thought was best for him (and consequently for themselves). They rejected Dershowitz's fluent appeal to Jewish law in favor of Callahan's hard-nosed — perhaps even cynical — pragmatism. Still, the balloting was close, and I later learned that the "swing votes" in the council were those of the more conservative Christians who, although they would love to have exonerated Jesus, felt that to do so would somehow contradict the Bible.

There had been no appeal of the original decision, and there was none of this one. The troublesome rabbi from Nazareth was condemned to death by crucifixion.

21

Dead Man Walking

On their way out they met a man from Cyrene, Simon by name, and pressed him into service to carry his cross.

Coming to a place called Golgotha (which means "Place of a Skull"), they offered him a drink of wine mixed with gall; but after tasting it he would not drink.

When they had crucified him they shared out his clothes by casting lots, and then sat down to keep watch. Above his head was placed the inscription giving the charge against him: "This is Jesus, the king of the Jews." — MATTHEW 27:32–37

O NLY A FEW VERSES in the Gospels are devoted to the passage of Jesus from Pilate's court, where he had been condemned, to Golgotha, where he was executed. But over the centuries this short time and space have evolved into depositories of legends, accretions, and elaborations too numerous to describe. That Jesus stumbled and fell; that he met and spoke with his mother one last time; that a woman named Veronica wiped his brow with her veil and his face was imprinted on it — these are all traditions that have evolved over the centuries.

More than a thousand years after Jesus' death, largely under the aegis of the Franciscans, these traditions were gradually organized into what eventually became one of the most familiar and best-loved devotional practices in the Christian world, the Stations of the Cross. It began in Jerusalem, and its early history is uncertain, but by the early years of the seventeenth century it is known that the Franciscans — whom the pope had made the custodians of the holy sites — were leading processions of barefooted pilgrims along what had become known as the Via Dolorosa every Friday evening. They would sing hymns and pause at various points to pray, usually an Ave Maria and a Paternoster. Soon eight regular stops, or stations, became customary, each identified with one of the events in Jesus' passage along the same streets. The pilgrims started in what was designated as Pilate's house, paused at the Ecce Homo Arch, and stopped at the spots where Jesus had fallen down, met his mother, and foretold the destruction of the city to the women of Jerusalem. They visited what they believed to be the prison of Christ in the Church of the Holy Sepulcher, and then ended at the hill identified as Golgotha.

The devotion was enormously popular with pilgrims, who carried descriptions of it home with them. Soon Christians in Europe began installing miniature versions of the Stations of the Cross both outside and inside their churches. The eight stations grew to fourteen, each embellished with pictures illustrating the event portrayed. Pope Clement XII finally fixed the number at fourteen in the early eighteenth century. People walking through the traditional Stations of the Cross were encouraged to imagine and share in the physical pain and emotional suffering of Christ at each stop. In this way the devotion bore a strong resemblance to the Jesuit *Spiritual Exercises*.

As the Stations of the Cross devotion spread, it stimulated stained glass depictions, sculpture, and countless paintings, both superb and tawdry. Even in relatively recent years, several great artists, such as Henri Matisse (1869–1954) and Barnett Newman (1905–1970), have attempted to capture its spiritual essence. But the fact that it traditionally occupies an extended space and that to be effective it requires viewers to move from one part to another has often rendered their efforts less than successful. The *Miserere* series by the French artist Georges Rouault (1871–1958), which was inspired by the Via Crucis but does not attempt to follow it directly, is probably the most successful.

The Stations of the Cross are an inspired combination of scant history and extraordinary religious imagination. One spring day I discovered its potency for myself. This happened after I had been teaching the course on Jesus for a number of years, but I wish I had come upon it sooner. I had flown to Jerusalem to give a lecture at the Tantur Ecumenical Institute, located on the Bethlehem road a few miles south of the old walled city. It was Holy Week, when the events of Christ's Passion are commemorated all over the world. There is no better place to be for that week than Jerusalem. Some Catholic friends in Jerusalem had invited me to join them on the Via Crucis on Good Friday. I hesitated at first, wondering what my Protestant forebears would have thought of such behavior. But then they were never in the Holy Land for Holy Week, so I guessed they would have understood.

As in days of old, we assembled at Pilate's house. It was a warm day, but not too hot. Small white clouds scudded across a clear blue sky. I was not barefoot, but I carried a candle in one hand and a tiny songbook in the other. The Via Crucis, or Via Dolorosa as it is called in Jerusalem, is actually a series of alleys. Souvenir stands, falafel shops, and pottery emporiums line both sides. The merchants hardly glanced up as we sang and shuffled by their stalls. At first I could not forget all the learned articles I had read about how historically inaccurate the route we were taking was. The street grid of Jerusalem has been altered at least a dozen times since the first century C.E., so no one knows where Jesus actually walked. Silting, rubbish, and new paving have buried the original streets far below the present level. There is some dispute about the location of Pilate's house, and therefore of the courtyard where Jesus was sentenced. We might have been three blocks or more from his original route. The procession ends at the Church of the Holy Sepulcher, but no one knows for sure if that is where the Crucifixion actually took place.

With the incense pots smoking, the rough cobblestones underfoot, the hymns swelling, the pictures at every stop, I felt all my senses being enlisted. I quickly gave my scholarly skepticism a brief respite. Slowly I began to appreciate the Via Crucis as a superb example of exactly what I had been telling my students the whole term. It was a masterpiece of the fusion of some history and a lot of imagination into a compelling narrative that countless thousands of people had appreciated. It was like much of the material we had been reading in the Gospels. Comparing ancient street maps with current tourist-and-pilgrim guidebooks suddenly seemed a little irrelevant. Soon I found myself wishing that every one of my students could be there with me. I could think of no better way to demonstrate to them the phenomenal power of narrative to awaken the imagination.

Walking along this narrow passageway in one of the world's oldest cities, therefore, I found myself identifying as I rarely have with Jesus. But I also found myself brooding on one of modern religious scholarship's most persistent problems: the vexed relationship between written history and mythic narrative. I could not entirely escape the question: What *really* happened here?

This question is not easy to answer, and the evidence is scant. But after many years of research the facts that underlie this endlessly elaborated event have become a little clearer. After Pilate had sentenced him to death, Jesus, like all condemned prisoners at that time, was forced to carry the cross to the place of execution, Golgotha, which lay outside the city walls. These processions along death row always attracted a curious crowd, just like Marie Antoinette's bumpy ride to the guillotine did. The mob can smell impending death, and a public spectacle is always alluring. A combination of the two is virtually irresistible. According to the biblical texts, most of those who lined the route heckled and jeered. Where were those who had welcomed the Son of David with palm fronds a few days earlier?

Undoubtedly there were still some in the city, but under the circumstances they must have been lying low. Although the Gospels themselves record very little of what happened during this agonizing forced march, they provide some tantalizing hints. For example, at some point it became evident to the soldiers in charge that Jesus had become too weak to drag the cross any farther. They enlisted a stranger who was just arriving in the city, one Simon of Cyrene, who was probably coming in for Passover and apparently had had nothing to do with Jesus, to carry it the rest of the way.

This single little incident reveals volumes about the arbitrariness and ad hoc brutality of the Roman regime. Crucifixion, death by slow torture, was clearly a means to terrorize the restive population. Death came from exhaustion, exposure, or suffocation. To impress passersby with the empire's might and reach, the bodies of those executed were usually left hanging in public places until they rotted or were devoured by dogs and birds of prey. The Romans showed little reluctance to use crucifixion. The historian Josephus writes that at the time of the Jewish rebellion against Rome and the consequent siege of Jerusalem, some thirty years after Jesus' death, they crucified so many of the Jews who were caught trying to escape from the city that there was not enough room for all the crosses or enough crosses for all the bodies.

For a crucifixion to take place, the condemned prisoner was compelled to carry not the whole cross but the crossbeam, or *patibulum,* to the place of execution. There his arms were tied or nailed to the crossbeam and it was attached to a permanent vertical pole. Usually a *titulus,* a sign proclaiming why the prisoner had been condemned, was nailed on the top of the pole or hung around the prisoner's neck. In Jesus' case the *titulus* bore a sarcastic mockery. It said, "Jesus of Nazareth, King of the Jews." The crime is now called *laesae majestatis,* or high treason, but what this placard said was, in effect, "This is what happens to anyone who claims to be the king of the Jews."

Historians who have patiently dug out the details of Roman military history and the Roman legal system have helped us immensely to fill in the gaps in the story of Jesus' execution. For example, forcing a hapless onlooker like Simon to carry the crossbeam bears out what historians of the period have often written, that the Roman army had the power to requisition goods and services from civilians arbitrarily. It also suggests that the scourging Jesus had undergone, a flogging using a cord whip studded with small pieces of bone or metal, had left him too weak to carry the crossbeam alone.

Secular history can be a valuable ally, and no one who has been exposed to its critical ways of thinking can ever fully escape its influence, even while trudging along the Via Dolorosa holding a candle. In truth, I do not believe we should try to escape this hard-won and invaluable way of understanding the past. But along with facts must come meanings, otherwise the facts make no sense. The challenge for the person who is both "modern" and "religious" in some sense, like many people today, is how the two go together.

The thinker who has addressed this issue most creatively is Yosef Hayim Yerushalmi in his classic book *Zakhor: Jewish History and Jewish Memory*. His thesis, simply put, is that as meaning-creating beings, humans absolutely need to remember in order to remain human. But memory relies on far more than an accurate recording of events. Facts need to be woven into patterns conveyed by narratives in order to be remembered. "The meaning of history is explored more directly and more deeply in the prophets than in the actual historical narratives; *the collective memory is transmitted more actively through ritual than through chronicle.*"

The bare fact is that a controversial rabbi named Jesus of Nazareth somehow made his way from his sentencing by Pontius Pilate, procurator of the Roman province of Judea, to the hill where he was put to death. The meaning of this event, which has been central to the lives of millions of Christians for centuries, is ritually enacted in the Stations of the Cross. Without the fact, the ritual would be an empty delusion. But without the ritual, the fact would be a useless fragment of trivia.

The Stations of the Cross is not only an inspired fusion of fact and meaning in a ritual narrative. It is also flexible enough to invite a wide variety of embellishments and interpretations. Some deepen faith; others border on sadomasochism. Mel Gibson's film *The Passion of the Christ* focuses obsessively on Jesus' physical pain. Processions that reenact Jesus' movement through the space and time of the Via Crucis sometimes carry the idea to excess. The fervent "Penitentes," who can still be found in the U.S. Southwest and in some other places, actually bind someone to a cross and draw real blood.

On a more positive note, some Latin American priests and lay leaders have recently reshaped the stations procession so that it stops at places in the community like police stations, sweatshops, or army barracks where the marchers believe some form of injustice still prevails.

One of the most audacious reinterpretations of the Stations of the Cross opened in December 2001 at MASS MoCA, the Massachusetts Museum of Contemporary Art, which is housed in a cavernous abandoned factory in North Adams, Massachusetts. It is Robert Wilson's *14 Stations*. At once bold, massive, and "immersive," it occupies a vast room the length of a football field. Like the original, this is not a Stations of the Cross one can appreciate merely by viewing it. *14 Stations* combines architecture, sculpture, music, landscape design, and sound and light into the setting for a participatory happening.

But there the surface similarity ends, while the deeper kinship begins to unfold. One enters Wilson's *14 Stations* through a wide, low-ceilinged building with a gleaming round metal well at its center. This is the judgment hall of Pilate. We can hear muffled sounds of condemnation rising from the well and surrounding us, but in a language we cannot understand. The effect is ominous and unnerving.

Then we step onto a boardwalk, suggestive of the nave of a church, with six wooden Shaker-style cottages lined up on either side. Each has a small window through which only one person at a time can peer. This technique makes what initially seems entirely too gigantic into an intensely personal experience. Inside of each cottage the viewer sees a scene evoked by one of the traditional stations, but expanded and intensified by Wilson's inventive imagination. When Jesus must shoulder the cross, we see a boulder floating in midair over a hand made of red wax. When he falls we see a lamb staggering on a floor of broken stone. When he meets his mother, another hanging boulder is completely pierced by a piece of pipe, and two small abstract figures face each other below it. When Simon of Cyrene is pressed into service to carry the cross, we see an empty white garment in the shape of a person. In Veronica's veil station, a beautifully garbed person in white linen holds an old-fashioned flatiron. When Jesus falls the second time, a cast iron stone seems to levitate. On a television screen on the floor, a man crawls slowly across the ground. A Roman soldier's helmet sits in the corner. When Jesus falls the third time, a figure crawls through bundles of rough branches. Again a table floats above. Where Jesus is stripped of his garments, there is no human form, but a large pipe runs through the back of the house to bring in light. Pairs of dice are scattered about, recalling how the soldiers cast lots for Jesus' robe. The death of Jesus on the cross is the most unsettling of this new version of the stations. A pack of eyeless red wolves, fangs bared, howl against a strangely lush background of peaceful mountains. Unlike the classical stations, this version includes a startling rendition of the Resurrection. An abstract figure is suspended upside down within a twenty-five-foot tepee of thatch and saplings. The shape suggests a church apse.

For some people this contemporary adaptation of the Stations of the Cross might seem irreverent, even blasphemous. For me, however, it made a completely different impression. The cumulative effect of Wilson's Via Crucis was one of awe and astonishment. The people around me who were also peering into the tiny windows and moving on to the next ones appeared absorbed or puzzled or shaken. When I walked through it a second time I tried to recall my feelings moving slowly along the Via Crucis in Jerusalem. I felt both a sense of continuity with that memory and an expansion. In one sense, Wilson had done with the traditional fourteen stations what the original had done with the few scattered verses in the Gospels. He had extended and deepened them. He had not falsified anything. A powerful narrative like the Via Crucis can absorb many layers of interpretation and elaboration, yet always seem fresh.

When I talked with people later about what they had felt as they walked through Wilson's *14 Stations,* the responses varied widely, but everyone seemed impressed or touched. One woman was nearly weeping. Not a single person I met felt Wilson's re-creation of the traditional devotion was disrespectful or irreverent. John Rockwell, who reviewed the work for the *New York Times,* reminded his readers that Wilson had first constructed it at the request of the officials of the Oberammergau Passion Play to help celebrate the fortieth anniversary of the play's presentation, and that his installation echoes photographs of the death camps at Auschwitz and Birkenau. I did not notice any such references, but I did appreciate Wilson's use of Shaker figures and pared-down furniture to evoke proportion and simplicity. In other words, Wilson had succeeded in making his symbolism sufficiently open so that each visitor, like the pilgrims of old, could bring his or her own expectations and hopes to the procession. Multiple readings are possible.

When I visited, both MASS MoCA and the artist were seeking a permanent home for *14 Stations.* Selfishly, I hope wherever it is installed it will be accessible to large numbers of people. I especially wish that future generations of students who enroll in courses on Jesus like the one I offered will have the opportunity to walk through it. I have never encountered a rendering of the Via Crucis that so effectively transports it into the contemporary mindset. True to the essence of the traditional devotion, and to the historical events it reenacts, it demonstrates brilliantly and reverently how fact, story, and ritual fit together in the human experience. It shows how augmentation is the essence of narrative. For Jesus himself, however, the walk along the alleyways of old Jerusalem was not a ritual. It led to a promontory that functioned both as a town dump and a hanging field.

22

Reason, Emotion, and Torture

The soldiers took him inside the governor's residence, the Praetorium, and called the whole company together. They dressed him in purple and, plaiting a crown of thorns, placed it on his head. Then they began to salute him: "Hail, king of the Jews!" They beat him about the head with a stick and spat at him. When they had finished their mockery, they stripped off the purple robe and dressed him in his own clothes.

— MARK 15:16–20

WHAT ROLE, if any, should emotions like anger, revulsion, fear, and outrage play in our thinking about moral issues? According to most ethical philosophers, from Plato to Kant to John Dewey, they should have no place at all. They corrupt our clarity of thinking and undermine our capacity to make sound judgments. This may often be the case. But in our era of long-distance warfare, proxy killing, and extortion by e-mail, abetted by the anesthetizing effect of constant media violence, we also have the opposite problem. Our capacity for sensing pain in others becomes numbed, deadening our ability to imagine what our actions may be doing to other people.

The trajectory from Guernica to Hiroshima presents a clear example of this muffling effect. Guernica is the name of a small town in the Vizcaya province of northern Spain on the Basque River. In April 1937 German planes sent to support Franco's forces bombed it heavily, killing a large number of civilians, including many women and children. The world responded with a wave of outrage, especially against the intentional slaughter of unarmed civilians. Pablo Picasso furiously painted what has become his best-known canvas, which bears the simple title *Guernica,* and the word itself became synonymous with injustice, cruelty, and the primal horror they arouse. Only six years later, however, the United States was heavily engaged in the intentional large-scale bombing of German and Japanese civilian populations. The campaign culminated in the firebombing of Dresden and Tokyo, in each of which a hundred thousand people — mainly civilians — were annihilated in one night, and finally in the atomic incineration of Hiroshima and Nagasaki. Children who were seven when Guernica was destroyed were only fifteen when Hiroshima was obliterated. But few Americans complained at the time. And no one painted any masterpieces of protest art, at least not for years afterward. This is how quickly outrage and the moral indignation it arouses cools into complacency.

A parallel coarsening of moral sensitivity may be under way today on the issues of torture. Once considered a relic of the Dark Ages, although it continued to be practiced, torture returned with a vengeance to the public eye under the twentieth-century dictators. Hitler's loyal henchmen introduced new and more modern methods. Mussolini force-fed his opponents quantities of castor oil. Stalin locked his prisoners in windowless cells piling up with their excrement. Latin American military juntas made effective use of electric shock, which leaves no visible scars. An international society for the abolition of torture was founded in France. Early in 2004 the world was shocked to see pictures of American soldiers torturing Iraqi prisoners.

Torture is obviously back on the agenda of moral concern. Therefore, it came as a surprise when a report began to circulate that the same Professor Alan Dershowitz who had so energetically defended Jesus of Nazareth against death by torture at our reenactment of his trial had published a book advocating the use of torture. How could he do it? It seemed incongruous.

As it turned out, the report was not true. What Dershowitz had actually written was that *since* torture has been, is, and will inevitably be used — often justified now as an effort to stem terrorism — its use should be scrupulously limited and carefully regulated. It should be brought out in the open and legally controlled. Otherwise it will retreat into cellars and dark backrooms, and avoid any accountability. To make his case he used the old example of the ticking bomb. Suppose, he argued, that law enforcement officials have in custody someone they *know for sure* has information that could prevent the terrorist bombing of, for example, a school or hospital that would kill five thousand innocent people. You have only a couple of hours at most to pry the essential information from the captive and save all those lives. But he or she refuses to talk. If the "ticking bomb" is a nuclear or biological or chemical weapon, this of course escalates the urgency. What would you do?

The ticking bomb scenario is only one example of a teaching technique Dershowitz often used in a class we taught together with the late Stephen Jay Gould. Dershowitz called them "Law School hypotheticals." I appreciated them because they provided an excellent example of how narratives can be used to teach moral reasoning. But I was also sometimes suspicious of them because, being hypothetical, they often sounded too formal and improbable, not real enough.

Dershowitz's own answer to the dilemma of the suspect who knows where the bomb is hidden was that virtually any police force in the world would resort to physical or psychological coercion to save so many innocent lives. Indeed, not to do so would be morally irresponsible. But, he continued — and this was the core of his argument that many missed — in order to prevent such torture from exceeding necessary bounds, and to prevent it from becoming indiscriminate and random, police should be required to apply for a "torture warrant," a one-time-only permission to apply coercion that would also specify precisely what method could be used. The warrant would have to be issued by a judge, and would be analogous to a search warrant. It would also limit what sort of torture could be used. In one sentence that many of his readers fixed on, sometimes ignoring the general thrust of his case, he suggested the insertion of sterilized steel needles under the prisoner's fingernails.

When I differed with Dershowitz about torture warrants in the class we were teaching together, I quickly learned how hard it is to engage in a reasonable discussion about this volatile subject. I began by reminding the class that there is a United Nations Convention Against Torture, which the Senate ratified in 1994, and which therefore has the standing of law in the United States. But legality and morality are not the same thing, and the purpose of Dershowitz's proposal was to place legal constraints on coercive interrogation. Still, for every argument there is what sounds like an equally plausible counterargument. Even such a wise and humane ethical thinker as Martha Nussbaum has said, "I don't think any sensible moral person would deny that there might be some imaginable situation in which torture [of a particular individual] is justified." But as everyone knows, people under torture are likely to say anything at all to stop the agony, and if the bomb is actually ticking, by the time what they say can be checked it will be too late.

There is also the "slippery slope" argument. Once torture of a limited kind is legalized by judicial warrants, it will almost inevitably spread to other cases and other kinds of pain infliction. The historical experience of France is sobering in this regard. Having legalized limited torture in its futile attempt to put down the Algerian rebellion, the practice spread quickly throughout the whole legal system. And it was a colossal failure. Not only did the French lose Algeria, their use of torture also poisoned Algerian attitudes toward their former colonizer for decades. Israel, which once allowed physical coercion, eventually decided to prohibit it. But even those who applauded that decision conceded that at times torture might have prevented at least some terrorist bombings. It often comes down to a matter of how much security a society is willing to risk in order not to sacrifice its basic values on human rights. Because these arguments sounded so confusing, our debate in class ended inconclusively.

The arguments also seemed to me a bit ethereal, so at the next session of the class I thought it was important to "de-abstract" the seven-letter word *torture*. Unfortunately, for someone like myself who has spent many years studying the history of religion and of Christianity, and who knows something about the Inquisition, moral and religious justifications for torture are not unfamiliar. Our libraries still shelve handbooks written for officials charged with extracting admissions of heresy or witchcraft. These how-to manuals list such classical devices as the rack, the wheel, red-hot irons, and the "iron maiden," a body-shaped cage with sharp spikes lining the inside. It is not particularly surprising, or comforting, to learn in reading about this grisly history that interrogators often succeeded by simply *displaying* their array of tools to the suspect. I described some of these classic techniques to the class, and even showed a couple of pictures.

But, I also pointed out, this is not just medieval history. Especially since September 11, 2001, and the "war against terror," torture has made a sensational comeback in many parts of the world. Although in the United States we might succeed in limiting physical torture to sterile needles under the nails, this would hardly be the case in many other countries, which would gratefully follow the American example in legalizing torture, but would continue to use their own proven routines. In addition, the United States now seems ready to transfer prisoners to countries that are less squeamish and let someone else do our torturing for us. On December 26, 2002, the *Washington Post* reported that the United States had already transferred detainees suspected of knowing something about terrorist attacks to countries such as Saudi Arabia, Egypt, and Morocco. But the methods these countries use have been publicly documented by the State Department itself. Suspects are routinely "stripped and blindfolded; suspended from a ceiling or doorframe with feet just touching the floor; beaten with fists, whips, metal rods or other objects; subjected to electric shocks." If a suspect is sent to Syria, which has happened in at least one case, he will find himself in a country where, according to the same U.S. State Department report, methods include "pulling out fingernails, forcing objects into the rectum . . . using a chair that bends backward to asphyxiate the victim or fracture the spine." These descriptions do not of course encompass the full range of torture techniques: long periods of solitary confinement, sometimes in total darkness; subjection to continuous bright lights and deafening noises; sleep deprivation; threats to families; and mock executions. Sadly, gang rapes of women prisoners, and sometimes men as well, have frequently taken place.

Still, the argument ebbed and flowed, with students voicing opinions on various aspects of the question. When, toward the end of the hour, we took a vote on the Dershowitz proposal, the class was split almost exactly fifty-fifty. Those who voted for it used the classical utilitarian logic. They argued that it was really a simple matter of mathematics: better to inflict pain on one person than to risk the lives of thousands. But I was still dissatisfied. I went back to the point I had made previously about having someone else do our torture for us, a practice with which the students had expressed almost unanimous dissatisfaction. I asked the class how many of them, if the judicial warrants policy were in effect, would be willing to insert the sterile needles themselves. Only a small number put up their hands. Then I asked those who favored the policy but would not do it themselves to formulate some moral justification for their action, other than mere squeamishness. A sullen silence followed.

Then I posed another question. Suppose, I asked, the suspect is not talking but you have his two children — aged four and seven — in the room. Would you threaten to torture them to get the information? After all, if it is mere mathematics, what is the temporary pain of two children compared to the possible deaths of five thousand people? Not a single person in the class was willing to hurt the children.

It is hard to debate and decide such questions in a reasonable way. Even the question of how "reasonable" one should be in discussing it becomes a factor. I was forcefully reminded of this when, after this class was dismissed, one student practically raced to the front of the classroom and pointed an angry finger at me. "What you have done," he said, "is to introduce *emotion* into what should be a *reasonable* discussion. You've tried to appeal to the students' emotions instead of their reason!"

The student was obviously overwrought, and his indictment of me was hardly lacking in emotion itself, but I tried to answer him as reasonably as I could. He was right, I told him. I had, in fact, introduced an "emotional element" into the argument, and I had done so on purpose because I thought it was needed. But, I told him, I did not accept his assumption that emotion and reason have no legitimate relationship to each other. If we drain all emotion from our reasoning, it becomes sterile and lifeless. If, on the other hand, we remove reason from our emotions, they become hysterical or sentimental.

Apparently a dedicated rationalist, the student disagreed, again not without considerable passion, evident in the rising color of his cheeks and the pitch of his voice. Emotion, he insisted, had no place in a classroom, so I had not played fair in this debate. I told him we would have to agree to disagree, smiled, and held out my hand for a shake. He hesitated, but then gripped my hand briefly and managed a miniature smile.

As I thought about this incident on my way home, I was grateful the student had come forward. There are probably classrooms in the world in which students would yawn and consult their watches even when the topic was torture. This man, on the other hand, was the kind of student one longs for. He not only felt I had violated the unspoken ground rules of academia, he was willing to confront me about it. He had also helped me understand both why the discussion had been so difficult and why the students had shifted ground so dramatically when I asked about their personal willingness to torture someone themselves or to torture children. The basic issue, I am convinced, is that in the torturer's eyes the prisoner to be tortured must first be turned into something less than a person. The victim must be converted into an enemy, a dangerous suspect, a non-Aryan, a terrorist, a less-than-fully-human creature. Only then can most human beings (there are probably exceptions) intentionally inflict unbearable pain on them.

Furthermore, this student had articulated, probably without fully realizing it, one of the central issues of the modern world and of academia in particular: What exactly is this "reason" by which we claim to be guided? What relation does it or should it have to love, awe, compassion? Or to anger and revulsion? Should all these human sentiments be sealed in airtight containers? In the West, until the thirteenth century, a much more ample concept of the nature of reason was common. The separation of these "emotional" elements from reason evolved only very slowly, and it seems possible that all parties have suffered from the divorce.

The life of Jesus and those around him is not only a history. It is also drenched with pungent emotions. They run the gamut from joy to pathos, from courage to cowardice, from soaring hope to the blackest despair. That is why his story still speaks to our imagination so powerfully, and thereby nurtures our capacity for moral choice.

❧ 23 ❧

It Had to Be Done

And when they reached the place called The Skull, they crucified him there, and the criminals with him, one on his right and the other on his left. Jesus said, "Father, forgive them; they do not know what they are doing."

They shared out his clothes by casting lots. The people stood looking on, and their rulers jeered at him: "He saved others: now let him save himself, if this is God's Messiah, his Chosen." — LUKE 23:33–35

IN MANY IMPORTANT RESPECTS the ethics of Judaism and Christianity are quite similar. Both emphasize the oneness of the human family and the responsibility we have for each other. Jesus continued and at times intensified the Old Testament prophets' defense of the poor and the powerless. But there is one matter on which the two traditions have diverged. Whereas Jewish thinking has emphasized actual deeds and their consequences, Christianity has often focused on intentions. Once, in the course of assuring his disciples that it was not so awful if they could not wash their hands before eating, Jesus said, "Out of the heart come evil intentions, murder, adultery, fornication, theft, false witness, slander. These are what defile a person, but to eat with unwashed hands does not defile" (Matthew 15:19,20). He seems to be saying that it is the heart, not the hands, that is the real source of a moral infraction.

The distinction is not absolute. Within the Jewish tradition, one of the Ten Commandments prohibits "coveting," which is an inner attitude; and Jesus condemned the pious people who ignored the beaten man on the road to Jericho. Whatever pity may have been in their hearts, they did not stop to help the mugging victims. But still, as the two traditions developed over the years, the distinction became a real one. For Christians this was evident several years ago when the Roman Catholic bishops of the United States condemned even the possession of nuclear weapons as a violation of the just war ethic. They argued that in order for these weapons to serve as a deterrent, a potential enemy had to be convinced that in certain circumstances we actually *intended* to use them. But even such an intention, they argued, was already immoral. The underlying premise is that evil intentions spawn evil deeds, and it is better to nip the foul flower in the bud rather than wait for the wicked action to blossom.

As the years passed, however, we began to see a certain convergence between these two ways of thinking about moral issues. Prodded by the need to reflect on actual policy options and their probable outcomes, Christian scholars began to probe more deeply into the possible consequences of actions, and not just what motivates them. Also, with the dramatic rediscovery of their mystical tradition, Jews have delved deeper into the inner self and its intricate labyrinth of impulses and desires.

I think this convergence is a healthy development. It is needed because once again our technology has outpaced our traditional modes of moral reasoning. There was once a time when evil thoughts and evil deeds took place at close quarters. There was a time when you needed to wield a club or a spear to kill your neighbor. Now we can do untold harm to multitudes of people at a great distance, and without feeling personally involved. In a brilliant book entitled *Evil in Modern Thought: An Alternative History of Philosophy,* Susan Neiman cites this impersonality as one of our gravest ethical dilemmas. It means, she argues, that we can no longer focus on evil *intentions* as a key to morality. We can now do great evil without intending to. What we need today is more *awareness,* a wider recognition of how the vast systems we are caught up in can do terrible things and how we can contribute to that evil without even being conscious of it. This is a disturbing idea. It means that the traditional debate about deeds and intentions needs to be rethought. "I didn't really mean it," should no longer exonerate us so easily, nor should "I had no idea of what I was doing." In our century to be unaware is to be less than moral.

This question came up with an unusual degree of forcefulness in the course on Jesus when we discussed his famous words from the cross: "Father, forgive them, for they know not what they do." I knew already that the students had strong feelings, if not always well-formulated ideas, on the topics we took up. They often stayed and continued to talk and argue with each other after the hour ended and I had left to go to another class. But this discussion did something else. It exposed the stubborn complexity of the moral world they live in more than any other we had had.

It started innocently enough when I asked the students if they were surprised or puzzled that Jesus was ready to forgive those who were at that very moment torturing him to death. As usual, their responses varied. Some said they were not surprised. That, after all, was the kind of person he was. Others confessed they simply could not understand it. They could not imagine themselves doing such a thing, so it made him less credible as a moral guide by seeming to put him out of reach. What puzzled all of them, however, was the phrase "for they know not what they do." How, they wanted to know, could they not be aware of what they were doing? It seemed entirely implausible. Also, just who was included in the "them"? Was it mainly the soldiers who mocked and beat him, or did it include the passersby who taunted him, the officials who had passed sentence on him, the spineless disciples who had fled, the collaborator who had betrayed him for a bribe? Besides, what if they *had* been aware of what they were doing, so that he could not have said, "they know not"; would he still have forgiven them? It was soon obvious that this single phrase from Jesus' lips was packed with layers of moral quandaries.

How, one student asked, could anyone engaged in something so blatantly cruel not be aware of what they were doing?

"Easy," another student answered. "We are rarely fully aware of the *full implications* of the things we do. There are always unforeseen consequences. Maybe that's what Jesus meant."

Another student pointed out that if by "them" Jesus was speaking of the Roman soldiers, we should remember that they were under orders. The Romans routinely used crucifixion as a form of punishment for people they adjudged dangerous to their rule. Maybe these soldiers had just gotten used to it, had become deaf to the moans of the victims. They had heard them before. The text says they were relaxed enough to throw dice for Jesus' tunic as he twisted and pleaded for water. Certainly prison officials today seem to be able to inject lethal chemicals into the veins of prisoners or strap them into a chair to receive a 20,000-volt jolt of electricity when a judge tells them to do so. Maybe these soldiers thought they were just carrying out a routine order.

As for the Roman officials and their local collaborators, maybe they really believed Jesus was a genuine threat to civil order and had to be dealt with in the customary fashion. Maybe they were doing their duty and did not feel the least uncomfortable. Still, most of the students were not satisfied. How could these people *not* know what they were doing?

Finally one young woman went back to a previous comment: Maybe what Jesus wanted to say was that they were not aware of the *full extent* of their actions, or of the long-range implications. They were small cogs in a large machine. So, in that sense they did not really "know." A chemistry student agreed: How could anybody ever be expected to accept responsibility for *all* the possible implications of what he might do? His remark sparked some further discussion, especially among the science majors, of how difficult — maybe impossible — it is to foresee how scientific discoveries might eventually be used. This led to some reflection about whether Alfred Nobel would have — or should have — given up devising dynamite if he had known how often it would be used in bombs. Another student who had seen a production of the play *Copenhagen* deepened the argument by recalling the moral dilemma faced by Niels Bohr,

Werner Heisenberg, and later J. Robert Oppenheimer and others who were inventing the first atomic bomb. Oppenheimer, for example, knew how destructive it was, but knew (or thought) the Germans were trying to make one too, so he went ahead with it. Later, however, he vigorously opposed developing the nuclear bomb.

The section discussion was still raging on when I had to leave, and when I came back an hour later most of the students were still at it, and they had not come to any consensus. I was not surprised. This text had propelled them into one of the most contentious moral issues of our time. Because advances in technology, especially in weaponry, remove individuals from the results of their actions, it allows human beings to do enormous evil without feeling the least bit involved. Pushing a red "fire" button at a target someone else has charted thousands of miles away is different from stabbing someone with a javelin. There is a quantitative gap between the battle-ax and the heat-seeking missile. Mass murder can become routine, even "banal" as Hannah Arendt once described it in the case of Adolf Eichmann.

I had learned a lot from the discussion of "they know not what they do." Clearly the students were becoming more and more aware of the bewildering complexity of many modern moral issues, but they still desperately wanted to "do the right thing." But I also noticed how quickly they cited plays, novels, biographies, films, even TV dramas in arguing their points. This confirmed again my deepening appreciation of the power of narrative in moral thinking, a power that is growing, paradoxically, just as some people think our capacity to craft narratives appears to be declining. Consequently I began to encourage the students to write stories or plays instead of the standard term paper most professors require at the end of the semester. When I began receiving such creative efforts, I wished I had started that practice earlier, and the next year's discussion on "Forgive them for they know not what they do" inspired some of the best ones. One student wrote a fictional counterhistory, an inventive account of what *might* have happened, but did not, after the execution of the rabbi from Galilee. It is such a good example of how an imaginative fictional creation can link the story of Jesus with our stories that I summarize the plot here.

Suppose, he wrote, that the terrified disciples, instead of scattering, had instead regrouped. Suppose these followers, led by the impetuous Peter, who had already defended Jesus with his trusty cutlass, stormed back into Jerusalem, where the word had begun to circulate about the murder of the man many of the Jews had welcomed so enthusiastically when he entered the city the previous week. Suppose these enraged Jews rallied crowds and seized Jerusalem by force of arms (as the Jews in fact did only forty years later during the Bar Kochba revolt). Now, having taken over perhaps even the whole province, suppose they rounded up those responsible for the illegal execution of Jesus, much as war criminals like Eichmann and Slobodan Milosević were sought out and brought to trial. The charge: crimes against humanity, in particular, torturing not only Jesus of Nazareth, but also hundreds, maybe thousands, of people to death.

Now, this counterhistorical fiction continued, imagine the defense. The corrupt Jerusalem religious and political elite — the shameless puppets of the Roman tyrants — would undoubtedly plead that they had only done what they considered necessary for the larger good of the people. Better that one man should die (or three or a hundred or a thousand) than that many thousands should perish under a crushing Roman repression of the revolt of the rabble Jesus seemed ready to inspire. "Look, we didn't really want to do it. No one takes pleasure in such things. But *we had no choice.* Someone had to do it, so we did."

Imagine the Roman opportunist Pontius Pilate in the prisoner's dock. At first he would undoubtedly reject the jurisdiction of the court (as Milosević did): Jewish rebels trying a Roman official! If he did choose to answer, he would have had a hard case to make, but he would undoubtedly have lied, claiming that he had merely given his official imprimatur to something the local Judean ruling clique wanted. He had done so, he would plead, because he needed them to maintain stability in this unruly province. He was doing what

Roman governors did everywhere, deploying the local ruling classes as vehicles for imperial authority and civil peace. Without their co-operation he could not have collected the taxes Rome naturally expected from her grateful subjects, and besides, everyone knew that Jews were notoriously hard to govern, that without the locals as intermediaries the whole place could easily have spiraled down into lawlessness and anarchy. But in the end, Pilate would have declaimed, proudly, that he was ultimately responsible to Caesar and Caesar alone. He did not recognize the authority of this fly-by-night tribunal of thugs and subversives.

One can also imagine the plumed centurions and sweaty grunts who had actually pounded in the nails. They would have looked astonished and said that of course they were only following orders, the classical Eichmann defense. They had never violated the rules of engagement taught them at boot camp. This has been the plea of ordinary soldiers for as long as armies have marched, and these dog-faces would not have been any different.

I found this counterhistory so intriguing that I did something I rarely do. I asked him if I could circulate it to at least some of the other students in the class as a way of provoking further conversation. He hesitated. He had not expected his paper to fall into the hands of his classmates. But he eventually agreed; so I had it copied and distributed it to the students in my discussion section with some of my own questions appended. I asked them to think about what reasons people they know, their own friends and family (not Roman legionnaires or Nazis), give today for doing things they have genuine moral reservations about.

Their answers were illuminating, if not terribly original. "Because it seemed unavoidable at the time" was one. Another was, "I dunno. I just couldn't help myself." Still another was, "Well, it was what seemed expected" or "It was just the way things are done." When I asked them for concrete examples, one student who had worked the previous year as an intern on the staff of a well-known senator in Washington recalled a telling incident. He reported that the senator (whom he rarely saw) was running for reelection that year, and that as an intern he fetched coffee and took notes at the meetings of the campaign staff. One day, he said, the polling data took a downturn, and the staff was faced with the decision about whether or not to "go negative," that is to prepare TV ads and press releases attacking the record — and the character — of his opponent instead of explaining the senator's own platform. The decision, he said, was particularly dicey because the senator had begun his campaign by promising to avoid negative campaigning. Now, however, he was unexpectedly slipping behind. What to do? The staff asked the senator to make the decision. But he told them he had picked them very carefully, and had full confidence in their judgment. He was sure they would do the right thing.

They "went negative." The senator won the election. But when it was over and reporters asked his aides why they had done so, their reply struck the same familiar chord. "We really did *not* want to do it," they insisted, "but *we had no choice*." Even the least sophisticated students in the class could detect the unspoken philosophical premises underlying this claim. Some inexorable fate or necessity had taken over. The campaign staff was being driven by an implacable kismet beyond their control. Or they believed they were. Or worse, they were not, but found this a convenient way to explain behavior they would otherwise have judged unacceptable.

The other phrase the campaign staff used later, the student recalled, was, "Too bad. But it had to be done." What is telling about this phrase, of course, is that it is in the passive voice. The subject of the sentence is now not the people who made the decision, but "it," the decision itself. Human agency and responsibility have disappeared. Also, since the senator was reelected, this seemed, in retrospect, to justify the decision the staff had made. Also, the former intern pointed out, since there is always rivalry and jockeying for power within senatorial staffs, the electoral victory strengthened the position of those on the staff who had pressed for "going negative" over those who had opposed it. Virtue, it seems, is not always rewarded, nor vice punished, at least not in the short run.

We did not come to any wholly satisfactory conclusion in our discussion of "Forgive them for they know not what they do." But our probes into the questions of agency, awareness, and responsibility were always valuable. At least they helped students to see that "the way it is done" is not always — maybe even rarely — the way it should be done. It stimulated them to imagine alternatives. Also, the way the students struggled with the issues made me even more aware that — like most of us — they were human beings who really did want to act morally and responsibly, but who would mostly live and work in institutions in which someone else made the rules and set the standard operating procedures. For that reason, despite their best intentions, they would not always be clear about what it would mean to "do the right thing," and might not always be able to do it even when they were. It was for this reason, I reminded them, that we should not focus exclusively on the "know not" part of this famous phrase, but should also remember that it begins with, "Forgive them."

My suggestion, however, did not resolve the dilemma. If anything, it pushed it into even deeper waters. "What do you mean by forgiveness?" they asked. When, they wondered, should we forgive people who do mean or even awful things to us or to others? Can we expect people we have hurt to forgive us? What does forgiveness have to do with being sorry, remorseful, or penitent?

These are all questions that sages have pondered for centuries, but it was fascinating to see how alive and immediate they were today for these young people, and I suspect for their elders as well. They are also unavoidable questions if one is studying the life of Jesus. The first words attributed to him in the oldest Gospel are, "The time has arrived; the kingdom of God is upon you." The next sentence is, "Repent, and believe the Gospel" (Mark 1:14). There is every indication that those who heard these words of Jesus recognized what he was asking for, although not all were willing to comply. All Jews of the time, even those with a minimal exposure to their religious heritage, would have known that repentance involves three elements: genuine regret for one's misdeeds, sorrow and remorse for the injury they have caused others, and a deeply felt desire to avoid repeating the offense. Without these three ingredients, genuine forgiveness, either by God or by one's fellow human beings, was not in the picture.

All this would have been familiar to most of Rabbi Jesus' hearers. The new element was the urgent tone of his demand for repentance. The coming reign of God, for which the pious prayed, was beginning now, and therefore the change of heart it required could not be postponed. As we have seen, Jesus' parables and sayings carry this same note of immediacy. Today, now, this moment is the time for repentance. The kingdom of God, albeit hidden and partial, is coming to birth in the midst of you.

For Jews today, God's demand for confessions and penitence is enacted during the Days of Awe between Rosh Hashanah and Yom Kippur. In what is staged as a cosmic courtroom drama, the people gather and confess not only their own transgressions, but also those of the whole people. At the last moment, just as the book of life is being closed, God's verdict is announced. Because God is ultimately compassionate, everyone is forgiven and afforded the opportunity to begin a new year with a clean page.

During the nearly two thousand years since the earthly ministry of Jesus, the various Christian churches have also developed highly complex liturgies of repentance and forgiveness. But the core of the Christian understanding is crystallized in the ancient invitation to the commemoration of the Lord's Supper (also called Communion or Eucharist), which eventually found its way into the Book of Common Prayer. It reads as follows:

> Ye who do truly and earnestly repent you of your sins, and are in love and charity with your neighbors, and intend to lead a new life, following the commandments of God, and walking from henceforth in his holy ways: Draw near with faith, and take this holy Sacrament to your comfort; and make your humble confession to Almighty God, devoutly kneeling.

It would be hard to find a more compressed summary of the Christian understanding of repentance and forgiveness. First, this invitation assumes that human beings are free. They are endowed by God with the capacity for choice and are therefore responsible for their actions. True, in some of its forms, the Christian idea of original sin seems to qualify this key premise. Yet, recognizing the paradox involved, the overwhelming consensus of Christian theology is that however free will may be blemished or weakened within the actual conditions of history, human beings nonetheless do have the ability to choose. Otherwise, the call for repentance would be meaningless.

This is not a trivial observation. Jesus' summons to repentance to all who came within earshot — the pious and the reprobate, the weak and the strong, the powerful and the socially marginalized — undercuts any kind of religious, psychological, or sociocultural determinism. It constitutes a firm rejection of any notion of karma or kismet that would make God or destiny or behavior in a past life or childhood mistreatment responsible for one's own actions. It suggests that although there can be mitigating circumstances, neither fate nor the psychological history of the person can be advanced as the sole reason for his or her conduct. Neither does it allow "it had to be done" or "nothing can be done about it" as excuses. It endows even the most victimized and oppressed peoples with a continuing and genuine responsibility, if only to struggle against whatever deprives them of their personhood. My offenses are ultimately mine. The *cogito ergo sum* of the Christian view of repentance is: Since I can repent, I am responsible.

The words "truly and earnestly" also carry an important message. They remind us that there is such a thing as inauthentic repentance. In our more secularized culture this spurious repentance often appears in the "public apology" that falls short of the real thing. The psychiatrist Aaron Lazare has pointed out that our public discourse is rife with such bogus apologies. A frequent form is, "I am really sorry that you feel that way" or words to that effect. The style of these utterances raises questions about whether they meet the standards of "truly and earnestly" preserved in the invitation to Communion. Public apologies are often marked by the systematic elimination of personal reference and a reliance on the passive voice. The "I" somehow disappears. They rely on phrases such as "injuries . . . may have been done" or "mistakes were made." This erasure of the subject betrays a continuing reluctance to accept personal responsibility.

The phrase "are in love and charity with your neighbors" means that the truly penitent person has *already* taken the first step toward reintegrating him or herself into the human community whose fabric has been torn by the betrayal of trust a transgression implies. Here the ancient Jewish emphasis on what was actually done continues to inform Christian practice. It is not enough just to *intend* to put things right. The word *are* is in the present tense. I must already *be* in love and charity with my neighbors, at least to some extent. Here reconciliation between a human being and his or her neighbors and reconciliation with God are indissolubly linked. During the Days of Awe before Yom Kippur, Jews are reminded that God can forgive those sins that we commit against Him, but that we must seek forgiveness from our human neighbors for the violations we enact against them. In the Christian view, this idea is modified to some extent. Since God is present in the neighbor, all sins, including those against the neighbor, are also sins against God. And since Christians usually retained the moral but not the ritual elements of Torah, it is hard to imagine a sin against God (in a Christian view) that is not also a sin against some neighbor.

The phrases "intend to lead a new life" and "walking from henceforth in his holy ways" suggest a determination on the part of the penitent person not to repeat the destructive conduct. But "intend" also allows for the weakness of human flesh. The invitation recognizes that we rarely live out even our most earnest intentions. Nonetheless, even though we fall short, we should still *have* those intentions. Further, the "new life" referred to is not one without moral guidelines. "Following the commandments of God" recalls not only the Ten Commandments but also the Golden Rule, which, in many forms of the Communion service, are read just before the invitation is issued. This reinforces the notion that these biblical principles are intended to provide moral parameters for the "new life" the penitent person now intends to live.

Finally, and perhaps most important, is the invitation to participate in Communion. It is, as it were, a readmission back into the family of God, gathered around a table that in Christian belief symbolizes the whole of humanity. It is the gateway through which one is welcomed back into a fellowship whose trust and confidence one has broken. It is an avenue to the restoration of the multiple relationships without which human life would cease to be human.

This linking of repentance and forgiveness with restoration to community echoes Jesus' linking his call to repentance with his announcement that the kingdom of God — the healed and restored human community — was "at hand." The point is vital to the Christian view of repentance. Genuine repentance is an integral element in the coming of the reconciled world of justice and peace that God wills for the world. Unlike Voltaire's famous observation that "Man was born free, but is everywhere in chains," the Christian phrase would be, "People were created to live together, but are everywhere divided and at enmity." The Christian liturgy of Communion is a symbol of the ultimate goal of a restored human community.

In many Christian theologies, this *restoratio humanii* is believed to be no less than the purpose of the Incarnation. Medieval paintings of the Crucifixion often show the skull of Adam at the base of the cross. The idea is that a new humanity is now taking shape on the spot where the first human being met his tragic denouement. Jesus spent his earthly ministry breaking the social and cultural taboos that had excluded certain types of people (prostitutes, lepers, tax collectors) from sharing meals with respectable, pious people. For Jesus, this was an act of symbolic restoration: inclusive table fellowship modeled an inclusive humanity. It prefigured the messianic feast foreseen by the previous prophets. The ultimate feast is unconditionally inclusive. As the Protestant theologian Karl Barth once remarked, the church should be "the provisional demonstration of God's intention for the whole human race."

It is important in both the Jewish and Christian traditions to avoid two extremes, which neither has always done successfully. The first is to make penitence and forgiveness so easy they come to mean nothing. It overlooks the stubborn fact that repentance, forgiveness, and reconciliation all belong together, and that each requires real effort. Sometimes Catholics have misunderstood the sacrament of confession as a license to repeat their misdeeds, since one can always confess again. Likewise Protestants have misread the idea of justification by grace as a permission to do as they please, since it is God's business to forgive. This amounts to what the Protestant theologian Dietrich Bonhoeffer once called "cheap grace." The other extreme, however, is to make forgiveness so terribly demanding that, as in the mind of Stavrogin, the poignant hero of Dostoyevsky's novel *Demons,* it becomes unreachable. If anything, I think our forebears, both Christian and Jewish, may frequently have made forgiveness too demanding. But I also fear that the "user-friendly" style of much contemporary religion may be sliding toward cheap grace.

In any case, although our extended dialogue as we pondered Jesus' words on forgiveness did not solve this old dilemma, I hope it left the students with the conviction that the kingdom of God Jesus announced was not for people who never did anything wrong. It was for "sinners," for those who — mostly — tried their best to do the right thing, often failed, but accepted the forgiveness of God and of others, forgave others, and themselves, and started over.

A World Without God?

Now from the sixth hour there was darkness over all the land unto the ninth hour. And about the ninth hour Jesus cried with a loud voice, saying, Eli, Eli, lama sabachthani? That is to say, My God, my God, why hast thou forsaken me? — MATTHEW 27:46

AMONG THE HUNDREDS of students who took Jesus and the Moral Life during the two decades I taught it, many came from serious, often quite pious, Christian families. They often questioned some of my interpretations of the Bible, but I encouraged them to stand up for their convictions. Some had been taught that Jesus had always felt close to God at every moment of his life, that his profound sense of God's presence never left him. But those students had a very hard time handling the verse quoted above. Jesus seems to be saying that, even in his hour of severest need, God had abandoned him.

Here is Jesus at his most human. If the painful experience of the absence of God is at times a part of a genuine spiritual life, which the great saints like John of the Cross have insisted that it is, then this is also Jesus at his most spiritual. It is also Jesus at both his most Christian and his most Jewish. Here he is quoting Psalm 22, often intoned by Jews, then and now, to help them through the most difficult trials.

This part of the story sounds very authentic. Jews have learned over the centuries how to cope with tragedies by turning to their scriptures, and this is just what Jesus was doing. He was at the nadir of his life, the point at which he shared the lot of humanity at its worst. He had suffered not just betrayal by a friend, public humiliation, appalling physical pain, the apparent failure of his mission, ridicule, and death, but also the awful sense that even God had deserted him at the time of his most searing need. Still, since most people, even devout believers, suspect at times that God has forgotten or ignored them, the realization that Jesus once felt the same way can strengthen and reassure them.

Although that thought may be helpful, it is hardly enough to go on for very long when things get tough. So it is important to realize that these words have a much wider resonance and that they sound a Jewish timbre far beyond one particular psalm. They focus on a point at which the Jewish story and the Christian story reverberate with each other in numerous ways. Maybe that is why the German theologian Dietrich Bonhoeffer, who was killed by the Nazis in the Flossenburg concentration camp, maintained that Jesus' cry of abandonment from the cross constitutes not just the core of the Christian message, but also the heart of the whole Bible. Again, it is how this text resonates with the Jewish larger story that makes his claim clearer. Bonhoeffer did not seem to be familiar with the Kabala, the great Jewish mystical text. But if he had been, he would undoubtedly have appreciated the kabalistic teaching about the *zimzum,* the "withdrawal" of God from the world in order to give the Creation breathing space and genuine freedom. The influential American Orthodox rabbi Irving Greenberg, though certainly not a kabalist, has said something very similar: "To the question, 'Where was God at Auschwitz?' the answer is: God was there — starving, broken, humiliated, gassed and burned alive, sharing the infinite pain as only an infinite capacity for pain can share it." Rabbi Greenberg's point is that if God did not swoop down to smash the ovens during that most monstrous of crimes, if instead he was among the victims, then we should not expect him to intervene to deliver us from our self-inflicted depredations in the future. This is at least one meaning of being "forsaken."

Bonhoeffer, who had opposed the Nazis from the start, was arrested in 1943 when the Gestapo began to suspect that he was secretly working against the regime (which he was). He was first incarcerated in Tegel, the military prison in Berlin. But later, when the attempt to assassinate Hitler failed on July 20, 1944, and the Gestapo suspected that he was involved in the plot (which he was), they moved him first to their own prison on Prinz-Albrecht Strasse in Berlin, then to Flossenburg, where he was hanged just a few hours before the American army liberated the camp.

I had been an admirer of Bonhoeffer's life and thought ever since, as a young theologian with a recently minted Ph.D. in hand, I lived for a year in Berlin and came to know a number of people who had worked with him. Later I also met Maria von Wedemeyer-Weller, the woman to whom he had become engaged but had never married. They had planned their wedding for after the war, which he did not live to see.

While he was locked in Tegel prison, Bonhoeffer spent much of his time reading and writing letters, some to his parents, some to his fiancée, and some to his best friend, Eberhard Bethge. A friendly guard helped smuggle them out. I am sure Bonhoeffer never expected the letters to be read by anyone else. But a few years after the war, Bethge decided the ones he had received included such daring and provocative insights that they should reach a wider audience. He assembled them and they were published first as *Prisoner for God,* then later as *Letters and Papers from Prison.* Within a few years this book became one of the spiritual classics of the twentieth century.

What makes Bonhoeffer's prison letters so powerful is that even though he knew he was facing certain death, and with it the loss of all he held most dear in life, including his forthcoming marriage, there is hardly a melancholy or lugubrious sentence in them. They stand along with St. Francis's canticles to Sister Moon and Brother Sun as among the most buoyant and life-affirming documents in all of Christian literature. Even his famous poem about his approaching death has an underlying joyful tone. Bonhoeffer adamantly opposed any kind of Christianity that appealed to human weakness or despair. In one of his letters he told Bethge he despised the idea of a God whom we experienced "only at the edges of human life, i.e., in death, sin and suffering." This seems a surprising assertion for a man bolted behind bars and facing virtually certain execution. Still, he went on, "I should like to speak of God not on the boundaries but at the center, not in weakness but in strength; and therefore not in death and guilt but in man's life and goodness."

But how could Bonhoeffer turn to the words Jesus spoke at the moment of anguish and death to make such a statement? Again, it is the resonance with the Jewish story that makes this clearer. Bonhoeffer believed that when God did not rush down like a Greek deus ex machina to save Jesus from the cross, he was signaling to human beings that we have indeed been "forsaken" in the sense of being left to work things out, or to fail, on our own. God will not compromise our freedom even to deliver us from the most tragic consequences of the worst of our hatred and greed. In another letter, Bonhoeffer told Bethge:

> [God] is weak and powerless in the world, and that is precisely the way, the only way, he is with us and helps us . . . the God who is with us is the God who forsakes us [Mark 15:34]. The God who lets us work in the world without the working hypothesis of God is the one before whom we stand continually [Letter of 16 July 1944].

So far this echoes the kabalistic teaching faithfully. Then Bonhoeffer adds a highly paradoxical Christian twist: "Before God and with God," he writes, "we live without God. God lets himself be pushed out of the world onto the cross."

This is pretty radical theology. But I had learned so much both from Bonhoeffer's writings and from the example of his courageous death that I decided to invite the students in my class to read some of his letters. They did. But then a problem I had not anticipated arose.

Bonhoeffer had insisted for many years in his previous teaching and writing that God was to be found in the secular world, not beyond it. But while he was in prison, Bonhoeffer discovered an unanticipated confirmation of his theology. He came to know and admire many brave men who were in no way "religious." Some were communists, others secular intellectuals, others simply ordinary people who had somehow aroused the ire of the Gestapo. Some were dismissive of religion, others simply indifferent. But what Bonhoeffer noticed was that, even in the midst of Allied bombing raids, and even faced with death sentences, they did not turn to "the consolation of religion."

Living month after month in close quarters with such fellow prisoners, Bonhoeffer began to notice some changes in himself. He began to believe that these men were harbingers of the future, non-religious or post-religious men, and that in fact history might itself be moving toward a time when religion would be left behind. How, he wondered, could the message of Jesus be communicated in such a time? Maybe, he conjectured to Bethge, religion has only been the "outer garment" of Christianity, one that it was now time to shed. But then, as he so pointedly asked, can we devise a "non-religious interpretation of Christianity" for a "world come of age"? Sadly, Bonhoeffer never had a chance to answer his own question.

When we tried to discuss Bonhoeffer I could see that the students were painfully conflicted. They admired his courage and his celebration of what he called *hilaritas,* the sheer joy of being alive in the world. They found his story gripping and many passages in his letters inspiring. But what in the world could he possibly have meant by a "non-religious interpretation of Christianity"? Wasn't Christianity itself a religion? Didn't many people claim it was the best or the highest or even *the only* true religion? Well, maybe it is or maybe it isn't. But surely it is *a* religion. What would be left of it if it were not a religion anymore?

During this conversation I came to the stark realization that my students, especially the younger ones, had moved beyond both Bonhoeffer's worldview and my own. They were not living in a post-religious era at all. They were living in an era in which religion seems to have made a surprising comeback in the latter decades of the twentieth century, a riposte that Bonhoeffer seems not to have anticipated. This "return of the sacred," as some scholars have called it, has not always been welcome. It has included religiously motivated terrorism as well as increasing church attendance in some parts of the world. It encompasses crystals and channeling and a variety of other fuzzy New Age pieties, as well as the Muslim renaissance, the spread of Buddhism to the West, and the rebirth of both Christian and Jewish theological scholarship. Students all over America now eagerly enroll in courses in religious studies and seem to relish perusing the great classics of the field. Religion may never actually have declined at all, but it is certainly "in" again.

Bonhoeffer, on the other hand, thought human history had passed through the "archaic age" of myth, had moved past the "metaphysical age" of religious systems, and was now entering what he called, drawing on a phrase from Kant, a "world come of age." He did not mean by this phrase that our era was any better or more virtuous, merely that we would no longer need the "God hypothesis" to explain the world. He warned that if God were called upon only to fill in the gaps in human knowledge, there would soon be no place left for him at all. There might be some people, he conceded, who would remain more or less religious, but they would constitute a smaller and smaller minority. Christianity would have to learn to address the "Third Man," the one who had left both myth and metaphysics behind, who was no longer in any historical sense religious. What was needed was a "non-religious interpretation of the Gospel."

It did not help when I explained to the students that Bonhoeffer was not just looking for this new expression of the message of Jesus so that he could convince someone else of the truth of Christianity. For him, it was a personal quest. He had never undergone what might be called a crisis of faith. If anything, his faith had deepened and matured during his imprisonment. But at the same time he increasingly recognized himself to be a "post-religious" man. In his impassioned letters he was trying to hold together two dimensions of his own life. He came to believe that there was no such thing as a spiritual realm, apart from the everyday world. He believed that the God who had, in one sense, "forsaken" the world was still alive and present in it. In fact, it was the very forsakenness of Christ on the cross that revealed *how* God is present. He is present suffering and struggling along with the despised and rejected people of the world, those whose lot is to be ignored, overlooked, and humiliated. Therefore the calling of the "post-religious" Christian is not to strive for transcendental salvation, but to enter joyfully into the "suffering of God in the world," and to strive for the renewal of Creation that only God himself could ultimately complete. With these words, and without knowing it, Bonhoeffer became one of the sources of inspiration for the liberation theology movement, which arose twenty years later.

My discussion with the students about "My God, my God, why hast thou forsaken me?" ended inconclusively. I had to concede that in the cultural climate of the late twentieth and early twenty-first centuries — a time swarming with a variety of religious movements, some healthy, some venomous — it was understandable why they could not wrap their minds around a "non-religious interpretation of Christianity." Bonhoeffer's cultural prediction may have been mistaken, or perhaps premature. But his portrait of how God is present in the seemingly "godless" secular world is still a powerful one. So I would not concede that Bonhoeffer is no longer relevant. True, we may never arrive in a fully non- or post-religious era. But if the kind of superficial religiousness that is engulfing us today continues to spread, then both serious Christians and serious Jews may find themselves insisting in a new way on the absence of the real God from such a world. Both the Jewish kabalists and the Christian mystics have taught that atheism is superior to the feeble complacency of so many people today.

Also, the divide between believers and nonbelievers may not be as wide, or as real, as many think. Even, or perhaps especially, the most truly religious people today have their dark nights of the soul, and they cannot escape being secular or even nonreligious at some moments or in some respects. And there are increasing numbers of nonbelievers in today's world who harbor gnawing doubts about the validity of their skepticism. We are all to some extent hybrids.

All in all, I have come to share Bonhoeffer's suggestion that Jesus' agonized cry, "My God, my God, why have you forsaken me?" is the most important verse in the Bible, and the most decisive moment in Jesus' life. If Christian faith teaches that in this man from Galilee God shared the most racking pain and the most overwhelming sorrow human beings can know, including death itself, then he must also have felt abandoned by God. He must have felt, in his own way, that he had lost his faith. Of course, this is a paradoxical statement. How can God feel abandoned by himself? But the fact that we cannot fully grasp such an idea does not make it any less powerful. It merely deepens the mystery of just how God was present in Jesus, and how God continues to suffer the grief and heartache of human existence. All the doctrines and theories that have been invented for nearly two thousand years have not even come close to explaining how such a thing is possible, and none ever will.

Once one of Bonhoeffer's fellow prisoners told him that his goal in life was to become a saint. But Bonhoeffer responded that, for him, being a saint was not an attractive prospect, that he simply wanted "to become a man," fully human. Of course, not all of Bonhoeffer's theological ideas were accurate. He was, like all of us, a creature of his time. Still, for me he remains a model of what it means to be a Christian in the twenty-first century. Maybe the prisoner in cell 19 of Tegel military prison was not a saint, but he came as close to being a fully human being as anyone I know of, and he still has something worthwhile to say to all of us.

25

The Easter Story

But very early on the first day of the week they came to the tomb bringing spices they had prepared. They found that the stone had been rolled away from the tomb, but when they went inside, they did not find the body of the Lord Jesus. While they stood utterly at a loss, suddenly two men in dazzling garments were at their side. They were terrified, and stood with eyes cast down, but the men said, "Why search among the dead for one who is alive? Remember how he told you, while he was still in Galilee, that the Son of Man must be given into the power of sinful men and be crucified, and must rise again on the third day." Then they recalled his words and, returning from the tomb, they reported everything to the eleven and all the others.

The women were Mary of Magdala, Joanna, and Mary the mother of James, and they, with the other women, told these things to the apostles. But the story appeared to them to be nonsense, and they would not believe them. — LUKE 24:1–11

WHEN I WAS A YOUNGSTER in a small town, Easter Sunday was always a memorable day. But not for the reasons the minister and the church elders obviously thought it should be. It was the only day when all the church congregations in town gathered in the dark before dawn for an ecumenical sunrise service. All the churches, I should add, except for the Roman Catholics. This was years before the Second Vatican Council in the early 1960s softened Catholic attitudes toward Protestants. I can still remember shivering as my bare feet hit the cold floor when I got up while it was totally dark, pulled on my clothes, crept quietly out of the house, and made my way to the park amid throngs of townspeople, some carrying flashlights. I was secretly a little pleased that at least on that one day we were out of bed even earlier than the Catholic playmates who got up every Sunday for the seven o'clock Mass and never tired of telling the rest of us how heroic they were and how easy we had it.

The gathering took place in a large open park also used for Fourth of July parades and the annual Volunteer Firemen's Fair. An obscure skirmish had been fought there during the Revolutionary War, and two rusting iron cannons were perched near a flagpole at one end. By the time I got there I could hear the combined choirs of the various churches singing, not just to set the tone but probably also to keep warm. There were already a few gray streaks on the eastern horizon, but it was still dark. The service was timed so that the sun would rise about halfway through it, which it usually did except when it was drizzling or the skies were overcast. No one seemed bothered by the quasi-pagan admixture of the rising of the sun with the Resurrection of the Son. I doubt that even the ministers realized something I did not learn until years later, that the word for the Christian holiday we now call Easter is derived from the name of a pagan goddess — Oester — who was associated with the east, where the sun comes up.

The Easter sunrise service could be strenuous. It always lasted longer than a regular service, in part because every minister in town had to be heard from, with an invocation, a prayer, or a word of welcome. Fortunately, they took turns giving the sermon, passing it around from year to year. Otherwise we might have been there until the sun set. Still, with a different preacher each year, I was able to detect some of the nuanced differences in the ways they interpreted the Easter story. That may have sown some of the seeds of what eventually became a lifelong fascination with theology and comparative religion. The service was also taxing because the only chairs were those elderly or infirm people had brought with them. The rest of us stood, so that by the time it was over, the benediction was pronounced, and the choir had sung its final "amen," I was quite ready for what I knew was coming next: the annual Easter Sunday all-church pancake breakfast.

This was always a sumptuous spread that took place in the basement of one of the larger churches. There were platters stacked with piles and piles of steaming brown and white pancakes, topped with ladles of maple syrup and chunks of butter, with crisp bacon on the side and orange juice in paper cups. The adults sipped at mugs of aromatic coffee drawn from shiny silver vats. The atmosphere was always cheery, but I am sure, at least for the young people, the festiveness had as much to do with the food and the ecumenical camaraderie as it did with the event we were celebrating. It was one of our few opportunities to mix at a church event with the boys and girls from other denominations from whom we were usually separated by niceties of theological distinction that did not seem all that vital. By the time I got back home, where my parents, who were not churchgoers, were just coming down to breakfast in their bathrobes, I felt buoyant, and a little self-righteous. I do not remember giving much thought one way or the other to whether the biblical text quoted at the start of this chapter, which I had just heard read, or the sermon that had just been preached were true. It just never entered my mind.

That began to change when I became a teenager and — as with all teenagers — people I knew began dying. Thoughts of my own mortality often upset me. My awareness of death was no doubt deepened when I began to work part-time for my Uncle Frank, who was the town's only undertaker, or "mortician," as he preferred to be called. I went out with his crew to pick up the bodies of people who had just died and bring them to his morgue. I watched him embalm some of them on a white table with a formaldehyde solution. I helped carry caskets to the cemetery. Some of the people he buried were old, some young, some were stout, some thin. But to me they all had one thing in common: They all looked *very* dead. Yet at the graveside, whatever minister was in charge always talked about the resurrection of the dead, and they were not just talking about Jesus.

They were talking about everyone — what is known as the "general resurrection."

I began to wonder. It was not long before I began to ask myself the question I had not asked as a youngster. Was what the Bible said, and what the songs and the ministers proclaimed, really true? And if there was eventually going to be a general resurrection, what was happening to all those dead people in the meantime? Now and then when a person died, someone in the church would say they were already in heaven, or had "gone to be with God." But that did not seem consistent with a general resurrection sometime in the distant future. Then, when I began to meet people who said there was no such thing as a life after death, that when you were dead you were dead, and that's that, the mystery deepened. Once in a while I would ask someone about what seemed to me a nest of contradictions, but I never got a satisfying answer. Eventually I just stopped asking.

The dilemma stayed with me when I went to college. In a sophomore philosophy course I wrote a term paper on the idea of the immortality of the soul in Plato, and got an A minus from the professor. I enjoyed attending a variety of different churches, so I heard a wide range of interpretations of life and death and resurrection. In my junior year I began reading the novels of Fyodor Dostoyevsky and was gratified to discover that he had not only wrestled with these questions his whole life, but that he considered them the most important things anyone could think or write about. By the time I graduated from college and began seminary, I knew three things. One was that the Resurrection of Jesus Christ, whatever it was, is not peripheral to Christianity but is at its core. Another was that I did not know what it meant or what I believed about it. Finally, I realized that I would probably never answer the questions I had, that I would have to live with an element of uncertainty, but that there were many thoughtful people — many of them exemplary Christians — who were in exactly the same situation.

Is it any wonder, then, that for the first couple of years that I taught Jesus and the Moral Life, I dodged the Easter narrative? Of all the stories told about Jesus, this one is the most potent and the most baffling. Yet for centuries many Christians — perhaps even most — have insisted that without it all the other stories lose their weight. Still, this outlandish tale of angels, grave clothes in an empty tomb, apparitions, and mysterious encounters between the man the Romans executed and his despondent followers defies all our everyday sensibilities. What are we to make of it?

At first I took the easy way out. I stopped the lectures about Jesus' life with the Crucifixion, then devoted the remaining few sessions to discussing some of the innumerable different interpretations of the moral significance of his life that have arisen in the centuries after his death. I passed over the Resurrection in part because I thought that talking about it in a core curriculum course at Harvard would be awkward, and might even seem inappropriate, especially with students from many different religious traditions present. I also knew how hard it would be to talk about an event that, unlike many other events in Jesus' life, stood on the borderline between the historical and the mystical. But then I changed my mind.

After a year or two I began to have a bad conscience about leaving out such a central element of the Jesus story. Even the most critical modern biblical scholars concede that undoubtedly the scattered and dispirited followers of Jesus experienced *something* after his crucifixion that convinced them that death had not finished him for good. Otherwise it is hard to imagine why they should have reassembled and insisted on continuing his hazardous work while the same brutal cliques that had put him to death were still in charge. The British New Testament scholar N. T. Wright catalogs half a dozen movements that were in some ways similar to the Jesus movement, and existed in the same historical period, but simply melted away after their leader's death or they selected a new leader. None of them claimed their leader was still alive. Furthermore, Jesus' followers ran the terrible risks of arrest and a death like their leader's precisely *because,* as they said time and again, they had encountered him as, in some sense, alive and in their midst. Their accounts of these meetings with a no-longer-dead Jesus are described in those passages scholars call the "Resurrection appearances." But because these experiences do perch on the precarious borderline of empirical history, they were impossible to portray in an ordinary vocabulary. Like any truly mystical experience, they could not be described in everyday language because everyday language describes everyday events. Mystical experiences always "break the language barrier," which is why mystics so often turn to symbols or song or silence.

But my own "resort to silence" did not satisfy the students, and ultimately it did not satisfy me either. The students let me know quickly, and in no uncertain terms, that having followed the story of Jesus with me from the manger to the grave, they were not going to permit me to skip so easily over its peculiar and baffling climax. And to my surprise, the objection came not just from the Christian students, who understandably wanted to hear my interpretation of Easter, which — with the possible exception of Christmas — finds more people in churches than any other celebration of the year. It also came from the nonreligious students and those from other religious traditions. Many of them had been drawn to Jesus as a rebel against the status quo, as a daring moral exemplar, or as an inspiring teacher of spiritual wisdom; still, they were puzzled, not just by this climax as it is told in the Gospels, but also by why it seemed so central in Christianity. No one had ever claimed that the Buddha or Confucius or Socrates or the Prophet Mohamet had returned from the dead. Why Jesus? I knew that somehow I was going to have to break the silence.

I also knew, of course, that the Easter story is sometimes no less problematical to Christians than to others. Many regular churchgoers do not know what to think of the Bible readings they hear on Easter, which sound to some like extracts from a Stephen King novel or the script for a Hollywood thriller, like the *Terminator* series in which the hero stubbornly staggers back time and time again even after he has been shot, incinerated, or blown to bits. One student told me that he attended church regularly but whenever he heard the Resurrection account read he could not help thinking of the scene in the Dracula films in which the pale "undead" count pushes open the lid of his coffin and climbs out to go on the prowl for some fresh blood. He quickly added that he knew it was wrong to think of Easter in the same frame with the prince of the vampires, but somehow he just couldn't help it. I was glad he had told me, because it reminded me once again that although today's worldview is quite different from the one in which these biblical accounts first circulated, there are also many troubling similarities, or at least what appear at first to be similarities. Like our first-century forebears, we in the twenty-first century are still both fascinated and horrified by death, and equally disquieted and intrigued when the dead do not stay dead. The idea of the Resurrection has been a "scandal" since it was first disseminated, but the reasons why it is hard to interpret change from age to age.

The young people of today are different from their twentieth-century grandparents, at least from the more "secular" of those elders. They no longer share the unshakable confidence in science that characterized the pre–World War I mentality. This sunny certainty about science had prompted that previous generation to reject the very idea of resurrection out of hand as simply nonsensical. Today's young people are not as wedded to the idea of a closed universe in which science has all the answers. They are open, sometimes uncritically, to possible other dimensions of reality that might impinge on or even penetrate the familiar one. They watch movies teeming with human-machine hybrids, time warps, dematerializers, and the million-dollar man. But this does not make the task of interpreting the Resurrection of Jesus any easier. Sometimes I am afraid it makes the danger of misunderstanding it even more acute. Jesus was not a benevolent first-century Terminator.

I also knew that, formidable as these obstacles were, there was another reason why I had been trying to steer around the Easter story: Classrooms, at least the ones I teach in, are not viewed as the proper venue for testimonies. What is supposed to go on in classrooms is "explanation." But not only did I not know how to explain the Resurrection to the class, I was not even sure what "explaining" it might mean. It eventually became clear to me, however, that all my excuses were, in the final analysis, unsupportable. By leaving out this part of the story I was not just being unfair to my students (albeit under cover of being evenhanded), I was also being intellectually dishonest, a little lazy, and cowardly. I realized that, at a minimum, I would have to sketch out some of the current interpretations of the Resurrection and suggest that they would have to decide among them on their own. I had a feeling that this was not going to satisfy them, and it turned out that I was right. But I set out to move from silence into at least some kind of conversation.

In preparing for this step I went back and carefully scrutinized the Resurrection accounts in the four Gospels, together with some of the many commentaries that have appeared about them. I knew that the Christians had not invented the idea of resurrection, that it was already present in the Hebrew scriptures. So I also went back to the passages there that deal with God's vindication of innocent suffering and of God's gift of new life, at times even to the dead. And I read the Jewish commentaries on these. Once again, the Jewish sages and the rabbis came to my aid.

Since I had not been talking about the Resurrection in class, I had not made a careful study of the key passages for some time, and when I did I was in for a few surprises. First, it immediately became evident that stories of raising the dead in the Old Testament *did not have to do with immortality.* They are about *God's justice.* They are expressions of a human hope that is born of a *moral,* not a metaphysical, impulse. They did not spring up from a yearning for life after death, but from the conviction that ultimately a truly just God simply had to vindicate the victims of the callous and the powerful. The prophet Isaiah declares this hope with particular eloquence. He looks forward in lyrical anticipation to the day when "the inhabitants of the world learn what justice is" and "the wicked are destroyed" because "they have never learned justice" (Isaiah 26:9, 10). But he goes on to foresee that even though the righteous now suffer and die, "your dead will live, their bodies will rise again. Those who sleep in the earth will awake and shout for joy" (Isaiah 26:19). The same sentiment is voiced in the poetic passage in the prophet Ezekiel about how God breathes across the valley filled with the bleaching bones of the vanquished casualties of imperial conquest, and they reconnect with each other and stand.

> The Lord's hand was upon me, and he carried me out by his spirit and set me down in a plain that was full of bones. He made me pass among them in every direction. Countless in numbers and very dry, they covered the plain. He said to me, "O man, can these bones live?" I answered, "Only you, Lord God, knows that." He said, "Prophesy over these bones; say: Dry bones, hear the word of the Lord. The Lord God says to these bones: I am going to put breath into you, and you will live. I shall fasten sinews on you, clothe you with flesh, cover you with skin, and give you breath, and you will live." (Ezekiel 37:1–6)

The Protestant theologian Jürgen Moltmann correctly notes that, for the Israelites, resurrection did not "refer to everlasting life or happiness"; rather, it was "a theological symbol to express faith in God's justice at the end of history . . . It was not a longing for life everlasting but a thirst for justice." Clearly the story of God's resurrection of the righteous rabbi from Nazareth is meant to be a continuation of these ancient stories of his people. As with so much else about Jesus, we misunderstand him badly if we remove him from the ongoing saga of his people.

Reading the Easter story in the context of this previous history makes one thing quite clear: It is at least as much a story about God as it is about Jesus. The Resurrection is not something Jesus does; it is something God does. Strictly speaking, the accounts do not say that Jesus awakened himself from the dead. Most of them say, "*God* raised him." As with Isaiah and Ezekiel, God is the principal actor in the drama. For obvious reasons this reminded me of the exodus story that Jews retell at every Passover seder. I had noticed when I participated in these celebrations that although Moses, along with his brother Aaron, led the Israelites out of their Egyptian captivity, Moses is scarcely mentioned in the Passover liturgy. This reflects the wisdom of the rabbis. They avoided casting Moses as the central figure because they wanted to make sure people realized that God was the real liberator. This rabbinical insight suggests yet again that we need to see Jesus not just against the Israelite background that went *before* him, but in light of the continuing Jewish history that came *after* him. As we will see in a moment, the Jesus story continued the old story, but added a new dimension.

The exodus from Egypt, kept alive by song and story for 3,500 years, is one of the most important events in human history. By liberating the Israelites from bondage, God not only humbled one despot, the Pharaoh, he also established a precedent that would pose a constant threat to any future tyrant as well. It has worked out just that way. The original exodus inscribed the conviction that people have a God-given right to be free within the Jewish psyche, and from there it eventually found its way into Christianity and into cultures all over the world. It started something irreversible in human history. When Benjamin Franklin was asked to design a great seal for the new American republic, he asked an artist to sketch the destruction of the Egyptian army at the Red Sea. (That design was eventually not the one chosen.) Black Americans identified completely with the exodus story. While still in slavery they sang "Let My People Go," and during the civil rights movement they sang "We Shall Overcome" because "God is on our side." The exodus is a key theme in liberation theology. It is completely understandable, therefore, why it provided the first Christians — all of them Jews — with the historical paradigm for the Easter story.

This is why for centuries Christians have spoken of Easter as a "second exodus." The idea is that in the original liberation of Jesus from the grip of death, God inflicted a mortal wound not just on human mortality but on the tyrannical forces that murder innocent people like him. The victory was not yet complete, just as the Israelites' escape from Egypt did not complete the destruction of despotism and servitude. But now both Jews and Christians could anticipate the final victory of God over all that deforms and destroys life, with confidence that the turning point had come and the decisive battle had been won.

At Passover, Jews eat the bitter herbs and the unleavened bread to make vivid the memory of their deliverance from captivity. Jesus told his followers to eat the bread and drink the wine "in remembrance of me." Memory is basic to both these observances because both commemorate massively subversive events; they become reminders of what one theologian has called the "subversive" memory that becomes the basis for hope, even in the worst circumstances. In short, the early Christians believed that the same God who had manifested himself in the exodus as the One who empowers human freedom had acted again at Easter, enlarging and deepening the scope of his liberating energy. This makes the Easter story, like the exodus, mainly a story about God.

Of course, the Easter story is also about Jesus. God, these puzzling old stories state, did not raise just anyone from the dead. He raised an innocent man who had placed himself alongside the misfits and the outcasts of his day, who taught people to love their enemies, who boldly confronted the rapacious elite, and who was tortured and killed — like so many others before and after him — by a depraved system of law and order. Furthermore, he was murdered *because of* who he was and what he did and said. He died because of the way he lived. It is also enormously significant that according to the Easter story, God vindicated a teacher of the Jewish law who had spent the night before his execution celebrating Passover. Christians often overlook this inconvenient fact, but this causes us to forget the corporate dimension of the exodus and reduce the Resurrection to an individual affair.

How Jesus died is very important. In the biblical texts he is not just described as "dead" but as "crucified." There is a difference. To restore a dead person to life might be seen to strike a blow at mortality. But to restore a crucified man to life means to strike an equally decisive blow at the system that caused his wrongful death, and the death systems that continue to cause the suffering and fatality of millions in what the Latin American theologian Jon Sobrino calls "a world of crosses." The Resurrection story points not just to the ultimate victory of life over death, but of God's shalom over cruelty, greed, and atrocities.

We need these three different searchlights to illuminate the Resurrection. Reading the Easter story against both its biblical background and its rabbinical foreground is a good start. But seeing the way both narratives have inspired freedom movements all through history brings the narratives up to date. Taken together, these three interpretive lenses help us glimpse what the New Testament writers were saying in the only language they had.

As I had anticipated, however, my students were still not content. We were left with the unanswered question both they and many church members raise. Yes, they say, it's a powerful story with an inspiring biblical pedigree; yes, it has empowered freedom struggles throughout history, but *did it really happen?* If it is true that "something" reinspired and regathered the shattered band of disciples and propelled them out into the world to carry on the work of the Nazarene, what was that "something"? Why did they notice it and no one else did? Was it some form of hallucination, a clever fiction, a wild rumor they started believing because they so much wanted to?

These are perfectly honest questions, and the only honest answer I could give my students was that I could take them only so far and no farther. The "Resurrection appearances" texts are inconsistent and discrepant. The original Gospel of Mark, the oldest of the Gospel accounts, ends by describing the arrival of the three women — Mary Magdalene, Mary the mother of Jesus, and Salome — to the tomb where the remains of Jesus had been laid. They planned to anoint the body with oils, an established mourning custom. They were worried about how they would move the large stone that had been used to close the entrance to the tomb, but as they approach they see that it has already been rolled away. Puzzled, they go into the tomb and find a young man in a white robe sitting there. They do not know what to say. The young man (he is not called an angel, just "a young man") says to them:

Do not be alarmed. You are looking for Jesus of Nazareth, who was crucified. He has been raised; he is not here. Look, there is the place where they laid him. But go and say to his disciples and to Peter: "He is going ahead of you into Galilee: There you will see him, as he told you." Then they went out and ran away from the tomb, trembling with amazement. They said nothing to anyone, for they were afraid. (Mark 16:6–8)

Astonishingly, this is where the account ends: "they were afraid." Period. The oldest and most authentic version of the Gospel of Mark simply stops here. In most editions of the New Testament today, other verses have been added, some of which are found in later manuscripts of the Gospel. However, the scholarly consensus is that they were tacked on because succeeding generations of Christians found it hard to live with this cryptic, unsatisfying — even disturbing — "nonending." Terrified women running away, too frightened even to tell anyone? What way is that to conclude the story of Jesus? Now what? What happens next?

The original Mark does not answer any of these questions. The women are simply told that to see him again they should return to Galilee, the impoverished land where Jesus had taught and healed and made himself controversial by talking about a new kingdom of God that would replace the divine Caesar's. There, where he had spent most of his life among the pariahs and the disinherited, is where they would find him.

This terse version of the Easter story has startling implications for the question of why some people could "see" the no-longer-dead Jesus and others could not. The story contains what philosophers call an epistemological point. It helps explain why some people find the idea that "Christ is risen" nothing but a far-fetched superstition, while for others it is the sustaining capstone of their lives (and there are many somewhere in between). As Jesus had frequently said in his teaching, the kingdom of God "does not come by observation." Likewise the Resurrection, as the continuation of God's vindication of the left out and the trampled upon, is something that by its nature is not observable or even remotely credible to impartial investigators. This is undoubtedly why the endless sifting through the scanty historical sources on Easter, which is obstinately carried on by amateur sleuths and scholarly analysts, convinces no one and is always so unsatisfying. These investigators will never prove or disprove something that is by definition not subject to the methods they employ. In order to "see" him, the women are told they have to go to where he will now — in some unspecified way — be carrying on with what he was doing before. One "meets" Jesus, the messenger of God who manifests God's reality, only by going where he is, to Galilee where he first initiated his audacious project. To "see God," Jon Sobrino has written, "one has to go to where God is."

In the other Gospels, the disciples encounter Jesus, but the accounts are not consistent. At times he appears, but the disciples do not recognize him, at least not at first. In the story of the road to Emmaus, two depressed followers meet a stranger who walks along with them but does not seem to know about the death of Jesus or the hopes they had attached to him. Only after they have sat down to eat with him do they recognize who he is. In another passage Jesus joins his disciples even though the doors and windows are barred. In another he sits on the beach and eats charcoal-broiled fish with them. St. Paul insists that he never met Jesus in the flesh, but that this Jesus spoke to him after he had been hurled to the ground while on the way to Damascus. Some of the disciples "see" Jesus. Some hear his voice but do not see him. Some, like Thomas, touch him. All the human senses are called on, stretched to and beyond their limits, to express something that by its nature transcends normal human senses.

Clearly these disparate reports are *not* describing a revivified corpse. But they are not talking about a ghost either. Within the limitations of human language, they are describing something the disciples believed was both utterly real and unique. Obviously the passages do not encourage us to think that we can do much better, or can locate and describe in some unambiguous way the "something" they are desperately groping to express. On this score I simply had to disappoint the craving of my students to find out "what really happened." I had to leave them to puzzle over these elusive reports as generations before them had done.

Still, two elements do seem to tie all these stories together. The first is that the confidence that Jesus was still alive did not originate in people hearing *about* an empty tomb or *about* the Resurrection and then *assenting* to the reports. St. Paul, for example, whose letters date from immediately after the Crucifixion, appears never to have heard about an empty tomb. Also, the confidence that Jesus was somehow alive began with an experience that convinced a dejected gaggle of followers that Jesus was still with them. Experience came first and narrative second. Then, of course, the two became intertwined so that for succeeding generations they became inextricable. The story began to trigger the experience. The experience sustained the story.

Second, in each of these encounters Jesus has the same message: *He wants them to keep on doing what he was doing,* to continue to announce and demonstrate the reality — albeit hidden — of the dawning reign of God, the birthing pangs of the age of shalom. He assures them that he will be with them as they set out to tell his story and the stories he told. This fusion of experience and assignment, encounter and project, is what keeps them going in a world that had already proven what it could do to nobodies who circulated such ideas.

For some theologians, this continuation of the work of Jesus in the life and work of his followers *is* the elusive "something" to which the Resurrection stories point. "Jesus Christ is risen" means Jesus lives in the lives and actions of those who once followed him, and still do. "The cause of Jesus," as some of them put it, "moves forward," and this is what the disciples were straining to say in their contradictory descriptions of their encounters with their crucified friend.

This sounds plausible, and it appeals to many people today. But its logic merely pushes the question back one more step. Jesus not only announced his "cause," the coming of God's shalom, he also acted it out — by dining with sinners and embracing lepers, for example. At times he even seemed to identify himself with it, for example, by riding into Jerusalem on a donkey. He was not just its publicist, he was its initiator. The disciples of course remembered this, and they were convinced not only that "the cause of Jesus" was continuing, that his struggles and his project would still go on; they also personalized it. They refused to separate the person from the program. They were also convinced that he himself was somehow living in their midst — albeit in a manner quite different from the way he had been with them before his death — and that was *why* the project could and would go on. This integral connection between Jesus and his mission, between the personality and the program, has generated countless attempts at explanation. None of them is totally satisfactory. They revolve around issues like the connection between the "Jesus of history" and the "Christ of faith," or between Jesus as prototype or archetype and the "spirit of Christ" that inspired succeeding generations. The link between Jesus and his "cause" also reminds us that for many, if not most, of those who have seen themselves as advocates of God's shalom, some personal experience of Jesus, and not just his message, has been a large part of their motivation.

None of this makes it any easier to believe in the Resurrection. In fact, I think the words *believe in* are misleading in this context. Confidence, hope, and trust are more appropriate perspectives on the Resurrection. If what lies behind, and shines through, the Resurrection stories is true, as Christianity teaches, it requires a huge step. It involves not just a sharply modified view of God and of Jesus, but also of the whole of historical reality. If God's vindication of Jesus had been a once-only exception to the closed web of cause and effect, it could be dismissed as an anomaly. It might not be all that significant. Sometimes even the inexplicable happens. But to see beneath the culture-bound language of the Easter story and into its inner reality involves more than accepting an isolated aberration. It is to make a life choice, to live by the hope that this is what reality is really like. Therefore hope, not belief, is what the story seeks to evoke, a hope that is not based on weighing possibilities but on one's own perception of what is most real in life — what some people call "God" — especially at times when there seems to be no way out.

Such a perception is even more radical than achieving Zen enlightenment. The whole world takes on a different visage. What once seemed hopeless is no longer so. What appeared to be final and crushing defeats become temporary setbacks. One begins to see possibilities where there were once only immovable obstacles. As Martin Luther King, Jr., used to say, you can only keep going against what seem to be impossible odds if you have "cosmic allies." To nourish the Easter faith is to allow oneself to hope that despite eons of injustice, pain, and death, in some way that now eludes our most vivid imagination, God's shalom will triumph in the end. This is a hope, though based on different grounds, both Jews and Christians can share.

But surely others can share the hope, too. The exodus motif originated with the Jews. It was embraced by Christians and applied to the Resurrection of Jesus. Both are about the final victory of God's shalom. But there is no reason why the same hope for a world where violence and hatred are abolished cannot be embraced by people of other religions and by those who do not adhere to any religious tradition. The exodus story suggests that God — that ultimate reality — stands on the side of all peoples who cherish this hope, not just the ancient Israelites. The Easter story means that God eventually vindicates the victims of all forms of persecution, not just persecution at the hands of the Romans. If these stories cannot be parsed to include the hopes of all peoples, then we are left with a tribal god who will be rightly dismissed by those who hold no church or synagogue membership card.

After I broke my silence about the Easter story, I told my students I did not expect them either to accept it or reject it on my authority. I warned them that it would make no sense at all unless they were personally involved, whatever they called it, in what Christians call the coming of God's reign, that often discouraging effort to establish what Jews call God's shalom in a world that seems constantly to defeat and frustrate it. I told them they need not expect to have anything like the "Resurrection experiences" reported in the Gospels (though I would not exclude the possibility), but that they should be alert in their own lives for analogies. I once saw a vivid poster in El Salvador of a contemporary pietà, a young woman weeping over the body of a young man whose body is riddled with bullet holes. But from the wounds spring twigs and tiny leaves: life out of death. We need new and daring metaphors for what the earliest Christians coded in the language of resurrection. They used the most potent vocabulary they had available, and we must do the same.

I also conceded that a classroom in a comfortable university where detachment and critical observation are what everybody expects might be the least likely place to ponder the Easter story, or to decide whether to live as though life will eventually triumph over death, and shalom over injustice. I said that my own Resurrection hope is not based on understanding it, which I definitely do not, but on something much deeper in my marrow. I told them that I was surest about it when I was locked in a southern jail during the civil rights movement and heard the young black people with whom I had been arrested singing "We Shall Overcome" at the top of their lungs in the next cell. If you want to meet God, you have to go where God is.

This, of course, is only my own interpretation of what the Resurrection story means. I *do* recognize that there are many other possible interpretations, and I would not discount any of them. In fact, "interpretation" is a very secondary matter. The "something" eludes all our theories and interpretations. But we have the *story,* and when the experience it conveys and evokes makes a real difference in our lives, the various theories all begin to sound less important.

Telling the Easter story in a classroom, or anywhere, is a risky enterprise. Still, despite my initial reluctance to talk about them, the highly fragmented and enigmatic narratives of the Resurrection make up a story no one can skip over. The Passover narrative from which this story emerged, the impossible-to-define "something" to which it points, and the way the world looks from the angle it creates, all provide an indispensable lens. But the story fails unless it opens the listener to an underlying reality that no story can adequately tell.

I was glad I had finally made the slippery move from silence to speech. In making it I even felt I shared a bit of the early Christian bewilderment and exasperation about how to tell other people what had happened to their friend and to them. But, like them, I was left with a lot of loose ends, and my students would not let me forget them. And one loose end in particular they simply would not let go of: What *did* happen to that *body?*

26

The Laughter of the Universe

If therefore they tell you, "He is there in the wilderness," do not go out;
or if they say, "He is there in the inner room," do not believe it. Like a
lightning-flash, that lights the sky from east to west, will be the coming
of the Son of Man.

Wherever the carcass is, there will the vultures gather.

— MATTHEW 24:26–28

YEAR AFTER YEAR the question of what happened to Jesus'
body always seemed to intrigue my students. I think I know
why. On top of all their assignments they also found time to
read paperback novels, and they often mentioned those with religious themes in class. Almost every year a featherweight "religious"
bestseller appears, and the plots are quite similar. The lead character, sometimes a renegade priest, shadowed by whiskey, memories
of a woman, or metaphysical doubt, stumbles upon something near
Jerusalem — a grave, an urn, or maybe even a skeleton that could be
that of Jesus. The news begins to leak out, but of course church authorities from the pope down try to hush up the sensational new
find. They realize that if the word gets around, their game is up.
The plot then wends its way through pages of predictable intrigue,
scheming prelates, shameless deceit, sexual hanky-panky, and cun-
ning cover-up. Such potboilers never come to a satisfying ending,
but that seems beside the point. It is the sensational premise that
intrigues readers, including many of my students, who regularly
showed me their marked-up copies of one of these Holy Land
thrillers and asked, "But what if . . . ?"

Apparently the early Christians also entertained some confusion about what had happened to the body of Jesus. Some of them answered in what is now called the Ascension: It is what might be called "the vertical solution." The risen Jesus leaves his disciples and goes (up) to be with God. Therefore there is no body to be found. But this is one of those cases in which paying attention to the work of the historical-critical scholars can be helpful. The truth is that the accounts of the Ascension in Luke and Acts have been edited, added to, and rewritten so many times that a complete critical edition of the New Testament requires nearly a full page of footnotes to list all the possible variants. Some of these alternatives have Jesus saying "Peace to you" as he leaves. Some do not. Some have him showing the disciples the wounds on his hands and feet, presumably to make sure they did not assume he was a ghost. Still others say "and he was carried up from them" or "and he was carried up to heaven." All this editorializing suggests that the question of what happened to Jesus after the Resurrection was also a disputed issue for his earliest followers. Many hoped that the idea of the Ascension would solve it. But apparently it didn't. The little word *up* made it into some translations, mainly older ones, but not into the newer ones that are based on better manuscript evidence. Consequently we are left to sort through the same problem they disagreed about.

The fatal flaw in the way the vertical solution is phrased is that it is constructed on a spatial metaphor. Some medieval paintings show the disciples gazing upward, jaws agape, at a pair of feet disappearing into a cloud. Whenever I projected this slide, the class invariably giggled. One student told me it reminded him of a takeoff of the space shuttle. Symbols that work superbly in one era can cause confusion and even evoke derision in another. Obviously we need to find new metaphors to convey the intention of these early believers. But what were they trying to say?

In the simplest terms, I think they were trying to express their conviction that the risen Jesus was neither a revivified corpse nor an ectoplasmic phantom, but something new and unique. They were convinced that although he was no longer with them in the way he once was, he was, nevertheless, still with them. For St. Paul and the earliest Christians, the most important thing about the Resurrection was that it was *just the beginning*. It was the first act in an immense re-creation and renewal of the entire cosmos. Therefore the *nature* of the Resurrection body was not insignificant. Years before Luke's account was compiled, St. Paul had written, against the fundamentalists of his time, "flesh and blood do not inherit the Kingdom of God." But he had also insisted, against the other side (the "spiritualizers"), that the Resurrection — that of Christ and that of all creation — involves what he called a "spiritual body." Paul Tillich helpfully explains that this curious phrase may sound like an oxymoron, but it is actually vital because it contains a "double negation." Its daring fusion of these two contradictory words — body and spirit — signals that we are in the realm of poetry and imagination. But, just as important, it also reminds us that our bodily corpuscles are inextricably linked in a vast interdependent web to the tiniest microbes and the vastest spiral nebulae.

The fact that Jesus continued to have a body after the Resurrection that heralded the beginning of the "new creation" meant for the early Christians that the new creation would not be *ex nihilo*. It would transform the *existing* world. "Spiritual body" is poetic. But it differentiates the idea of resurrection from that of immortality, which is exclusively spiritual, and from reincarnation, which perpetuates ordinary bodily continuity in another life form. Human bodies are enmeshed both in history and in nature. The poetic symbol "spiritual body" says that whatever new world God is creating will not cancel out the world we live in now. Christianity is not about pie in the sky by and by, but a "kingdom come on earth."

This casts a helpful light on our ecological plight. Human beings and animals and plants are indeed all in peril together on spaceship Earth. But so is the ship itself, and the cosmic sea through which it plies, in peril. All are made of the same stuff, and have a common destiny. Any ultimate fulfillment of history cannot focus exclusively on human history, to say nothing of one's own personal history. It must be a hope for a reality that existed quite well for several billion years before *Homo sapiens* appeared, and a hope for even such tiny neighbors as the outermost moon of Jupiter. "Don't get any exaggerated delusions about your place in the big picture," says the voice from the whirlwind to Job. "Where were you when I laid the earth's foundations of the world while the morning stars sang in chorus?" A modern paraphrase might read, "Where were you when the spiral nebulae began to cool or when the triceratops roamed the earth?" This puts us as human beings in our place. The Christian view of the future, initiated in the Resurrection, includes both the earthworms and the black holes. There was a time when this entrenchment of the human in the loam and rock of the universe was not acceptable rhetoric. But since the rise of the ecological movement, with its emphasis on the interdependence of every molecule, it no longer sounds so strange. It even makes Jesus' words at the Last Supper, when he holds a piece of bread and says, "This is my body," sound more sensible. His body, like our bodies, was an inextricable part of the universe. Perhaps that is why the prescient Jesuit paleontologist Pierre Teilhard de Chardin could speak of the earth as the altar on which the mass of life is constantly celebrated.

I learned, however, to be careful when I linked Jesus or the Resurrection to ecology. Concern for the earth is rightly one of the most popular causes among students today, and they were looking for ammunition wherever they could find it. I wanted to give them all the help I could, but I sometimes worried that in their welcome rediscovery of our indissoluble oneness with the soil and the seaweed, they were sometimes asking too much of Mother Earth. They looked to her not just as our mother but also as our savior, a role for which the earth is plainly not suited. I feared that exalting the earth into a goddess, Gaia, as some students did, had become an ill-advised overreaction to her thoughtless devastation by bulldozers and power saws. Desecration had been replaced by sacralization. But deifying Mother Earth fails to appreciate that she shares our finitude and our mortality. Like all of us, sooner or later, she too is fated for destruction. She will eventually burn to an ash in the explosion of the dying sun.

The earth is not God, but God's creation. Our hope should not be *in* her but *for* her. Again, as St. Paul (not a literalist) says, it is not just human beings, and not just our home planet, but the whole creation that "groaneth and travaileth" as, along with us, it awaits its total liberation from death and bondage as well as from the humiliation it has suffered at human hands (Romans 8:18–24).

Admittedly this is a sweeping vision. But why should we settle for less? Christian eschatology in the final analysis is nothing more or less than the confidence that the same Unnamable One who called the worlds into being, freed the Israelites from the sweatshops of Egypt, initiated on Easter the ultimate vindication of the victims of all sweatshops, and promised the liberation of the cosmos from its captivity to death is still present among us. Sweeping indeed, perhaps too much so. But that is what the Christian hope is. We can discard it if we must. There are thoughtful people who have done so. But we should not whittle it down to something manageable and lackluster.

If the early Christian ideas of how Jesus left were confused and divergent, views about what would come next were even more so. The Gospel of John teaches that renewal of the Creation, having begun with Jesus, is now continuing. No further intervention seems in store. Other Gospel writers looked for a rapid return of Christ, perhaps even within the lifetime of the authors. We discussed some of these competing visions in Chapter 17, on Armageddon. But the belief that persisted, and eventually found its way into the historic creeds of the churches, states that he "will come again in glory." For most people this is at best a confused concept. A cluster of symbols — "Second Coming," "Coming Again," "Return of Christ," "Glorious Appearing," "Judgment Day" — all dance in disordered pandemonium in their minds. The four Gospels themselves do not agree on any of this, and some theologians insist that the whole idea of a *second* coming, as though Christ does not continue to be present in the world, is misleading and possibly even a mistranslation.

The key Greek word in question is *parousia*, which can mean many things. It means "return" or "arrival," but it can also mean "presence," or "appearing." Jürgen Moltmann in his *Coming of God* says, "To translate *parousia* as 'coming again' or 'second coming' is wrong, because it presupposes a temporary absence. The Christian message, he says, is that God has come, and that God has never left. There is convincing evidence for this reading. Paul, in the First Epistle to Timothy, uses the word *parousia* to refer to the earthly life of Jesus. In the fourth chapter the King James Version translates *parousia* not as "coming," but as "appearing." Jesus himself, in the concluding verses of Matthew, sends his disciples out and promises them, "I am with you always, to the close of the age" (Matthew 28:20).

Unfortunately, the idea of a second coming has done considerable harm in Christian usage. It plays into the ever-inventive hands of prognosticators and end-time schedule scribblers. *Appearing* seems to be the better term because it suggests the presence — perhaps someday in a new and fuller way — of one who has been here all along.

Still, I am not ready to discard the idea of "return" completely, and I had no choice but to admit my uncertainty to my students. The reason is that the themes of exile and return are so central to the biblical faith, and especially since Jews still live by them, I am reluctant to abandon them. They strike a resonant note to many ears today. We do often experience God as absent as much as present. Can we hope for a time when God will be fully present? Again the wisdom of the Jewish sages helps. Through centuries of reflection on persecution and expulsion, some rabbis came to the startling and profound insight that *God is also in exile*. God himself (or herself, and in this case, as we will see, "herself" is better) shares in the dislocation and alienation of the world's peoples. But along with God's exile, the rabbis also taught that the *shekinah*, the relational Spirit of God, the feminine side of the deity, stays with us faithfully even in our exile. In the Jewish vision, however, exile and return, absence and presence, are not temporal. They are inevitable facets of human experience, and they are always with us.

This is an area in which Christian theology can enter into a more profitable partnership with Jewish thought. The idea of a temporal second coming that will happen next week, next year, or next millennium inevitably feeds reckless speculation, like the *Left Behind* series. The Jewish idea of the *shekinah,* on the other hand, suggests a parallel to the Christian conviction that the hidden God, the *deus absconditus,* is nonetheless with us, but in a way God chooses, not in the way we might prefer. Rather than seeing the *parousia* as the "coming again" of an absent one, we can see it as the manifesting of the one who has been present with us all the time, albeit often unrecognized, like the Jesus on the road to Emmaus whose disciples did not recognize him until they ate together at the end of the journey. We experience the God who "returns" as having been with us all along, especially among the misfits and losers in the great rat race — among whom we might least expect to find him or her.

The idea of a second coming, as we saw in Chapter 17, is always tied up with conjecture about the end of the space-time continuum, the "world as we know it." These are the kinds of Big Questions late adolescents love to think about. Every year many of my students wanted to write their term papers about them, usually bringing in some recent theory about the expanding universe shrinking back to its original pinhead size, or a colossal black hole swallowing everything into its inner vacuum. I was usually reluctant to encourage them to dart off in this direction. After all, this was a course in moral reasoning, not cosmology. But I sometimes softened and let them go ahead, if only to see what they came up with.

Still, their instincts were not entirely wrong. They were thinking about eschatology, which, as someone once wisely said, is not about the end-time. It is about the end *of* time, the transcending of the cramped temporal container within which we mortals must think even though we sense there is something else and something more. As a child in church, I lustily sang a gospel song with the line, "When the trumpet of the Lord shall sound and time shall be no more." But what could it mean, I wondered, that "time shall be no more"? I sometimes became so absorbed musing about that extraordinary phrase that the sermon, which often had seemed endless, flew by. Time had, at least temporarily, disappeared.

I still ponder that phrase. Indeed, here we reach the limits of theological discourse, where stories explode into poetry. It is impossible to conceive of a "time" when "was," "is," and "will be" shall be no more. This is one reason why I believe any Christian view of the details of the ultimate destiny should be robust in scope but modest in detail. We can sing about it, but we cannot describe it.

Christian language about resurrection, ascension, and return is now passing through a time of crisis. I believe the underlying reality these ancient formulas point to is true. But by now the imagery is so obsolete it has become misleading. We desperately need a new language, but we cannot simply concoct it. When it comes, it will spring, as it always has, from the borderline between the conscious and the unconscious, where imagination and the mundane mingle, where myth and history intersect.

As the semester drew to a close, I always wanted to leave the class with both an appreciation for the classical symbols and a recognition of our need for new ones. But how could I do it? Giving a lecture, however eloquent, on the need for a new idiom seemed contradictory. That is why we have artists and composers, and especially poets. I also wanted them to carry away as a final impression the realization that "the moral life" is much larger than moral reasoning. I tried various strategies from year to year. For a while I projected the score of Handel's "Hallelujah Chorus" on a screen, played a tape of the Mormon Tabernacle Choir singing it, and invited the students to stand and join in if they liked. Most of them did, and some years we had a chorus of several hundred voices shaking the walls of the lecture hall. After a few years, however, an associate dean delicately suggested to me that this might not be an entirely appropriate activity in an academic course. Then for a couple years I simply asked them to sit and listen while I played excerpts from Mozart's *Requiem*. Later still I tried poetry, especially what the great laureates had said about how things — including the semester and the world — end. I read from Robert Frost, who wrote that from what he knew of desire, the world would probably end with fire, and from T. S. Eliot, who thought it would happen not with a bang but a whimper. It was Dante, however, who surpassed them all. In *The Divine Comedy* he depicts his gradual ascent from the inferno through the *purgatorio* to the gates of heaven. There is no reason, however, why we cannot read it as his inspired fantasy on the course of human history. But even though he had proven himself to be an unrivaled master of vivid description in the early cantos, as he approaches the full presence of God, visual images seem to fail him, so he modulates to another key. As he draws near the highest celestial sphere, he says that he heard a sound he had never heard before. Pausing, he listens. *"Me sembiana un riso del universo,"* he writes. It sounded "like the laughter of the universe."

As my own association with the class was drawing to a close in its latter years, I liked to read these lines, first in Italian and then in English, on the last day of the semester. It rolled all the themes into one. Like the parables, it was a surprise climax. It was a masterpiece of imagination. It celebrated a hope that words could not capture. I could think of no better way of ending the course. The whole universe laughing? The solar system, the Milky Way, the hundred billion galaxies that surround our earthly protons, all bent over in convulsions of hilarity? A laughter that somehow catches up an entire history of sobs and cries of pain? The last laugh of the God of life after so many deaths and defeats? Was it too much to hope for? Maybe so, but why hope for anything less?

Postscript

WHENEVER I HAD FINISHED the last lecture, graded the last exam, and read the last term paper for Jesus and the Moral Life, I inevitably underwent the academic equivalent of postpartum depression. I missed the students, the zesty give-and-take of the discussions, the continuous eruption of new moral quandaries, and the constant upsetting of my expectations about what would happen next. After a few weeks I usually regained my normal balance, and soon began thinking about how I would approach the course the next year. Given the relentless flood of books about Jesus, and articles about newly emerging ethical questions, there was a stack of reading to do and a lot of conversations to pursue. As the years went by I would often meet ex-students and alumni who wanted to chat about their memories of the course. Some offered criticisms and suggestions, which I tried to take into account.

Then, after nearly twenty years, when I decided to "retire" the course, I had to cope with a new kind of sadness, something closer to mourning, or what in Portuguese is called *saudade,* a kind of bittersweet sorrow. A couple of times I stepped into one of the large classrooms where, for twenty years, I had lectured twice a week. As I should have known, these excursions into nostalgia did nothing to assuage my grief. Eventually I decided to take a more constructive approach. I would evaluate how — or whether — taking the course had actually affected the moral reasoning of the students. I had given out hundreds of grades in the course. Now it was time to grade the course itself.

I used a very unscientific approach. Whenever I ran into an ex-student who had taken the course, I fired a small barrage of questions. I went back to the original objectives of the Moral Reasoning division of the core curriculum, and to my own convictions about the basic components of the moral life. Given the inconvenient fact that moral choices rarely announce themselves as such, but come to us garbed in other kinds of decisions — financial, clinical, political — had the course helped the students to recognize a moral decision when it appeared?

Most ex-students thought it had. We had talked about family relationships, politics, genetics, money, sexuality, class, intergenerational conflict, medical procedures, race, ecology, torture, violence and nonviolence, death and dying, leadership styles, and dozens of other topics. In fact, some students told me we had covered too many issues too quickly, and they were glad they had been able to devote their term papers to exploring one of them more thoroughly. Still, I thought the course deserved a fairly high grade for helping students see an issue as a moral one.

What about being able to decide what was the "right thing to do"? That was a trickier matter. In the light of the stories by and about Jesus, we came to a rough consensus on some issues. But on many other questions we did not. It was clear that different students would have different ideas of what "the right thing" was in any given case. Maybe the course had helped them eliminate a certain amount of unreflective behavior, but in a world where there are always innumerable imponderables, it was clear that they had all had to learn to live with the realization that even our best-informed decisions might be wrong. Oliver Cromwell famously wrote in 1650 in his letter to the Assembly of the Church of Scotland, "I beseech you, in the bowels of Christ, think it possible you may be mistaken." Three hundred years later Judge Learned Hand said that he wished those words could be inscribed "over the portals of every church, every school, and every courthouse, and, may I say, of every legislative body in the United States."

It is widely recognized that Cromwell's admission that he might be mistaken did not prevent him from taking decisive actions, many of which now appear hasty and heartless. His cruelty to the Irish is still remembered by their descendants today. Still, if the course had helped students to learn that other people might sincerely arrive at decisions about what was right that were quite different from their own, that was an important gain.

Students often told me that although they had begun the course feeling tongue-tied about moral choices, even the ones they cared about deeply, the discussions had done two things. They had taught them how to present their beliefs in a more coherent way, and had pushed them into reexamining even their firmest convictions, to "think it possible" that they too "might be mistaken." Their comments made me recall some of the early reservations I had had about offering such a course. The colleagues who had told me that careful discussion and study could hone students' skills in moral reasoning had been right, at least in part. The course, it seems, had raised the level of moral discourse, if only a little bit, and only for those students who took it seriously. But I was even more convinced that my strategy of building on the real-life choices people face, especially the ones the students themselves confronted, and not hypothetical cases, had saved the course from becoming merely a theoretical parlor game. The students knew that these issues were not just "case studies"; they were indeed the real thing. I decided that the course probably deserved a fairly good grade in this respect, if not an A plus.

But what about the Big Question: moral courage? Having learned to recognize moral choices and to sort out what they believed was the right thing to do, would they have the inner fiber to *do* it? Would they summon the fortitude to bear the consequences of unpopular decisions, to remain steadfast when opposition and ridicule engulfed them?

It was hard, if not impossible, for my ex-students to answer this. Clearly it was an important objective of the course, but the real results would appear only much later. What would happen when, fifteen or twenty years after their graduation, they were faced with a hard moral choice, recognized it, decided on the right action . . . but then were tempted to choose an easier way? These might be choices that no one else would know about. No classmates would challenge them in an obsolete ROTC building. No professor would put question marks in the margins of a term paper. One of the lessons I had tried to get across to them was how important it is to continue discussing moral choices with other people, but they might not always be willing or able to do so. In some cases, of course, they would fail the moral courage test. Other people might ultimately find out about their lapse, but even more frequently they would have only their own consciences to answer to. What would they do?

This was obviously an area in which only one of the grading options given us by the college registrar seemed fully appropriate: "incomplete." That grade is reserved for students who, on reasonable grounds and with previous approval, postpone handing in a term paper or taking an exam. Usually, however, an "incomplete" must be completed before the end of the following semester. In this case, however, we would all have to live with a permanent incomplete, not just for the students, but also for the course itself.

The question "What would Jesus think and what would he do if he returned today?" has spawned a deluge of theory, fiction, and chatter over the years. Some of it has been downright silly. Most of it is not very helpful. Much of it fails because those asking the question have an obvious ax to grind. It also fails because most people do not remember that Jesus was a rabbi, and therefore had a characteristic way of approaching issues — posing more questions and telling stories rather than delivering definitive answers. Still, the underlying question — what would he do today? — is not as silly as some sophisticated critics think. But to respond to it requires a huge step beyond the parameters of most biblical scholarship and ethical theory.

It requires a leap into situations Jesus never faced: a leap of imagination. I do not believe those who claim the human faculty for imagining is dead or dying today. There is too much evidence to the contrary. It may be weakened, but it can be nourished and strengthened. If imagination is fed a rich diet of stories, it can once again be brought to bear on the moral questions we grapple with throughout our lives.

After some years of evaluating whether the Jesus course had made any real impact on the students, I had an even thornier question to confront: How had it influenced me? This was a hard one, because the figure of Jesus had been important to me for as long as I could remember, and my relationship to him had always been (I use the word quite consciously) a friendly one. As a child I had sometimes pictured God as a bearded old man with a frowning countenance. I never envisioned the Holy Spirit at all. And Mary I knew only as Jesus' mother. But my favorite gospel song had always been "What a Friend We Have in Jesus." That was the term for Jesus I liked: *friend*. It was even better than "Savior" or "Lord." I knew these were significant designations too, but "friend" topped the list.

During my years of study and teaching I have read many criticisms of envisioning Jesus as a friend. To some it appears to be overly intimate, glib, or childish. Psychologists warn against clinging too long to the babyish habit of having an invisible playmate or a "magic helper." Some theologians deprecate using "friend" for Jesus because it diminishes the majesty and transcendence of the divine. But I was never swayed by these arguments. We have only human language and our experience of human bonds to express ourselves, and these supply the metaphors we must draw on to talk about Jesus: everything from lover to king, and from "lily of the valley" to "bright and morning star." Among all these, I still think that "friend" comes closest, not just to conveying how I experience my relationship with Jesus, but to the core of Jesus' message itself.

I am not the only one. Even though the term *friend* has its sophisticated critics, it also has its equally sophisticated defenders. A friend is one who loves and accepts us despite our faults, enjoys our company, and sticks with us in the most trying times. Karl Barth, the most prominent Protestant theologian of the twentieth century, once remarked that his entire multivolume theology could be summed up with the phrase, "God is *for* us." The theologian who influenced me most, Dietrich Bonhoeffer, described Jesus simply as "the man for other men." I think both men were right. The entire message of Jesus is that God has freely chosen, like the best of friends, to "be with" all human beings, especially those who would otherwise be friendless, to the bitter end.

The biggest challenge, both personally and intellectually, I had to grapple with as I taught the course was that Jesus had meant so many different things to so many different people. Scholars like Jaroslav Pelikan and Charlotte Allen have skillfully cataloged the staggering variety of "takes" that have emerged over the centuries, some to fade quickly, others to persist to the present. Recently Stephen Prothero has charted the evolving renderings of Jesus that have sprung up in American history. Who remembers now that the man from Nazareth was once construed as both the exemplary paradigm of a pared-down ethical deism (by Thomas Jefferson) and as a nearly crazed apocalyptic visionary (by Albert Schweitzer)? Bruce Barton portrayed him as a talented super-salesman, a tycoon in the making. One writer even suggested that Jesus had never existed as a person, that the name was applied to a psychedelic weed imbibed by a wandering band of first-century nomads. I remember times when both the students and I were troubled and puzzled at what seemed to be the endless plethora of identities conferred on this one man. Some seemed frivolous, some demeaning. Was there any limit? How could anyone make anything of such a chaotic jumble?

As the years went by, however, I noticed two things about this theological disarray. The first was that although interpretations of Jesus seemed to multiply, there were some that just did not stick. Hitler's philosophers tried briefly to make Jesus into an anti-Semite, but won only the most fervent Nazis to such a bizarre concept. Followers of Castro once circulated a poster of Jesus carrying an automatic rifle, but only a handful of people were taken in, and the poster is now a collector's item. This gave me a certain confidence that Jesus may be supple, but he is not endlessly elastic. Somehow we keep coming back to the biblical stories, the ones he told and the ones that were told about him. And Jesus always seems to survive all the distorted portraits.

The other thing I noticed was that this proliferation of interpretations is not just a recent development. There was never a time when there were not many versions of Jesus in circulation. Christians have never been unanimous about who he was, and this is one of the healthiest features of Christianity: It has never been univocal. I am glad we have four Gospels, not one. They describe a Jesus who is recognizably the same person, but they do not agree on everything about him. They are different not just because they were written for different audiences, but because Mark's understanding of Jesus differed in some ways from Matthew's, and Luke's differed from John's. If we had only one gospel it would be a terrible loss. We would feel hemmed in and coerced. The possibility for creativity and change we need in our understandings of Jesus would be stymied, and it would deny the heart of Jesus' message, which invited reciprocity and imaginative response, and still does.

It is also enormously significant to me that the church has lost whatever monopoly it once had, or claimed to have, to control interpretations of Jesus. He does not belong to any ecclesiastical institution. He never did. If now he "belongs to the world," that is as it should be. If Muslims and Buddhists, feminists and humanists want to claim him, that is entirely appropriate, so long as they recognize that their versions cannot be the definitive one either.

I am not really worried about depictions of Jesus as a hallucinatory plant, a bouncy business magnate, or even a well-intentioned psychopath. I am confident Jesus can shake off these strange grave clothes and stun even the best-armed sentinels of the tombs in which they have buried him. The forceful question the angel asks the three women who appear at the grave on Easter Sunday is still the appropriate one: "Why seek ye the living among the dead?"

After decades of writing, thinking, and teaching about him, I can honestly report that I still think of Jesus as a friend, but I find him ever more elusive and impossible to pin down. Every so often he takes me by surprise. I catch a glimpse of him sometimes on wintry afternoons strolling through Harvard Yard; chatting with sophomores, Ph.D. candidates, and faculty members; dunking doughnuts in coffee with the maids and janitors; helping the students who run the homeless shelters in the church basements to make up the beds for another cold night. Sometimes I see him as one of the shivering homeless men or women who wander into those shelters. But why should I be surprised? He is where he always was, doing what he was always doing: teaching, chatting, eating and drinking without regard to rank. Today, like then, he meets the same mixture of welcome and hesitation, skepticism and rejection. He runs the constant risk of real trouble with both the religious and the political establishments. But he gently forces people to look at life differently and maybe even to live it differently.

Jesus did come to Harvard, but not just once. I am sure he was there long before I taught Jesus and the Moral Life, and that he did not leave town when I closed the books on the course. He is still there, still elusive, still hard to pin down. But he is a persistent one, that rabbi. He just won't let up.

NOTES

ACKNOWLEDGMENTS

INDEX

Notes

Introduction

page

4 *the most famous example:* Even atheists have been drawn to the moral example of Jesus. The original German title of the book by Milan Machovec, translated into English as *A Marxist Looks at Jesus* (London: Darton, Longman and Todd, 1976), was *Jesus fur Atheisten.*

4 *the claims of both these groups:* See also Jarif Khalidi, *The Muslim Jesus: Sayings and Stories in Islamic Literature* (Cambridge, Mass.: Harvard University Press, 2001), and Beatrice Bruteau (ed.), *Jesus Through Jewish Eyes: Rabbis and Scholars Engage an Ancient Brother in a New Conversation* (Maryknoll, N.Y.: Orbis Books, 2001).

1: He Was Then, We Are Now

16 *a prominent role in the Qur'an:* The best of these efforts to recover the "historical Jesus" is that of Dominic Crossan, *The Historical Jesus: The Life of a Mediterranean Peasant* (San Francisco: HarperSanFrancisco, 1991). More recently Crossan, along with Jonathan L. Reed, has published *Excavating Jesus: Beneath the Stones, Behind the Texts* (San Francisco: HarperSanFrancisco, 2003).

19 *the exaggerated expectations of its audience:* For a fascinating exchange between two scholars who use similar methods but come to somewhat different conclusions, see Marcus Borg and N. T. Wright, *The Meaning of Jesus* (New York: HarperCollins, 1999).

19 *it also left him as one:* One important exception to "leaving" the historical Jesus is the work of Marcus J. Borg, one of the key figures in

the Jesus seminar. See his *Meeting Jesus Again for the First Time* (San Francisco: HarperSanFrancisco, 1994).

2: Rabbi Jesus on the Scene

25 *stands taken:* Edith Wyschogrod, *Saints and Postmodernism: Revisioning Moral Philosophy* (Chicago: University of Chicago Press, 1990), p. xxii.

25 *"of the mind and not others":* Martha C. Nussbaum, *Poetic Justice: The Literary Imagination and Public Life* (Boston: Beacon Press, 1995), p. 9. Nussbaum says she is here drawing her argument from Wayne Booth's *The Company We Keep: An Ethics of Fiction* (Berkeley and Los Angeles: University of California Press, 1988), pp. 70–77. See also Nussbaum's *Upheavals of Thought: The Intelligence of Emotions* (New York: Cambridge University Press, 2001).

27 *only "Bible" Jesus ever knew:* It should be recalled also that the vast majority of people at the time of Jesus were illiterate, and therefore they knew this "Bible" not by reading it but through the oral tradition.

3: A World Full of Stories

32 *"is one long story":* Quoted in Noam Zion and David Dishon, *A Different Night* (Jerusalem: The Shalom Hertman Institute), p. 45.

35 *"those who do not believe":* Umberto Eco, *Five Moral Pieces* (New York: Harcourt, 2001), p. 29.

35 *"miss the better story":* Yann Martel, *Life of Pi* (New York: Harcourt, 2002). The quotation from *Self* is from "The Man, or the Tiger?" a review by Pankaj Mishra in *The New York Review of Books,* 27 March 2003, p. 17.

36 *his native Romania at the time:* For a chilling glimpse of Eliade's role in Romania before and during World War II, see Mihail Sebastian's *Journal 1935–1944: The Fascist Years* (Chicago: Ivan R. Dee, 2000).

38 *into four levels:* This method was first devised by my colleague Ralph Potter and used in his unpublished doctoral dissertation, "The Structure of Certain American Christian Responses to the Nuclear Dilemma, 1958–1963." The dissertation is deposited in Widener Library, Harvard University.

39 *"are actually produced":* Don Cupit, *What Is a Story?* (London: SCM Press, 1991), p. ix.

40 *"as though it's the only one"*: Arundhati Roy, *The God of Small Things* (New York: HarperCollins, 1998).

41 *"the ability to exchange experiences"*: Walter Benjamin, "The Story-teller," in Hannah Arendt (ed.), *Illuminations* (New York: Schocken Books, 1968), p. 83.

43 *"of stories that are not our own"*: Paul Elie, *The Life You Save May Be Your Own: An American Pilgrimage* (New York: Farrar, Straus and Giroux, 2003), p. 472.

44 *"where it belongs"*: Ibid., p. 472.

4: The Ballad of the Begats

51 *not have been great scholars:* See Dan Cohn-Sherbok, *Fifty Key Jewish Thinkers* (London and New York: Routledge, 1997).

5: Picking Just the Right Woman

57 *"with brown/blue eyes"*: This ad is actually quoted in an article by Connie Zong, "Donors Wanted: The Ivy League Factor in Egg Donations," *The Harvard Science Review,* Vol. 18, No. 2 (Spring 2002), p. 20.

60 *who will carry it until birth:* Ms. Zong describes this procedure at greater length, including the full names of the drugs used, in "Donors Wanted," p. 21.

62 *"take root in her heart"*: Quoted in Sally Cuneen, *In Search of Mary: The Woman and the Symbol* (New York: Ballantine Books, 1996), p. 99.

64 *"against victimization and for survival"*: Ibid., p. 25.

6: Exiles from Eden

68 *around the nearest tree:* See Gary A. Anderson, *The Genesis of Perfection: Adam and Eve in the Christian and Jewish Imagination* (Louisville, Ky.: Westminster/John Knox Press, 2001), for a finely researched account of the many interpretations of the Adam and Eve story. Adam's words, in the passage from Milton, quoted by Anderson on p. ii, are:

> O goodness infinite, goodness immense!
> That of all this good of evil shall produce,
> And evil turn to good; more wonderful
> Than that which by creation first brought forth
> Light from darkness!

71 *"how they looked to me as well":* Martin Buber, *Tales of the Hasidim, Book II* (New York: Schocken Books, 1947), p. 207.

71 *Matthew 19:6:* I have quoted here from the King James translation of the Bible, the one from which the words used in wedding services are most frequently taken.

72 *the story of Mary and the angel:* Maybe I discouraged them too quickly. More recently in his absorbing book *Enough: Saving Humanity in an Engineered Age,* Bill McKibben has demonstrated how many important moral choices are involved in these new techniques (New York: Times Books, 2003).

74 *"with a lovely spirit":* Quoted from David Curzon (ed.), *The Gospels in Our Image* (New York: Harcourt, Brace and Company, 1995).

74 *is not so bad after all:* A highly original exploration of the idea that the Incarnation represents an effort by God to overcome a crisis in his own life can be found in Jack Miles, *Christ: A Crisis in the Life of God* (New York: Alfred A. Knopf, 2001).

7: The Gurus and the Usual Suspects

79 *had previously been acknowledged:* See Marc Hirshman, "Rabbinic Universalism in the 2nd and 3rd Centuries," *The Harvard Theological Review,* No. 932 (Spring 2002), pp. 101–115.

8: Riffing on Simeon

86 *with Jesus is disputed:* Even the historicity of Simeon himself is questioned. My colleague Professor Ellen Aitken thinks that, on balance, he must be viewed as an imaginative creation of Luke himself.

87 *"moments of our own day":* Jacob Neusner, *The Classics of Judaism* (Louisville, Ky.: Westminster/John Knox Press, 1995), p. 94.

88 *"went ahead and violated them":* Ibid., p. 413.

90 *"thy actions by what is certain":* Louis Ginzberg, *Legends of the Bible* (Philadelphia and Jerusalem: The Jewish Publication Society, 1992), p. 239.

9: Beat the Devil

94 *leader would he be:* I am grateful to my colleague Brent Coffin for suggesting this very plausible explanation of what the temptation scene represents.

100 *I plunged ahead:* It is important to recall here that the idea of the Incarnation is the best-known but not the only way Christians have explained the presence of the Spirit of God in Jesus. See, for example,
Roger Haight's brilliant *Jesus: Symbol of God* (Maryknoll, N.Y.: Orbis
Books, 1999) and John Hick, *The Metaphor of God Incarnate: Christology
in a Pluralistic Age* (Louisville, Ky.: Westminster/John Knox Press,
1993).

101 *"no cultivated apathy can feign":* See Hugo Rahner, quoting Bishop
Sailor in *Ignatius the Theologian* (New York: Herder and Herder, 1968),
p. 89.

102 *and the* Odyssey *demonstrates:* Angels have provided a fascinating object
of reflection for theologians for centuries. Thomas Aquinas taught
that angels are not subject to the contradiction between particularity
and universality. Paul Tillich called them "concrete poetic symbols of
the structures or powers of being." The discussions about "archetypes" among psychologists and the dramatic reemergence of the de-
monic in twentieth-century literature demonstrate that the language
may change but the fascination continues. See Paul Tillich, *Systematic
Theology,* Vol. I (Chicago: University of Chicago Press, 1951), p. 260.

10: The Campaign Begins

107 *and applauded his eloquence:* Or were they growling rather than
purring? In his highly readable *The Gospel According to Jesus* (New York:
HarperCollins, 1991), p. 203, Stephen Mitchell claims that the expression "Mary's son," which they used, refers to their belief that he was
illegitimate, and that their other expressions meant something like,
"Who does he think he is?" and "Where does he get this stuff?"

110 *a loud trumpet* (Yobhel *in Hebrew):* Notice that the inscription on the
Liberty Bell in Philadelphia is taken from this section of Leviticus:
"Proclaim liberty throughout the land and to all the inhabitants
thereof."

11: Jesus Retells His People's Story

117 *Anna Kamienska:* Translated from the Polish by David Curzon
Graznya Drabik in David Curzon (ed.), *The Gospels in Our Image: An
Anthology of Twentieth-Century Poetry Based on Biblical Texts* (New York:
Harcourt, Brace and Company), p. 80.

123 *crushing their spirits:* See Francine du Plessix Gray, *Simone Weil* (New York: Viking Penguin, 2001).

124 *wimp or doormat or passive:* I am grateful to Warren Carter's fine book *Matthew and the Margins: A Sociopolitical and Religious Reading* (Maryknoll, N.Y.: Orbis Books, 2000). See especially pages 128–137.

125 *"to live faithfully and expectantly":* Ibid., p. 133.

126 *given such an ostensibly:* Ibid., p. 135.

126 *between humankind and the natural world:* Ibid., p. 135.

12: Salt and Lamps

135 *"which in effect is complete non-cooperation":* Quoted by Sharon Dobbins from Gandhi's *Nonviolent Resistance* in "The Principles of Equity and the Sermon on the Mount as Influence in Gandhi's Truth Force," *The Journal of Law and Religion,* Vol. 6, No. 1 (1988), p. 135. See also Glen Harold Stassen and David P. Gushee, *Kingdom Ethics: Following Jesus in Contemporary Context* (Downers Grove, Ill.: InterVarsity Press, 2003).

13: The Rabbi Teaches Torah

140 *"of their own":* See Michael Lerner's chapter "Fresh Eyes: Current Jewish Renewal Could See Jesus as One Like Themselves" in Beatrice Bruteau (ed.), *Jesus Through Jewish Eyes* (Maryknoll, N.Y.: Orbis Books, 2001), p. 146.

142 *"his own people's piety at its best":* Sherman Johnson, *The Interpreter's Bible,* Vol. 7 (New York: Abingdon Cokesbury Press, 1951), p. 309.

145 *of the Lower East Side:* See Adrian House, *Francis of Assisi* (Mahwah, N.J.: HiddenSpring/Paulist Press, 2001), and Robert Ellsberg (ed.), *Dorothy Day, Selected Writings* (Maryknoll, N.Y.: Orbis Books, 1991).

14: Parables and Zen Slaps

158 *"only through our once experiencing it":* D. T. Suzuki, "Satori, or Enlightenment," in William Barrett (ed.), *Zen Buddhism: Selected Writings of D. T. Suzuki* (Garden City, N.Y.: Doubleday Anchor, 1956), p. 83.

159 *a story with a surprise ending:* See especially Chapter 5 in Amos N. Wilder, *The Language of the Gospel: Early Christian Rhetoric* (New York: Harper and Row, 1964).

15: The Crooked CEO and the Spoiled Brat

168 *by refraining from doing so:* One good example of this "explaining" can be found in Matthew 13:36. It depicts the disciples taking Jesus aside after he has told his well-known parable of the sower. But many scholars view this as an addendum, and a rather self-serving one since it suggests that the disciples are privy to some inside information others do not have.

16: Why the Crowds Came

175 *he did not attend:* See Herbert Benson, *The Mind/Body Effect: How Behavioral Medicine Can Show the Way to Better Health* (New York: Berkeley Publishing, 1979), and, with Margaret Stark, *Timeless Healing: The Power and Biology of Belief* (New York: Scribner, 1996).

17: The Armageddon Syndrome

187 *the* Left Behind *series:* As of this writing there are eleven titles in the series: *Left Behind, Tribulation Force, Nicolae, Soul Harvest, Apollyon, Assassins, The Indwelling, The Mark, Desecration, The Remnant,* and *Armageddon.* All are written by Tim F. LaHaye and Jerry B. Jenkins, and published by Tyndale House, which is located in Wheaton, Illinois.

188 Scarlet and Purple, The Mark of the Beast, *and* In the Twinkling of an Eye: These books were published in London by W. Nicholson and Sons beginning in 1913.

189 *differ from age to age:* Crawford Gribben, "Before Left Behind," *Books and Culture,* July/August 2003, p. 9.

189 *in fifty-four languages:* Hal Lindsey, *The Late Great Planet Earth* (Grand Rapids, Mich.: Zondervan Publishing, 1970).

189 *the establishment of the state of Israel:* See Paul C. Merkley, *The Politics of Christian Zionism 1891–1948* (London: Frank Cass, 1998).

191 *of the* Left Behind *novels:* Reported in an article by Joan Didion, "Mr. Bush and the Divine," *The New York Review of Books,* 6 November 2003, p. 81. This figure, Didion says, includes hardcover books, trade paperbacks, mass market paperbacks, compact discs, audiobooks, e-books, and comic books.

192 *nothing can be done to avoid it:* See Gershom Gorenberg, *The End of*

Days: Fundamentalism and the Struggle for the Temple Mount (New York: The Free Press, 2000), pp. 55ff.

193 *no longer to be in the running:* Probably hundreds of thousands of pages of speculation have been written about the mystery of "666." The most plausible theory is that the numerological equivalent of the name Nero Caesar, when written in Hebrew, adds up to 666. Nero was the notorious persecutor of the early Christian community to whom the author of the book of Revelation was writing.

194 *a large backlog of negative images:* See Laurie Goodstein, "Seeing Islam as 'Evil' Faith, Evangelicals Seek Converts," *The New York Times,* 27 May 2003, p. 1.

198 *all too real:* Robert Jay Lifton, in *Superpower Syndrome: America's Apocalyptic Confrontation with the World* (New York: Nation Books, 2003), describes the origin and the danger of apocalyptic rhetoric.

18: The Transfiguration and the Prophet's Night Journey

207 *"just come out of a bath":* Quoted in Kanan Makiya, *The Rock* (New York: Pantheon, 2001), p. 181.

19: Bridge Burning and Street Theater

213 *who had made the conquest possible:* My colleague Professor Allen Callahan pointed out this clear Roman precedent to Jesus' entry into Jerusalem.

20: Trial and Retrial

221 *to supply a frame of meaning:* For a superb account of this complex mixture of history and prophecy, not just in the accounts of the trial but throughout the Gospels, see Paula Fredriksen, *Jesus of Nazareth* (New York: Random House, 1999).

221 *in operation at the time:* John Dominic Crossan's *Who Killed Jesus?* (San Francisco: HarperSanFrancisco, 1995) is especially valuable because it uncovers some of the roots of anti-Semitism in the way the narratives of the trial of Jesus are compiled.

224 Pontius Pilate: Ann Wroe, *Pontius Pilate* (New York: Random House, 1999).

225 *"the tyranny of hard choices":* Ibid., p. xiv.

226 *clear and present danger to Roman rule:* See Richard Horsely, *Jesus and the Spiral of Violence: Popular Jewish Resistance in Roman Palestine* (San Francisco: Harper and Row 1987). See also his *Jesus and Empire* (Minneapolis: Fortress Press, 2003).

21: Dead Man Walking

229 *pictures illustrating the event portrayed:* Karen Armstrong, *Jerusalem: One City, Three Faiths* (New York: Ballantine Books, 1996), p. 336.

233 "through ritual than through chronicle": Yosef Hayim Yerushalmi, *Zakhor: Jewish History and Jewish Memory* (Seattle and London: University of Washington Press, 1982). The quotation is found on p. xvii in the foreword by Harold Bloom. I have added the emphasis.

233 *and draw real blood:* See Alberto Lopez Pulido, *The Sacred World of the Penitentes* (Washington, D.C.: The Smithsonian Institution Press, 2000).

234 *some form of injustice still prevails:* For a fictional description of such a combination of protest march and Stations of the Cross, see Ana Castillo, *So Far from God* (New York: Penguin Group, 1993).

236 *the play's presentation:* The Oberammergau Passion Play has been presented every ten years since 1633. After World War II its producers were rightly criticized for the stereotypical portrayals of Jews, but since then the script, makeup, costumes, and staging have been completely overhauled.

22: Reason, Emotion, and Torture

239 *What would you do:* Professor Dershowitz's position can be found in his important book, *Why Terrorism Works: Understanding the Threat, Meeting the Challenge* (New Haven, Conn.: Yale University Press, 2002).

240 "[of a particular individual] is justified": Quoted in Eyal Press, "In Torture We Trust," *The Nation*, 31 March 2003, p. 11.

241 "subjected to electric shocks": Ibid., p. 12.

242 "or fracture the spine": Ibid., p. 11.

244 *have suffered from the divorce:* See the interesting treatment of the gradual stripping from "reason" of these qualities that were once considered integral to it in John Milbank, "The Last of the Last: Theology, Authority and Democracy," *Telos*, No. 123 (Spring 2002), pp. 5ff. Paul Tillich also discusses this same question in *Systematic Theology*, Vol. 1 (Chicago: University of Chicago Press, 1951), pp. 53–54 and 72–74.

23: It Had to Be Done

246 *one of our gravest ethical dilemmas:* Susan Neiman, *Evil in Modern Thought: An Alternative History of Philosophy* (Princeton, N.J.: Princeton University Press, 2003).

24: A World Without God?

260 *"for pain can share it":* Irving Greenberg, *The Jewish Way: Living the Holidays* (New York: Summit Books, 1988), p. 320.

261 *liberated the camp:* See Andre Dumas, *Dietrich Bonhoeffer: Theologian of Reality,* translated by Robert McAfee Brown (New York: Macmillan Company, 1968). The standard biography is Eberhard Bethge, *Dietrich Bonhoeffer: Theologian, Christian Contemporary* (New York: Harper and Row, 1970).

261 Letters and Papers from Prison: Dietrich Bonhoeffer, *Letters and Papers from Prison* (New York: Collier Books, 1971).

262 *"in man's life and goodness":* Ibid., p. 311.

262 *"stand continually (Letter of 16 July 1944)":* Ibid., p. 360.

264 *"non-religious interpretation of the Gospel":* The author, forty years ago and under the influence of Bonhoeffer, wrote *The Secular City* (New York: Macmillan, 1965) as an attempt to address the theological questions of a "world come of age."

265 *which arose twenty years later:* See the introduction to *The Power of the Poor in History* (Maryknoll, N.Y.: Orbis Books, 1983), in which Gustavo Gutierrez, the "father" of Latin American liberation theology, acknowledges his debt to Bonhoeffer.

25: The Easter Story

271 *claimed their leader was still alive:* N. T. Wright, *Jesus and the Victory of God* (Minneapolis: Fortress Press, 1996), p. 110. Wright lists, for example, John the Baptist, Eleazar ben Deinaus, and Bar Kochba, among others.

272 *symbols or song or silence:* See Sarah Coakley, "Not with Eyes Only: The Resurrection, Epistemology, and Gender," in Center of Theological Inquiry (ed.), *Reflections* (Princeton, N.J.: Center of Theological Inquiry, 2003).

273 *just couldn't help it:* As an unapologetic fan of the original Dracula film, I must add here that many film critics see it as a perversely clever

inversion of certain elements in the Christian story, such as resurrection and being kept alive by drinking blood.

274 *decide among them on their own:* Roger Haight in his *Jesus: Symbol of God* (Maryknoll, N.Y.: Orbis Books, 1999) includes an excellent survey of these interpretations. See p. 119.

275 *"thirst for justice":* Quoted in Jon Sobrino, *Christ the Liberator* (Maryknoll, N.Y.: Orbis Books, 2001), p. 26.

276 *"God is on our side":* See Michael Walzer, *Exodus and Revolution* (New York: Basic Books, 1985).

276 *for the Easter story:* Sobrino, *Christ the Liberator,* pp. 66ff.

280 *"to go to where God is":* Ibid., p. 35.

26: The Laughter of the Universe

288 *the vastest spiral nebulae:* Paul Tillich, *Systematic Theology,* Vol. 3 (Chicago: University of Chicago Press, 1963), p. 414.

292 *into its inner vacuum:* For a thoughtful exploration of these themes, see M. A. Corey, *God and the New Cosmology: The Anthropic Design Argument* (Lanham, Md.: Rowman and Littlefield Publishers, 1993).

292 *what they came up with:* See J. Polkinghorne and Michael Welker (eds.), *The End of the World and the Ends of God: Theology and Science on Eschatology* (Harrisburg, Pa.: Trinity Press, 2000).

Postscript

297 *"every legislative body in the United States":* Quoted from Learned Hand's *Morals in Public Life* in John Bartlett and Justin Kaplan (eds.), *Bartlett's Familiar Quotations,* 16th ed. (Boston: Little, Brown and Company, 1992), p. 615.

300 *others to persist to the present:* See Jaroslav Pelikan, *Jesus Through the Centuries* (New Haven, Conn.: Yale University Press, 1985), and Charlotte Allen, *The Human Christ: The Search for the Historical Jesus* (New York: The Free Press, 1998).

300 *sprung up in American history:* Stephen Prothero, *American Jesus: How the Son of God Became an American Icon* (New York: Farrar, Straus and Giroux, 2003).

300 *a tycoon in the making:* Bruce Barton, *The Man Nobody Knows: A Discovery of the Real Jesus* (New York: Triangle Books, 1940).

Acknowledgments

Because this book grew out of many years of teaching, I wish I could list the individual names of the thousands of students who, over two decades, contributed to what it eventually became. I obviously cannot. But in the best of all worlds, they would be included as full coauthors. I frequently quote them without using their names, not just to preserve their anonymity, but because in many cases I have forgotten exactly how they said things or which one made what astute remark. Frequently I have also forgotten just where I heard something. Was it during a question-and-answer exchange after a lecture, or was the comment made in a discussion section? Or did it come up at an informal chat over a double cappuccino in a local bistro? These occasions do tend to merge. I also admit that I may have expressed ideas here that I once thought of articulating in class, but perhaps never did. After so many years, I do not remember. Many of us conceive the most brilliant retorts only when we get home, and then, after a few years, it is sometimes easy to think we actually made them. Such is the plight of aging. Still, I think these ideas remain worthwhile, or I would not have included them.

I also wish I could mention all the friends and colleagues with whom I have enjoyed conversations. From them I have gained insights that, after seeping into my own intellectual repertory, eventually surfaced in this book, again mainly without attribution. It is very hard to be entirely original. But I am especially grateful to my friend and colleague Allen Callahan, an accomplished scholar of the New Testament and early Christianity. He and I once offered a course on Jesus together, and I learned an immense amount from him. He also generously read the manuscript for this book and offered numerous astute suggestions that rescued it from many obtuse errors. Whatever is historically accurate in the book is due to his guidance. Where there remain boners, they are exclusively of my own creation.

It is of the nature of acknowledgments that they can go on forever. Who in my life has not at some point contributed to my spiritual and intellectual development, even without recognizing it? But instead of registering names, I want to express my gratitude to one young woman who took my course the first year I offered it, but whose name I never knew. Let her stand in as the symbol for all the other unnamed sources and inspirations.

It happened this way: When I first began to teach a course on Jesus in Harvard College I was acutely worried and terribly apprehensive. I had never taught such a course to undergraduates before. Would anyone sign up? Would I be able to deliver? Underlying these gnawing doubts there lingered another more profound one: Was a course like this really needed?

A kind of answer came during the very first weeks. A large number of students did enroll. Good, so far, but I was still uncertain. Then, I think during the second week, an earsplitting fire alarm rattled the walls of the aging building where I was teaching. I had been warned that this sometimes happened, so I stopped abruptly and told the students to walk — not run — to the exits, all located in the rear. I grabbed my notes, stepped off the platform, and followed them. But then I noticed a tall young woman with a black ponytail struggling down the aisle toward me and against the crowd, waving her notebook over her head and shouting something I could not hear above the clamor of the alarm. I pointed to the rear doors behind her and yelled, "Fire alarm! Go-to-the-exit! The *exit!*" But she continued to thrash toward me, jostled by the throng pushing in the opposite direction. Finally she got close enough so that I could hear what she was saying: "But what's the *assignment?* What-is-the-*assignment?*"

As it turned out, there was no fire. It was a false alarm. But I was mightily impressed with that student. Admittedly she may simply have been a little wacky. However, I chose to interpret her impetuous behavior in another way. Here, I told myself, was someone who seemed willing to brave the flames rather than leave without knowing what her reading was for the next session. I let her madcap act assure me that there was indeed a need for such a course, and that I was at least beginning to meet that need.

Of course, not everyone who eventually took the course matched her excessive zeal. But after many years I still fondly remember that young woman in the ponytail and owe her a genuine acknowledgment. She may have been more than a little overeager. But she shared many qualities with the students I came to know during the years I taught that course, and others like it, and with countless people I have met beyond the classroom. Like her, they were dissatisfied with both the frigid moral haughtiness they encountered on the one side, and the wimpy "well whatever" laxity they found on the other. They shared a hope that learning more about Jesus of Nazareth might bring some clarity to their moral thinking. But also, perhaps like her, many of them discovered that this man Jesus, believed by many people to be the foremost moral influence in history, is hard to get hold of. He frequently seems distant, maybe because we so often look for him in the wrong places. This book is intended for these dissatisfied seekers. I also hope it serves as a belated thank-you to the ponytailed lass who, without even knowing it, encouraged an apprehensive professor to give it his best shot.

Index

COMMON PRAYERS

Faith, Family, and a Christian's Journey
Through the Jewish Year

"An especially welcome primer [which] leaves one, finally, in the presence of the holy and with a deepened appreciation for life and ritual." — *Los Angeles Times*

AS A MEMBER OF AN INTERFAITH HOUSEHOLD, Harvey Cox has had ample opportunity to reflect upon the essence of Judaism and its complex relationship to Christianity. In a book organized around the Jewish calendar from Rosh ha-Shana to Yom ha-Atzma'ut, Cox illuminates the meanings of Jewish holidays as well as milestone events such as death and marriage. He describes in elegant, accessible language the traditions' personal, historical, and spiritual significance and the lessons they offer all of us.

ISBN-13: 978-0-618-25733-1
ISBN-10: 0-618-25733-0